THE MIRACLES AND TRANSLATIO OF SAINT JAMES

Books Two and Three of the
Liber Sancti Jacobi
A Translation, with Introduction,
Commentaries and Notes by
Thomas F. Coffey and
Maryjane Dunn

Italica Press
New York & Bristol
2019

Copyright © 2019 by
Thomas F. Coffey & Maryjane Dunn
Italica Press Medieval and Renaissance Texts Series
Italica Press, Inc.
99 Wall Street
Suite 650
New York, New York 10005

All rights reserved. No part of this publication may be reproduced, stored in a retrieval system, or transmitted, in any form or by any means, electronic, mechanical, photocopying, recording, or otherwise, without prior permission of Italica Press. For permission to reproduce selected portions for courses, please contact the Press at inquiries@italicapress.com.

Library of Congress Cataloging-in-Publication Data

Names: Coffey, Thomas F., translator, editor. | Dunn, Maryjane, translator, editor.
Title: The miracles and "translatio" of Saint James : Books Two and Three of the Liber Sancti Jacobi / a translation with introduction, commentaries and notes by Thomas F. Coffey and Maryjane Dunn.
Other titles: Codex Calixtinus. English. | Codex Calixtinus. English. Book Two. | Codex Calixtinus. English. Book Three.
Description: New York : Italica Press, 2018. | Series: Italica Press medieval & renaissance texts series | Includes bibliographical references and index. | In Latin and English.
Identifiers: LCCN 2017027719 (print) | LCCN 2018034007 (ebook) | ISBN 9781599103259 (ebook) | ISBN 9781599103235 (hardcover : alk. paper) | ISBN 9781599103242 (pbk. : alk. paper)
Subjects: LCSH: James, the Greater, Saint--Cult--Spain--Santiago de Compostela. | Christian pilgrims and pilgrimages--Spain--Santiago de Compostela.
Classification: LCC BT685.5 (ebook) | LCC BT685.5 .C63513 2018 (print) | DDC 282/.4611--dc23
LC record available at https://lccn.loc.gov/2017027719

Cover Illustration: St James the Greater. Workshop of Santiago de Compostela, Spain, c.1410. Jet. The Cloisters Collection, 1965. Metropolitan Museum of Art, New York, Accession Number 65.67.

For a Complete List of Titles in
Italica Press Medieval & Renaissance Texts
Visit our Web Site at
http://www.italicapress.com/index003.html

ABOUT THE EDITORS

THOMAS F. COFFEY holds a B.A. in French and an M.A. and Ph.D. in Medieval Romance Philology, with German, Greek, and Spanish as support languages. He taught various levels of French, German, and Spanish at Creighton University in Nebraska, and English and French in Nordrhein-Westfalen, Germany. He has published in English, French, and Latin and has worked extensively on medieval texts in the areas of rhetoric, French history, and the Inquisition.

MARYJANE DUNN is an associate professor of Spanish at Henderson State University, Arkansas. She has followed the pilgrimage to Santiago de Compostela both personally (first walking the Camino Francés in 1979) and professionally in her scholarly work, focusing on the realities of medieval pilgrimage as well as on its allegorical and literary depictions.

Together they are currently working on an English translation of Book I of the *Codex Calixtinus* to be published by Italica Press.

IN MEMORY OF
LINDA KAY DAVIDSON,
FRIEND, COLLEAGUE, AND
FELLOW PILGRIM
† OCTOBER 24, 2017

Contents

About the Editors	v
Illustrations	ix
Preface	xi
Acknowledgments	xviii
Abbreviations	xix
Introduction	xxi
Saint James the Greater in the New Testament	xxi
Saint James In Early Christian Writings	xxiii
Saint James in Spain	xxviii
Naming the *Liber Sancti Jacobi*	xxxvii
The *Codex Calixtinus* and Salamanca MS 2631	xli
Twentieth-century Editions and Translations of the *Liber Sancti Jacobi*	xlii
The Miracles of Saint James: Book II of the *Liber Sancti Jacobi*	xliv
The Authors of the Miracles	xlvii
Chronology and Dates of the Miracles	xlix
Geographic and Regional Distribution of the Miracles	liv
Aspects of Saint James in the Miracles	liv
Feast Days and the Miracles	lvii
The *Translatio* of Saint James: Book III of the *Liber Sancti Jacobi*	lix
Notes on the Translation	lxvii
The Miracles of Saint James	1
The *Translatio* of Saint James	69

APPENDICES 97
   1. Pseudo-Abdias: The "Passion of James" 97
   2. Song on the Altars of the Twelve Apostles 106
   3. O Word of God Revealed by the Mouth of the Father 107
   4. *Pasionario Hispánico*:
      Saint James, Brother of John 110
   5. *Pasionario Hispánico*:
      About Torquatus and His Companions 118
   6. Agreement of Antealtares 122
   7. History of Compostela: Discovery and *Translatio* 127
   8. The "Veneranda dies":
      How the *Translatio* of this Apostle Occurred 132
   9. Feast Day of Saint Luparia 135
BIBLIOGRAPHY 137
INDEX 151

Illustrations

1. The Holy Door. S.A.M.I. Cathedral of Santiago de Compostela. The Holy Year of Mercy, September 2016.   x

2. The beheading of Saint James and the Scribe Josias. *Bible historiée dite de Pampelune*, Bibliothèque virtuelle des manuscrits médiévaux (BVMM). Amiens, Bibliothèque Municipale. MS 108, Folio 208R.   xx

3. Saint James as Pilgrim. Church of Santa Marta de Tera, Camarzana de Tera, Zamora, Spain. 12th century.   lxx

4. Martín Bernat. The *Translation* of the Body of Saint James the Greater at the Palace of Queen Lupa. (1480–90). Prado Museum.   lxxii

5. "Whatever is written in the first two books up to the sign that is similar to this, which denotes Jesus Christ, may be sung or read in churches." The Chi Rho, Book I of the *Codex Calixtinus*. Archivo-biblioteca de la Catedral de Santiago de Compostela. Folio 2r.   4

6. Saint James Matamoros. Tympanum in the south transept. S.A.M.I. Cathedral of Santiago de Compostela. 13th century.   23

7. One of two cave entrances on the Pico Sacro, commonly known as the "Dragon's Lair." Boqueixón, Galicia, Spain. May 2016.   82

1. The Holy Door. S.A.M.I. Cathedral of Santiago de Compostela. The Holy Year of Mercy, September 2016.

PREFACE

In the twenty years since our first English edition of *The Miracles of Saint James* was published in 1996, the interest in the pilgrimage to Santiago de Compostela has grown astronomically if measured by the number of pilgrims to Santiago de Compostela: from 23,218 in 1996 to 100,377 in 2006 to 278,232 in 2016.[1] No longer is there simply "The Way" or "The Camino," instead there are multiple recognized routes — the *Camino primitivo*, *Camino del norte*, *Camino inglés*, *Ruta de la plata*, *Vía sanabrés*, *Camino portugués*, *Camino portugués interior*, *Camino catalán*, and the *Camino madrileño* — and more are being (re)discovered. Of course these routes only apply to the pilgrimage after it crosses into the Iberian Peninsula; the marked routes across Europe are simply too numerous to mention. Truly, for many, the pilgrimage to Santiago de Compostela has returned to its earliest roots whereby one simply closes the door to one's house and sets off, creating a personal pilgrimage journey.

Making a pilgrimage is in vogue worldwide. New sites and new places where persons may receive some direction and blessing and sense of connectedness are emerging[2] while earlier sites are

---

1. At least some of the increased pilgrimage traffic of 2016 was due to the opening of the Puerta Santa (Holy Door) as part of Pope Francis's declaration of a special Holy Year of Mercy, December 8, 2015–November 20, 2016 (Fig. 1). If one goes back even farther, the numbers are even more dramatic. Linda Davidson (co-author of the first Miracles translation) was a member of a pilgrim group sponsored by Indiana University, organized and led by David Gitlitz in 1974, when 108 certificates for completing the pilgrimage were awarded. I was a pilgrim-participant for a similar trip led by Gitlitz and Davidson in 1979 under the auspices of the University of Nebraska when a total of 231 were given out.

2. Some new sites, such as the Jeju Olle Trail in South Korea, are modeled after the pilgrimage to Santiago de Compostela, "Established in 2007 by the Jeju Olle Foundation, the Jeju Olle Trail now spans over 376 km (234 miles) of beautifully maintained and managed walking and hiking trails. The founder, Suh Myung Sook was inspired by her spiritual journey along

experiencing a resurgence of interest. The motives given for walking on the pilgrimage routes to Compostela have become widely varied: exercise, adventure, curiosity, study, spiritual growth, self-exploration, inexpensive vacation, in addition to the more traditional religious reasons such as to fulfill a vow or request a favor. The pilgrimage to Santiago de Compostela as a specific devotional act in order to worship before the tomb of Saint James is becoming rare. Many pilgrims post on blogs or social media that "Saint James's spirit is on the Camino" not relegated to his church. Some pilgrims prefer to spend only minimal time in Compostela, continuing their journey on to Finisterre or Muxia on the Atlantic seacoast. In 2013 I was asked by a receptionist at the Seminario Menor hostel in Santiago de Compostela if I planned to "do a complete Camino and finish in Finisterre," an idea so popular that there is now a separate Credential printed by the Concello de Negreira (the municipal government of the area in La Coruña, Spain) for those walking onward.

In some sense, however, the pilgrimage to Santiago de Compostela has also returned to its medieval role of creating a nexus between Church and State, although sometimes contentious. Since the 1987 creation of a *Credencial de peregrino* (pilgrim's credential) by the Primer Congreso Internacional de Asociaciones de Amigos de Santiago (First International Congress of Associations of the Friends of Santiago), there has been controversy over who controls the Camino, as well as the coveted "*Compostela*,"[3] a document granted by the Pilgrim's Office of the Cathedral of Santiago de Compostela recognizing the completion of the pilgrimage at Compostela. The

---

the El Camino de Santiago Trail in Europe, and brought back to Korea the ancient rejuvenation tradition of taking a long journey to cleanse one's soul and find spiritual tranquility." Melina Taylor, "South Korea promotes Jeju Olle Trail as major tourist destination," *American Trails Magazine*, http://atfiles.org/resources/international/Korea-tourism-Jeje-Olle-Trail.html (accessed July 2018). Other sites, such as the ancient Kumano Kodo trails of southern Japan are being (re)discovered by persons of all beliefs as a ritualized, spiritual hike to one, two or three sacred (Shinto) shrines.

3. This is the name used for the certificate itself. It was changed in 1988 from *Compostelana* to *Compostela*. Throughout *Compostela* (in italics) will refer to the document rather than the city of Santiago de Compostela.

PREFACE

Archicofradía Universal del Apóstol Santiago, (the oldest and most important society dedicated to Saint James) based in Compostela has traditionally supported the Christian (Catholic) pilgrimage, at times in opposition to the less structured, more open spiritual journey (of any or no specific faith) undertaken by many modern hikers along the routes.

In 2009 the Pilgrim's Office decreed that pilgrims must walk the last 100 kilometers (or cycle or ride horseback 200 kilometers) of the journey, collecting a minimum of two "sellos" (stamps) per day on an officially approved credential in order to receive a *Compostela*. Meanwhile the government of Galicia stepped in to create low-cost pilgrim hostels (*albergues*) clearly signaled on their *Pasaporte de peregrino* (pilgrim's passport) and valid along eight different pilgrimage routes as they cross into Galicia, all the while reminding pilgrim–tourists they must also carry an official church-based credential in order to qualify for a six-euro bed for the night and a *Compostela* at the end of their journey.

With the heightened interest in Santiago de Compostela and the route(s) to this site have also come at least two diverging popular emphases: religious and touristic. Before 1986 there were few firm rules about who could be classified as a pilgrim and receive the *Compostela*.[4] In the mid-1990s the Pilgrim's Office began issuing a "*Certificado de bienvenida*" (certificate of welcome) to pilgrims who did not profess to have travelled "for religious or spiritual reasons" and thus were not eligible to receive a *Compostela*. This issue of documentation or "proof" of being a pilgrim has confused who should be classified a pilgrim and who should oversee these decisions.[5] The cathedral itself is a building in contention, since it

---

4. For a detailed discussion of the definition of a pilgrim and the controversy of the issuance of the *Compostelana* / *Compostela*, see Maryjane Dunn, "Historical and Modern Signs of 'Real' Pilgrims on the Road to Santiago de Compostela," in Samuel Sánchez y Sánchez and Annie Hesp, *The Camino de Santiago in the 21st Century: Interdisciplinary Perspectives and Global Views* (London: Routledge, 2015): 13–35.

5. Steven Gardener, Carlos Mentley, and Lisa Signori discuss the ownership of the modern Compostela pilgrimage in greater detail in "Whose

serves both as a religious center and as a living museum: tourists and pilgrims alike take excursions to the rooftop and the excavations beneath, all while religious services are conducted in the nave as well as other chapels. Attendance at services appears to be high, especially on those occasions when the giant incensor (the *Botafumeiro*) is being used, but attendees must frequently be reminded over loudspeakers that a religious ceremony is underway and to please put cameras away and be quietly respectful of others. In the summer of 1986, pilgrims attending mass were very noticeable: in their boots and walking shorts and sleeveless tops and carrying their backpacks, they stood out from the rest of the residents and tourists attending services. In 2016 signs were posted that no backpacks were allowed inside the cathedral, forcing pilgrims to check their gear prior to entering the church, creating an invisible barrier between the euphoria of arrival and the pilgrim's visit to the tomb of Saint James.

The pilgrims often share online with family and friends the travails along the route and the excitement of arrival at Compostela, as well as their highly personal reflections. There is an enormous amount of digital ink expended in describing their experiences in blogs, tweets, online forums, and electronic or print books, sometimes self-published. With so much information it is hard to imagine why anything new needs to be published, and yet, so much of what is written about the Camino de Santiago pilgrimage experience today lacks any historical grounding. With that in mind, this book is intended to introduce pilgrims and would-be pilgrims to Saint James — who he was, how he was called to be an Apostle, his role amongst the disciples, his work after Christ's crucifixion, and his own martyrdom. We want to explain his relationship with the Iberian Peninsula and clarify the pseudo-history, folklore, and local stories, often promoted along the routes and often repeated without any clear understanding of the nature of legend and its dissemination.

For instance, virtually all pilgrims who write about their pilgrimage experiences on the *Camino francés*, when arriving in

---

Camino Is It? (Re)defining Europe on the Camino de Santiago," in Sánchez y Sánchez, *The Camino*, 57–77.

PREFACE

Santo Domingo de la Calzada (La Rioja, Spain) feel obliged to retell the fanciful tale of the Hanged Pilgrim, motivated by the presence of a "holy chicken coop" within the main sanctuary of the cathedral there. Some embellish the tale with superstitious elements like the good luck bestowed by the rooster crowing during mass. Few pilgrims realize that this miracle is recorded in Book II, chapter 5 of the *Codex Calixtinus* about a German family travelling to Compostela. There the miracle is recorded as taking place at Toulouse in France, not in Santo Domingo. I have also twice observed on the *Via sanabrés* on the last night before reaching Compostela that pilgrims were unaware that they were so near a site connected to Saint James's final resting place. In both 2013 and 2016, as I stayed in Outeiro / Vedra, Lugo, Galicia, I hired a taxi driver — there was only one in the whole area — to drive me to the upper base of Pico Sacro, but the driver eventually made three or four trips to carry some twenty pilgrims to join me at the peak, eager to hear the story from a local storyteller and guide, as well as an American scholar. These events proved that modern pilgrims would welcome an accessible translation of Book III of the *Liber Sancti Jacobi*.

With the increase in the number of pilgrims, there has been a growth in scholarly interest and publication in the pilgrimage routes and in the pilgrims who travel them. In *The Pilgrimage to Santiago de Compostela: A Comprehensive, Annotated Bibliography*,[6] Linda Davidson and I sought to give, at a minimum, adequate bibliographical citations to everything written before July 1993 that contained a reference to the Santiago pilgrimage in its title. We amassed 2941 items. Today, a quick search on Amazon brings up 2081 entries, and these do not include journal articles. In more traditional research-based scholarship, the emphasis has moved beyond investigations of old manuscripts and excavations of ancient sites. For sociologists and anthropologists, the numbers of pilgrims afford tremendous research possibilities. Scholars in other disciplines are adding their expertise as they use the Camino de Santiago, both historical and modern, as their laboratory for making comparisons

---

6. New York: Garland Publishing, Inc., 1994.

with other religious pilgrimages, for observing the effects of long-distance hiking on the body, for considering the economics of travel, or for studying how jurisdictional rights and laws (both canon and civil) affected (and affect) the pilgrimage.

Amid all this interest, secular and religious, experiential and scholarly, it is important to come to terms, individually and culturally, with the biography of Saint James the Apostle and his place in the development of medieval Spain and medieval civilization. Whether the pilgrim's motives are religious, touristic, scholarly, or strictly personal, knowing the background of the phenomenon will enrich the experience. Who was the historical Saint James the Greater? How did the cult of Saint James develop in the furthermost corner of Europe? What did the medieval pilgrims who walked to Santiago know and believe about him? Where did those who walked these roads come from? Why did they come?

The pilgrimage to Compostela is graced with an exceptional witness from the early days of the route: the *Liber Sancti Jacobi* (LSJ). This twelfth-century manuscript offers a compendium of individual items that collectively form an encyclopedia of the medieval pilgrimage and the cult of Saint James, and that separately display the nascent stages of several literary forms. Book V, for example, is a pilgrim's guide to the route, with appropriate cautions and recommendations. It is a unique twelfth-century travel guide, likened to Frommer or Fodor guidebooks of the twentieth century.[7] Book IV, once thought so spurious that it was removed from the manuscript, contains an early version of the Roland and Charlemagne story, with material not found in the other early versions that have come down to us.[8] Books I, II, and III deal directly with the cult of Saint James, offering hymns and sermons for masses and other liturgies, miracle texts, and a story of the transfer of Saint James's body from the Holy Land to Galicia.

---

7. Paula Gerson, "France and Spain On Five *Nummus* A Day: A Medieval Travel Guide," *Topic* 35 (Fall 1981): 9, n. 1.

8. Kevin Poole, *Chronicle of Pseudo-Turpin: Book IV of the* Liber Sancti Jacobi (New York: Italica Press, 2014), xxix.

PREFACE

In this book, Tom Coffey and I have translated into English Books II and III of the *Liber Sancti Jacobi:* the "Miracles of Saint James" and "The Great *Translatio*[9] of Saint James." We, along with Linda Davidson, have previously published Book II, the collection of the saint's twenty-two miracles, along with the codex's introductory letter and its most famous sermon, the "Veneranda dies."[10] Twenty years later, we feel that these miracles would be well served by a new edition, revised and updated with additions from Salamanca MS 2631, which is now available in facsimile. It is also important to consider these miracles in connection with Saint James's martyrdom and the subsequent transfer of his body to the Iberian Peninsula as it is told in Book III. These two books of the *Liber Sancti Jacobi* give the reader a good understanding of the saint's power and importance as their compiler or author would have his audience know them. They reflect the significance of Saint James and of Santiago de Compostela as a major medieval Christian pilgrimage site.

As a scholar of the pilgrimage and as a pilgrim along the Road to Santiago for over four decades, I have watched and participated in the increase in pilgrimage studies and interpretations as well as in the number of pilgrims. Tom Coffey brings a background in medieval philology to bear upon the text. This fortuitous combination of talents, abilities, and interests has benefited the project that required a knowledge of Latin and French–Cluniac vernacular literary styles and conventions, and a knowledge of the geography and history of the period as well as a familiarity with the Road itself.

Maryjane Dunn
February 2017

---

9. Throughout this work we retain *Translatio* (Latin, capitalized and in italics) when referring to the story told in Book III.

10. Thomas Coffey, Linda Davidson and Maryjane Dunn, *The Miracles of Saint James* (New York: Italica Press, 1996).

ACKNOWLEDGMENTS

The English translation below of Book II, *The Miracles of Saint James*, is largely unchanged from the 1996 edition. We are extremely grateful to Linda Davidson, who, although she was unable to be a full-fledged collaborator on this current edition, consulted with us on many points, provided encouragement, gave her blessing to our using and modifying the miracle translations from our first book, and made numerous suggestions and edits to this preface and introduction. We regret that she did not live to see its publication.

We especially wish to thank Beth Farwell, Associate Director for Central Libraries, Baylor University for access to the facsimile copies of both the *Codex Calixtinus* and the Salamanca Manuscript 2631, which are housed in the Central Libraries Special Collections at Moody Memorial Library, as well as the Baylor University's Digital Projects Group, Electronic Library, which provided scans of important pages of both facsimiles.

We wish to thank the staffs of the Reinert Alumni Memorial Library at Creighton University, the Pius XII Memorial Library and the Vatican Film Library at St. Louis University, and the Huie Library at Henderson State University for their help in providing materials. Thank you also to George Greenia for his prompt responses and suggestions to our queries.

We are indebted to Tiffany Carter, Assistant Director of the Writing Center at Henderson State University, for her careful assistance in proofing the draft of this book.

The photo of the "Dragon's Lair" (Figure 7) on the Pico Sacro was taken by Katie Smith — a Henderson State University student who participated in the "Henderson on the Camino 2016" program — and is used with her permission. All other photos were taken by Maryjane Dunn during her pilgrimages to Compostela in 2013 and 2016.

ABBREVIATIONS

AASS	*Acta sanctorum.*
BHL	*Bibliotheca Hagiographica Latina.*
CC	*Codex Calixtinus.*
HC	*Historia compostelana.*
Herbers	*Liber Sancti Jacobi: Codex Calixtinus.* Ed. Klaus Herbers and Manuel S. Noya. Latin transcription.
Kaydeda	*Liber Sancti Jacobi.* Facsimile.
LSJ	*Liber Sancti Jacobi.*
Moralejo	*Liber Sancti Jacobi: Codex Calixtinus.* Spanish translation (1951 ed.).
PG	*Patrologiae cursus completus: series graeca.*
PL	*Patrologiae cursus completus: series latina.*
Salamanca	*Codex Calixtinus de la Universidad de Salamanca.* Facsimile.
Whitehill	*Liber Sancti Jacobi.* Ed. W.M. Whitehill. Latin transcription.

2. The beheading of Saint James and the Scribe Josias. *Bible historiée dite de Pampelune,* Bibliothèque virtuelle des manuscrits médiévaux (BVMM). Amiens, Bibliothèque Municipale. MS 108, Folio 208r.

INTRODUCTION

About that time King Herod laid hands on some from the church to harm them. He had James, the brother of John, executed with a sword. When he saw that this pleased the Jews, he proceeded to arrest Peter too. (This took place during the feast of Unleavened Bread.) Acts 12:1–3

These few verses from the Acts of the Apostles of the Christian New Testament describe an event that has had social, cultural, historical, political, and religious repercussions for over 2000 years. From the report of his ignominious death as the first martyred apostle to his reputed burial in what is now Santiago de Compostela, the story of Saint James the Greater, favored apostle of Christ, has captivated writers and readers to the present day.

SAINT JAMES THE GREATER IN THE NEW TESTAMENT

The texts that narrate the life of this first martyred apostle are limited. There are great gaps between the manuscripts that tell of his beheading in Jerusalem and those that tell of the flourishing of his cult and the pilgrimage to his tomb in the northwestern corner of the Iberian Peninsula. Many of these documents offer only cryptic allusions. In the mid–eleventh century, however, the *Liber Sancti Jacobi* (Book of Saint James, LSJ) was compiled to educate and correct pilgrims who traveled to Compostela. Its purpose was to provide "sermons in a simple manner…so that these things might be accessible to the unlearned as well as the learned,"[1] to offer a collection of music for the celebration of his feast days, and to honor Saint James the Greater (in Spanish *Santiago el Mayor*), the fourth apostle to be chosen by Christ, after [Simon] Peter, Peter's brother Andrew, and James's brother, John.[2]

1. Coffey et al., *Miracles*, 5.
2. Mt 4:18–22, Mk 1:16–20.

The earliest and most widely accepted Christian writings about James are found in the three synoptic Gospels (Matthew, Mark, and Luke) and the Acts of the Apostles. With the exception of the story of Herod's beheading of James in Acts 12:1–2, his brother John is always present with him. In Lk 5:1–11, we read that James and John were fishermen on Lake Gennesaret (the Sea of Galilee) and partners of [Simon] Peter, and after experiencing the miracle of the great catch, they "left everything and followed him [Jesus]." The story of James's calling differs slightly in Mt 4:21–22 and Mk 1:19–20, which say that he and his brother John were preparing their nets in their father Zebedee's boat when Jesus saw them and called them into his service. James, along with his brother John as well as Peter, was specifically named as witnessing the transcendental moments of Jesus's life: his Transfiguration,[3] his raising of Jairus's daughter,[4] and his agony in the Garden of Gethsemane.[5] James and John — or their mother on their behalf — boldly asked a favor of Jesus: that they be allowed to sit in glory at his right and at his left, a request denied by Jesus who said it was not in his power to grant.[6] James was outspoken in at least one other instance, when he entreated Jesus to let him call down fire to punish a Samaritan village that would not welcome them on their way into Jerusalem.[7] It is not surprising that Jesus gives James and John the sobriquet "Boanerges" (Sons of Thunder) for their impetuous and imperious natures.[8] In the end, however, James was to be counted among the most faithful; Luke specifically names him as present along with the other disciples at the post-Ascension gathering during which the apostles voted for Matthias to replace Judas to complete their group.[9] And finally, it is Luke who tells us in Acts that James became the first of the apostles to be martyred, in Jerusalem by Herod Agrippa, in 44 CE.[10]

3. Mt 17:1–13, Mk 9:2–13, and Lk 9:28–36.
4. Mk 5:21–42 and Lk 8:40–56.
5. Mt 26:36–46 and Mk 14:32–42.
6. Mk 10:35–45 (the brothers' request) or Mt 20:20–28 (their mother's request).
7. Lk 9:51–56.
8. Mk 3:14–17.
9. Acts 1:12–26.
10. Acts 12:1–3.

INTRODUCTION

This is the Christian New Testament history of the life of Saint James the Greater. The story of Saint James in all his guises — apostle, pilgrim, or Moorslayer[11] — evolved over nine centuries, was created and embellished by several authors, and spans the eastern and western parts of the Early Christian world. Saint James's legend provides insight into the pilgrimage to Santiago de Compostela and its significance in medieval religion, history, and culture. During the early centuries of Christendom, however, Saint James was not a particularly important figure, when compared to Paul with his numerous writings and notable status in the Early Church, or the noted preacher Peter, whose church in Rome became the symbol and political center of western Christendom.

Saint James In Early Christian Writings

For nearly seven centuries, Saint James played no significant role either in the liturgy or in the formation of the Early Christian

---

11. Many do not link "Santiago" with the English version of his name "Saint James." The epithet Santiago "Matamoros" (Saint James the Moorslayer) has generally been replaced today with the appellation "Caballero," variously translated as Knight or Gentleman. As early as 1995, the Santiago Cathedral began to refocus Saint James's importance away from his Moorslayer image and back towards his original, more benign, apostolic image, as seen in the change of the seal on the *Compostela*, the document awarded for completion of the pilgrimage. Prior to 1995 the seal depicted Saint James atop his charger wielding a sword with a battle flag; since 1995 the seal has depicted the casket and star as seen under the altar of the cathedral. In 2004 church officials removed José Gambino's polychromed wood statue of Santiago Matamoros from the main area of the church after the bombing of the Atocha train station. Xosé Hermida, "La Catedral compostelana retira una imagen de Santiago 'Matamoros,'" *El País*, 2 May 2004 (https://elpais.com/diario/2004/05/02/cultura/1083448804_850215.html (accessed July 2018). The officials had said it would be housed in the cathedral museum, but public outcry led to its reinstatement in the main church, albeit with flowers and cloths arranged so that visitors do not see the "Moors" (actually Turks) beheaded and being trampled under the horse's hooves. Isambard Wilkinson, "Public Outcry Forces Church to Keep Moor Slayer's Statue," *The Telegraph*, 22 July 2004, https://www.telegraph.co.uk/news/worldnews/europe/spain/1467621/Public-outcry-forces-church-to-keep-Moor-Slayers-statue.html (accessed July 2018).

church, especially not the western Church. He left no letters, and there are few accounts before the seventh century that document his activities or speeches. His name appears in early lists of the twelve apostles, but there is often confusion, or ambiguity, about where James preached and where he was buried. Adding to the uncertainty is the confusion between the several saints named James in the Christian New Testament and Early Church — James the Greater (the apostle and brother of John), James the Lesser (the apostle also known as James, son of Alpheus), and James the Just (also named by some as the brother of Jesus and apocryphally as the first bishop of Jerusalem and to whom are attributed the first three New Testament books of James).

Saint James does not figure prominently in extant early Christian writings, and much of what is written is only a shadow of a record.[12] In Eusebius's *The History of the Church* (c. 315) we read the beginnings of the story of Josias (although he is not named) who was converted by James, and martyred alongside him, as told in Clement of Alexandria's (d.c. 215) lost work called *The Outlines*.[13]

---

12. See Jan Van Herwaarden, "Saint James in Spain up to the 12th Century," in *Wallfahrt kennt keine Grenzen,* ed. Lenz Kriss–Rettenbeck and Gerda Möhler (Munich: Schnell & Steiner, 1984): 235–47 for a discussion of the importance of Saint James in religious histories. In "The Origins of the Cult of St. James of Compostela," in *Between Saint James and Erasmus* (Leiden: Brill, 2003): 311–54, Van Herwaarden also discusses the sources of the Saint James legend. Robert Plötz ("Peregrinatio ad Limina Sancti Jacobi," in *The* Codex Calixtinus *and the Shrine of St. James,* ed. John Williams and Alison Stones, Jakobus–Studien 3 [Tübingen: Gunter Narr, 1992], 37–50) also summarizes these historical documents and provides an overview of the early importance of the pilgrimage to Santiago de Compostela. In *Santiago: Trayectoria de un mito* (Barcelona: Edicions Bellaterra, 2004), Francisco Márquez Villanueva examines the origins of the mythological connection between Saint James and Spain, which has shaped the history, politics, religion, and cultural identity of the peninsula through the eighteenth century.

13. This work is often referred to by its Greek name *Hypotyposes* or *Outlines* [ὑποτύπωσες]. Only fragments such as those written down by Eusebius survive.

INTRODUCTION

At that time, namely in the reign of Claudius Augustus, Herod the king set out to afflict some from the Church, and he killed James the brother of John with a sword. Concerning this James, Clement directly relates something worthy of memory in the seventh book of the "Outlines," just as he had received it from great men. For Clement says: "The one who had brought James to trial, when he saw James, confessed the faith of Christ freely and affirmed that he was also a Christian, having been moved by the perseverance of the man [James]. Therefore, both were led to death at the same time. And when this companion asked this same James that he be given forgiveness, James, with very little delay, said: 'Peace be with you' and immediately kissed him. Thus at the same time both were cut through at the head and perished. Then just as the divine Scripture transmits, Herod, when he saw that the death of James was most welcome to the Jews, also approached Peter whom he placed in chains and who was about to be sentenced to capital punishment, except that by divine power, Peter, with the help of an angel appearing at night, was liberated, against all hope, from the chains, and was sent out for the ministry of preaching. And certainly they attained these things for Peter through some heavenly providence." [14]

This very early story of the converted guard weaves in and out of the Saint James legend across the centuries. In some versions he is named Josias, in some he is called a scribe. Some stories contain more details: for example, Saint James asks for a glass of water and baptizes him with this water. Although there is no mention of this character in Acts, the illustrated tale appears in the Pamplona

---

14. Eusebius of Caesarea, *Ecclesiastical History* 2.9 (PG 20:157–58). This and subsequent quotes are included as functional, not critical, translations from readily available sources.

XXV

picture Bible,[15] showing James baptizing Josias (who is named in the text) followed by their beheading (fol. 207v and 208r, Fig. 2).

The first stories of James's activities post-Pentecost do not associate him with Spain. These tales appear in multiple versions of the early Eastern hagiographic tradition — a few of these tales, such as the conversion of the guard, transfer to the western European tradition, while others do not. Some early Arabic or Coptic texts say that James traveled with Peter to "the country of Lydia" (modern day Turkey)[16] or "the city of India"[17] where they cured a blind man, escaped arrest through a series of miracles, and cured a young boy, later converting and baptizing his father, the judge Theophilus, along with the rest of the family. When in a separate chapter these manuscripts tell of Saint James's death, he is described as having preached to the Twelve Tribes of Israel.[18] This version of Saint James's post-Crucifixion activities and the miracles associated with them are not included in the *Liber Sancti Iacobi*, nor are they found in the *libelli* or saints' lives that grow into the liturgical *Pasionario Hispánico*.[19]

15. Created by order of King Sancho VII of Navarre, completed c. 1197, and housed in Amiens, Bibliothèque municipale ms. 108. See http://bvmm.irht.cnrs.fr/consult/consult.php?reproductionId=15143 (accessed July 2018). This manuscript and its slightly later sister manuscript are available in facsimile, in François Bucher, *The Pamplona Bibles: A Facsimile Compiled from Two Picture Bibles with Martyrologies Commissioned by King Sancho el Fuerte of Navarra (1194–1234): Amiens Manuscript Latin 108 and Hamburg MS. I, 2, Lat. 4°, 15* (New Haven: Yale University Press, 1970).

16. S.C. Malan, trans., *The Conflicts of the Holy Apostles, an Apocryphal Book of the Early Eastern Church, Translated from an Ethiopic MS* (London: D. Nutt, 1871), 172.

17. Agnes Smith Lewis, *The Mythological Acts of the Apostles, Translated from an Arabic MS in the Convent of Deyr-es-Suriani, Egypt, and from MSS in the Convent of St. Catherine on Mount Sinai and in the Vatican Library* (London: C.J. Clay and Sons, 1904), 30.

18. Malan, *Conflicts*, 172–78. Also Lewis, *Mythological Acts*, 30–34.

19. Appendix 4.

INTRODUCTION

Other elements of these stories, however, are associated with another collection of saints' lives credited to Pseudo-Abdias, a supposed bishop of Babylonia, who narrated the now famous story of Saint James's conversion of the magician Hermogenes. The Abdias texts incorporate the contest between the magician Hermogenes, his pupil Philetus, and Saint James; the conversion of the guard (named Josias); and the story of Saint James's beheading in the time of Abiathar the priest — all elements found in Book III (*Translatio*) of the LSJ. While there has been some disagreement about the origin and date of these stories[20] of the conversion of Hermogenes and of the guard Josias, they represent a distinct narrative that in no way links Saint James with the Iberian Peninsula, although both accounts were well known by the time of composition of the *Liber Sancti Jacobi* and are included (although in a rather garbled narrative) in the Prologue of Book III. Later books of saints' lives, especially Jacobus de Voragine's *Legenda aurea*, expand upon the story of the dispute between Hermogenes and Saint James.[21]

---

20. See Appendix I for the English text of the Pseudo-Abdias, "De historia ac rebus gestis Jacobi majoris Apostoli." The early editions of the Pseudo-Abdias passion texts by Johann Albert Fabricius (*Codex apocryphus Novi Testamenti*, 2 ed. [Hamburg: Schiller & Kisneri, 1719]) and Richard A. Lipsius (*Die Apokryphen apostelgeschichten und apostellegenden* [Braunschweig: C. A. Schwetschke und Sohn, 1883]) assigned a very early date (second century) to these collections of saints' lives. Manuel Díaz y Díaz ("Xacobe en Compostela: primeiros testemuños literarios," in *Escritos jacobeos* [Santiago de Compostela: Universidade de Santiago de Compostela, 2010], 226–27) proposes that these passion stories, especially the *Passio Iacobi*, actually originated in the Narbonne region of France during the early sixth century. He posits ("La *Passio Iacobi* – Trabajo inédito" in *De Santiago y de los Caminos de Santiago* [Santiago de Compostela: Xunta de Galicia, 1997], 17–18) that there were two recensions of the Pseudo-Abdias collection — one Spanish, the other western European — of which the Spanish version is distinct from the one included in the *Codex Calixtinus*.
21. *The Golden Legend: Readings on the Saints*, trans. William Granger Ryan (Princeton: Princeton University Press, 1993): 2:4–5.

Saint James in Spain

The stories of the conversions of both Hermogenes and Josias place James in the area of Jerusalem between Pentecost and his death in 44 CE; none of the earliest known apocryphal texts substantiate a connection between Saint James and the Iberian Peninsula during those years. Until the seventh century, there is no written record or mention of Saint James the Greater being directly associated with, or preaching in, Spain. Tracing the development of the story of Saint James as it is connected to the Iberian Peninsula prior to the compilation of the LSJ is extremely complex and includes both Church and secular sources spanning Europe and Asia Minor that exist in multiple intertwining manuscripts with major or minor variations in wording. Excellent, detailed discussions of the transmission of the legend and its early links with the Iberian Peninsula may be found in Plötz, Díaz y Díaz, Van Herwaarden, Herbers, and García Turza.[22] As generally agreed, the primary writings that have the most direct bearing on Saint James's legend as it is linked with Spain are:

1. *Breviary of the Apostles.* Anonymous (sixth century).

This text is considered the first to connect Saint James with the Iberian Peninsula, i.e. the West, as it assigned missionary fields to the apostles[23]:

---

22. See the bibliography for multiple articles by these scholars. Javier García Turza's article, "The Formulation, Development and Expansion of the *Translatio* of St James," in Antón Pazos, ed., *Translating the Relics of St James From Jerusalem to Compostela* (London: Routledge, 2017): 88–122, appeared in print only a few weeks before this manuscript was completed. We are gratified that García Turza generally agrees with our chronology of the development of Saint James's story as it relates to the Iberian Peninsula and recommend this article for anyone wishing to understand the relationship between the texts and the secular and ecclesiastical political situation of the time.

23. Robert Plötz, "*Peregrinatio*," 40–41; Van Herwaarden, "The Origins of the Cult of St James of Compostela," in *Between Saint James and Erasmus: Studies in Late Medieval Religious Life* (Leiden: Brill, 2003) 317–18.

INTRODUCTION

4. James, whose name means supplanter,[24] son of Zebedee and brother of John, went to the western parts of Spain and preached, and, after being killed with a sword by Herod, was buried and has rested in the Achaia marmarica. Eighth calends[25] of August.[26]

With this text begins the quixotic search for the meaning or place of "Achaia marmarica," variously interpreted as a geographic place, the location of James's sepulcher, or as a description of his tomb, a phrase that ultimately becomes *"parvam arcuatam domum"* or "small arched house" in chapter 2 of the *Translatio.*[27]

---

24. Text should read *supplantor* but *supplantus* is supplied in the Latin of the text. The name Jacob (from which James derives) means "he who replaces" or "he who overthrows."

25. "Calends" [Latin *Kalendae/Kalendas*, etc., depending on case] is part of the old Roman system of specifying dates from certain fixed points in the month: Calends, Ides and Nones. Calends is a fixed point denoting the first of every month, the day before would be *Pridie Kalendas,* and the day before that would be *III Kalendas,* hence December 30 in the modern calendar would be III Kal. Ianuarii. For a detailed description of the liturgical dates of the feast days of Saint James, see Vincent Corrigan, "Music and the Pilgrimage" in *The Pilgrimage to Compostela in the Middle Ages: A Book of Essays* (New York: Garland Publishing, 1996), 43–45. There are two references to the saint's *translation* in Book II, at the end of the miracles of chapters 1 and 20. Throughout we have retained the references to "calends," "ides," and "nones." See the Introduction LVII for information about the saint's feast days.

26. *Breviarium Apostolorum.* Translation is from the Latin found in Theodor Schermann, *Prophetarum vitae fabulosae* (Leipzig: Teubner, 1907), 208.

27. Part of the extensive scholarship about this term and its meaning and implications includes: Manuel Díaz y Díaz, "El lugar del enterramiento de Santiago el Mayor en Isidoro de Sevilla," *Compostellanum* 1.4 (1956): 881–85; Casimiro Torres Rodríguez, "Arca Marmórea," *Compostellanum* 2.2 (1957): 323–39; and "Notas sobre 'Arca Marmórea,'" *Compostellanum* 4.2 (1959): 341–47; also José Guerra Campos "Notas críticas sobre el origen del culto sepulcral a Santiago de Compostela," *Ciencia tomista* 88.279 (July–Sept. 1961): 417–74 and 88.230 (Oct.–Dec. 1961): 559–90; finally Juan José Cebrián

XXIX

2. *On the Birth and Death of the Fathers.* Isidore of Seville (c. 560–636).

This treatise is considered to be the first peninsular document to mention of Saint James preaching in Spain. The words "achaia marmarica" are interpreted as "intra marmaricam"[28]:

> James, son of Zebedee and brother of John, the fourth in order, wrote to the twelve tribes that are in the dispersion of the peoples, and he preached the Gospel and spread the light of preaching to the peoples of Spain and of the places of the West. By order of Herod he was killed and he has lain in repose and buried in marmarica.[29]

Isidore seemingly accommodates the earlier texts that stated that James had preached to the Twelve Tribes of Israel by suggesting an epistolary relationship with them; there is no record of James writing to any groups.

3. *Song on the Altars of the Twelve Apostles.* Aldhelm of Malmesbury (c. 639–709).

This is the first known work to acknowledge a connection between Saint James and the Iberian Peninsula.[30] For the English and Latin of this text, see the Appendix. The possibility raised by Aldhelm that Saint James was sent forth at Pentecost to preach on the Iberian

---

Franco, *Los relatos de la traslación de los restos del Apóstol Santiago a Compostela.* (Santiago de Compostela: Instituto Teológico Compostelano, 2008).

28. Whether Isidore himself used this phrase is not yet established. It is possible that it may be an eighth–century interpolation to his *De ortu et obitu Patrum.* For a focused discussion on the relationship between the Saint James legend and Isidore of Seville's writings, see Manuel Díaz y Díaz, "La leyenda hispana de Santiago en Isidoro de Sevilla" in *De Santiago y de los caminos de Santiago* (Santiago de Compostela: Xunta de Galicia, 1997): 87–96.

29. Isidorus Hispalensis, *De ortu et obitu partum,* 71.125. PL 83:151.

30. Van Herwaarden dismisses the idea that there is an association between the Anglo-Saxon and Spanish Christians ("Origins," 318–19).

INTRODUCTION

Peninsula was quickly followed in other works by the complex idea that he was entombed in what is now Santiago de Compostela, either immediately following his decapitation or several centuries later.

4. *O Word of God Revealed by the Mouth of the Father.* Beatus de Liébana (c. 730–c. 800).

This hymn,[31] probably falsely ascribed to Beatus de Liébana, served as part of the Mozarabic liturgy of the early Hispanic church, linking Saint James with his December 30 feast day, celebrating both his calling and the *translation* of his body. For the English and Latin of this text see the Appendix.[32] After listing each of the apostles and their mission fields, strophes 7–10 focus on Saint James, and, by some interpretations, suggest that his cult is already well developed and that he is considered the patron of Spain or *Hispaniae*. The Mozarabic ritual kept December 30 as Saint James's feast day, and it is only with the introduction and acceptance of the Roman rite in the late eleventh century that his principle feast day moved to July 25.[33] "O Dei verbum" links Saint James even more tightly to the Spanish Peninsula, as it is also an acrostic in honor of King Mauregatus of Asturias (r. 783–88, d. 789)[34]

---

31. The hymn exists in two manuscripts — from Toledo and Santo Domingo de Silos. Van Herwaarden ("Origins," 320–27) provides a detailed explanation of the differences between these two manuscripts and describes the connection between this version and earlier eastern texts via the imagery of the twelve precious stones and their connection to Syrian elements.

32. *O Dei verbum Patris ore proditum*, PL 1306–07.

33. Today many consider this hymn proof that Saint James is, and always has been, the patron saint of Spain as defender of Christendom in his most militant aspect. See for example "El himno 'O Dei verbum,'" *Pro iter agentibus: Boletín de la asociación gaditana del Camino de Santiago "Via Augusta"* 16 (Sept. 2011): 16–19, which also provides a Spanish translation of the hymn. (www.asociaciongaditanajacobea.org/pia16.pdf (accessed July 2018).

34. Also known as "the Usurper." As the illegitimate son of Alfonso I, he challenged the reign of his nephew, Alfonso II "the Chaste." See Joseph O'Callaghan, *A History of Medieval Spain* (Ithaca: Cornell University Press, 1975), 100–11 and 306–13 for a concise explanation of the liturgical, religious, and political situation of this period. Mauregatus is also believed to have defended the Church from the heresy of adoptionism (a non-Trinitarian belief in

who was seen as a defender of Hispanic Christendom against the Moslem invaders.

5. *Martyrology.* Usuard (d. 877).[35]
This is one of the first martyrologies to tell of the *translation* of James's body to Galicia:

> Eighth calends of August, Day 25 [of July]. Feast of the death of the apostle James, brother of John the Evangelist; he was decapitated by King Herod. His most sacred bones were transferred from Jerusalem to the Spains, and buried in their farthest limits, and they are worshipped with frequent veneration of those peoples.[36]

Although his martyrology mentions Saint James's *translation*, James is listed under the Roman liturgical feast day of his Passion on July 25. His words are also the first to link Saint James with an at-least incipient cult in Galicia.

6. *Martyrology* (c. 900). Notker Balbulus (c. 840–912).
This martyrology shows the biography–legend of Saint James having acquired most of its elements: James preached both in Palestine

---

which Christ is viewed as fully man, adopted by God as his son via his baptism). Since the fourth century there were concerns about heresies in the Galician region. The theory has been proposed that the actual remains in the tomb in Compostela are really those of Priscillian (d.c. 385), bishop of Avila, who was ultimately executed for spreading an extreme asceticism and non-Trinitarian doctrines. For more information about adoptionism and the cult of Saint James, see Henry Chadwick, *Priscillian of Avila: The Occult and the Charismatic in the Early Church* (Oxford: Clarendon Press, 1976).

35. Usuard was a Benedictine monk at the Abbey of Saint-Germain-des-Prés near Paris. He traveled to Spain in 858 to bring relics back to the abbey. AASS, July, VI, 459.

36. Usuardus, *Martyrologium*, PL 124:295–96.

and Spain, he died in Jerusalem at the hands of Herod, his body was brought for burial to Galicia, where a cult of followers was established, and miracles took place:

> Eighth calends of August.[July 25] Feast of the Death of Saint James the Apostle, son of Zebedee and brother of John the Evangelist; he was beheaded at the order of King Herod in Jerusalem, as the book of the Acts of the Apostles teaches. The most sacred bones of this holy apostle were transferred to the Spains and buried in their farthest limits, namely near the British Sea, and they are revered with the frequent veneration of those peoples. Not without merit, since through his corporal presence and teaching and through the efficacy of his miraculous works, these same peoples were converted and brought to the faith of Christ. Even the most blessed apostle Paul promised that he would go there for establishing the faith of these people.[37]

These six works offer only minor information about Saint James and his relationship to the Iberian Peninsula and are not primarily concerned with increasing his fame or spreading the story of his life. In most cases, he is not singled out, but rather the information is imparted along with that about Christ's other apostles. It is apparent, however, that during the ninth and tenth centuries, the cult of Santiago and the pilgrimage to Santiago de Compostela had become established and well-known.

7. *Letter of Pope Saint Leo.* Anonymous (ninth or tenth c.).
It is not until the diffusion of this text that details are added to explain the circumstances of Saint James's martyrdom and the *translation* of his body, the actions of his disciples, and his subsequent

---

37. PL 131:1125–26.

burial in what is now Santiago de Compostela. This letter had prodigious dissemination throughout Spain and France and exists in numerous forms.[38] There are several well-known manuscripts that contain some version of the letter, which ranges in length from a paragraph to a page.[39] In the expanded versions, many of the more fanciful and well known images arise — the dragon and wild cattle of the Pico Sacro, the renaming of the mountain Illicinus, the multiple named disciples (generally three) that entwine with the legend of the Spanish saint Torquatus and the Seven Apostolic Men, and the woman who opposes these disciples.[40]

The letter is mentioned in reference to James's *translation* in the *Agreement of Antealtares*:[41] "as we learned in the witness of Pope Saint Leo."[42] The *Translatio* of Book III infers that the letter is the true story of the transfer of James's body: "I did not want to leave out the *Translatio* of Saint James from our codex, as such wonders and treasures are written down in it to the honor of our Lord Jesus Christ and of the apostle; and these things in no way differ from the letter which bears the title of Saint Leo."[43] While chapter 2 of Book III follows the letter's story, it is not the only account of James's passion and *translation* in Book III.

---

38. Manuel Díaz y Díaz groups the text in two distinct redactions: an older form, lacking embellishment and written in a less formal, oral style, and an embellished version that brings in additional elements and shows literary narrative influence. See "La *Epistola Leonis Pape de translatione sancti Iacobi in Galleciam*," in *Escritos jacobeos* (Santiago de Compostela: Universidad de Santiago de Compostela, 2010), 133–81; rpt. from *Compostellanum* 43.1–4 (1998): 517–68.

39. Díaz y Díaz ("La *Epistola*") provides the Latin of six texts denoted as Limoges, Picosagro, Escurialense, Gemblacense, Casanatense, and Fécamp. Because chapter II of the *Translatio,* included in this work, is a version of the letter we have not included a separate translation of the letter in the Appendix.

40. Appendix 6.
41. Appendix 6.
42. Below, 122.
43. Below, 70.

INTRODUCTION

8. The *Pasionario Hispánico*.⁴⁴ Anonymous (pre-eleventh c.).
A passionary is a compilation of narratives of variable length that recount the life, martyrdom, *translation,* and/or miracles of saints. The *Pasionario Hispánico* is a collection of stories of the early saints of the Iberian Peninsula, which was used as part of the pre-eleventh-century Mozarabic liturgy. Through the entry for Saint James in the *Pasionario Hispánico* various elements from the Eastern tradition (the stories of Hermogenes, as well as Josias) circulated in Spain, but it says nothing about his preaching in Spain or having disciples there. It is, in fact, very similar to the text of the *Passio Iacobi* in the Pseudo-Abdias.⁴⁵

The most important role of the *Pasionario Hispánico* in Saint James's legend is the melding of his story with that of Saint Torquatus and his followers, "*Torquatus et comitum.*"⁴⁶ It introduces us by name to the seven men who in later manuscripts are designated as the disciples of Saint James: Torquatus, Tisefons, Isicius, Indalecius, Eufrasius, Secundus, and Cecilius. Their narrative includes an adventure very similar to one of chapter 1 of the *Translatio*: inadvertently they send some of their group to obtain supplies in the town of Guadix, where the townspeople are celebrating the feast of Jupiter, Mercury, and Juno. The disciples anger the pagans with their preaching and must escape across a bridge. The bridge collapses while the pursuers are crossing, killing them, an act witnessed by a noble woman, Luparia, who converts to Christianity. By the time Book III is written, these disciples and the story of the collapsing bridge are fully incorporated into Saint James's *Translatio.*

---

44. Angel Fabregau Grau published a two-volume Latin study and edition of the *Pasionario Hispánico* (Madrid: Consejo Superior de Investigaciones Científicas, 1953–55). An excellent, newer critical edition with a Spanish translation is *Pasionario Hispánico* by Pilar Riesco Chueca (Seville: Universidad de Sevilla, 1995). This edition, however, does not contain the *Passion of Saint James*, although it does contain that of Torquatus.
45. Appendix 1.
46. Appendix 5.

9. *Agreement of Antealtares.*[47] Anonymous (c. 1077).

In 1077 a land agreement was made between Bishop Diego Peláez and the abbot of San Pedro Antealtares and Fagildo, the abbot of the chapel under which lay James's tomb. In setting out the basis for this land settlement, the document begins, not just with the *Translatio*, but with the first written record of the *inventio* (discovery) of Saint James's tomb that occurred in 830. Based on this manuscript, the discovery took place during the reign of Alfonso II "el Casto" (the Chaste) of Asturias (c. 760–842, r. 783 and 791–842)[48] and before the death of Bishop Teodomiro (d. 847). The legend has been embellished in later texts but all of the essentials appear in this manuscript. The tomb is revealed by angels to the hermit Pelayo who lived nearby. Other faithful persons living in the parish of Saint Felix of Lovio see strange or divine lights in the sky. After some deliberation they bring the bishop of Iria, Teodomiro, to the site. The bishop, after three days of fasting, accompanied by a crowd of faithful, finds the sepulcher of the apostle under a marble cover *(sepulcrum marmoreis lapidibus contectum invenit)*. Filled with joy, he goes immediately to report what they have found to King Alfonso.

These last two works (the *Letter of Pope Saint Leo* and the *Concordia de Antealtares*) provide all the basic information upon which the legend of Saint James and his burial in Santiago de Compostela has been fabricated, providing details of the *translation*, the disciples, and the miraculous discovery of the tomb. The story of the *translation* as it appears in the *Pasionario Hispánico* provides the basis for the account in the prologue and chapter 1 of Book III, carrying forward the Hermogenes and Josias tales from the Pseudo-Abdias / *Passio Iacobi* narratives.[49] Interestingly, although the *inventio* of the tomb, as well as the *Concordia*'s account of the discovery occurred well before the compilation of the LSJ, this story is not included in any of its books.

---

47. *Concordia de Antealtares.* See Appendix 6.
48. The reign of Alfonso II of Asturias was interrupted by the reign of his uncle King Mauregatus. See above, n. 34.
49. See above, XXVII and Appendix 1.

INTRODUCTION

Naming the *Liber Sancti Jacobi*

Sometime during the year 1172, a monk named Arnaud du Mont from the monastery in Ripoll wrote to his house asking permission to stay in Compostela to copy a portion of a manuscript that he thought worth having in Ripoll. The text he sought to copy is commonly known today as the *Codex Calixtinus* (CC), a name based on its supposed author, Pope Calixtus II (born Guy of Burgundy c. 1065, pope 1119–24).[50] The CC is considered the earliest surviving complete manuscript of the LSJ.

The original name of this particular manuscript, as well as those that have been copied from it, is not necessarily its true or original name. The introductory letter, purportedly by Pope Calixtus begins, "From the Material comes the Title. This book is called James,"[51] giving rise to the long-standing confusion between the name of the Compostela-housed manuscript (CC) and the name for its contents (LSJ).[52] Some scholars prefer to call the work simply the *Iacobus,* taking that title from a statement in the manuscript itself, "…this codex called Iacobus contains.…"[53] While the Ripoll

---

50. Throughout we use the name "Calixtus" — as does the manuscript — to refer to the person or persons who authored, recorded, or compiled Books II and III.
51. Coffey et al., *Miracles*, 3.
52. Joseph Bédier was the first to propose that the manuscript housed in Compostela be denominated *Codex Calixtinus,* while the compilation itself be called the *Liber Sancti Jacobi.* See "La Chronique de Turpin et le pèlerinage de Compostelle," *Annales du Midi* 24 (1912): 18, n. 1.
53. Coffey et al., *Miracles,* 13. Manuel Díaz y Díaz, "El texto y a tradición textual del Calixtino," in *Pistoia e il Cammino di Santiago: Una dimensione europea nella Toscana medioevale,* ed. Lucia Gai (Naples: Edizione Scientifiche Italiane, 1984): 23–55, furthers this argument. The study made by Díaz y Díaz, María Araceli García Piñeiro, and Pilar del Oro Trigo, *El* Códice Calixtino *de la Catedral de Santiago: Estudio codicológico y de contenido* (Santiago de Compostela: Centro de Estudios Jacobeos, 1988) is indispensable for information about the LSJ and the CC. Also useful are Klaus Herbers, *Der Jacobuskult des 12. Jahrhunderts und der* Liber Sancti Jacobi. *Studien über das Verhältnis zwischen Religion und Gesellschaft im*

manuscript gives us a date for one copy of the *Liber Sancti Jacobi,* it does not give us a certain fixed date for the *Codex Calixtinus* now housed in the Compostela Cathedral library.[54] Variations in the full-text manuscripts of the *Liber Sancti Jacobi* suggest that the *Codex Calixtinus* is not necessarily the source of all subsequent copies of the LSJ.

The LSJ contains five books, each with a different focus. Book I, the longest, contains the liturgical material and music for the saint's feast days. Book II, divided into twenty-two chapters, narrates the miracles worked by the saint after his death. Book III, the shortest, narrates the miraculous *translation* of James's body after his martyrdom in the Holy Land to his final resting place in Galicia. Book IV, commonly referred to as the "Pseudo-Turpin Chronicle," links Charlemagne to the pilgrimage to Compostela, as it describes Charlemagne's and Roland's battles against the Moors on the Iberian Peninsula, instigated by Charlemagne's dream vision of Saint James.[55] Finally, Book V provides the famous twelfth-century guide to the four French routes that lead toward Compostela, describing the perils and sights the pilgrim may encounter while following them. It also names the monuments to see and necessary activities to do once the pilgrim has reached Compostela and includes cautions

---

Hohen Mittelalter. Historische Forschungen 7 (Wiesbaden: F. Stiner, 1984) and the collection of articles based on the 1985 conference on the *Codex Calixtinus* at the University of Pittsburgh (see John Williams and Alison Stones, eds., *The* Codex Calixtinus *and the Shrine of Saint James* (Tübinger: Gunter Narr, 1992).

In earlier days, the Latin "i" was used for both the semivowel "j" and the vowel "i." In the Renaissance, the practice arose to use "i" for the vowel and "j" for the semivowel. In general, we have returned to the practice of using "i" in both cases for modern transcriptions; however, the use of *Jacobus* and *Jacobi* are firmly fixed in the Renaissance convention.

54. Díaz y Díaz, "El *Codex Calixtinus*: Volviendo sobre el Tema," in Williams and Stone, *Codex Calixtinus,* 1–9.

55. For an English translation, with introductory material, see Kevin Poole, ed. and trans., *Chronicle of Pseudo-Turpin: Book IV of the* Liber Sancti Jacobi (Codex Calixtinus) (New York: Italica Press, 2014).

about bad food and water found along the way, as well as warnings about, and colorful descriptions of, local inhabitants.[56]

It is generally believed that each of the LSJ's five books was written at a different time. The *Translatio* is clearly a compilation of a long and varied array of lists, liturgical works, and legends; several chapters of the *Miracles* are ascribed to authors other than "Calixtus"; the Pseudo-Turpin draws on a wide range of literary genres. It appears that the LSJ was probably assembled into its final form sometime between 1140 — the latest miracle placed in the work is dated 1139 — and 1172 when Arnaud du Mont made his copy. The compiler's identity may never be determined. Even the identity of the authors of the individual hymns, sermons, and miracles is doubtful, although many pieces are attributed to historical figures. The LSJ opens with a letter from "Calixtus" addressed to Diego Gelmírez[57] in Compostela and William, patriarch of Jerusalem.[58] Although the letter is ascribed to Pope Calixtus II, he had died well

---

56. For an English translation, with extensive introduction and notes, see William Melczer, *The Pilgrim's Guide to Santiago de Compostela* (New York: Italica Press, 1993). A critical study of Book V with a facing page Latin / English text is also available: Paula Gerson, Annie Shaver-Crandell, Jeanne E. Krochalis, and Alison Stones, *The Pilgrim's Guide: A Critical Edition* (London: Harvey Miller, 1998).

57. Diego Gelmírez (c. 1069–c. 1140) was bishop of Compostela (c. 1100–1121), and later archbishop (1121–40) until his death. His see was raised to archdiocesan status in 1121 and subsequently to metropolitan status by Pope Calixtus II. The metropolitan status was contested and even lost on a number of occasions. There are several pieces of correspondence between Gelmírez and Pope Calixtus in PL 163. For a detailed biography, see R. A. Fletcher, *Saint James's Catapult: The Life and Times of Diego Gelmírez of Santiago de Compostela* (Oxford: Clarendon Press, 1984); and Anselm Gordon Biggs, *Diego Gelmírez, First Archbishop of Compostela* (Washington DC: Catholic University of America Press, 1949).

58. There are multiple people with the name William to whom this letter might have been directed in the Holy Land. Given the compilation date of the mid–twelfth century, the most likely candidates are the first patriarch who served 1128–30 or William of Messina, who served from 1130–45 (and died in 1185).

before the LSJ was compiled.⁵⁹ On folio 192 within the appendix to the manuscript, the names of Aymeric Picaud and a companion named Giberga are mentioned as having been the one(s) to carry the manuscript to Compostela. Some scholars ascribe to Aymeric Picaud authorship of the entire work, some just of Book V, while others consider him to be only the scribe or the person who delivered the manuscript to Compostela.⁶⁰

Scholars' opinions vary widely about the purpose of the LSJ. Some view it as an exaltation of the saint's cult and propaganda for the pilgrimage route and the aggrandizement of Compostela. Others have pointed to the complex twelfth-century political–religious alliances and relationships on the peninsula, including the pervasive role of the French religious order of Cluny in the establishment of monasteries along the road. Another reading of the text centers on a recurring concern about the Reconquest efforts on the peninsula. This argument is less persuasive as only the miracles 1 (the siege of Zaragoza by the Christians) and 19 (the fall of Coimbra to the Christians) speak directly to events of the Reconquest. Saint James's appearance to Charlemagne and his help in the fall of Pamplona in Book IV, the *Pseudo-Turpin Chronicle,* seem to be a more important

---

59. Pope Calixtus II (1119–24). Before his election as pope, Guy (or Guido) was archbishop of Vienne. A noble by birth and a reformer by inclination, he is probably best known for attempting reconciliation with the Holy Roman emperor and for his role in effecting the Concordat of Worms. His works are contained in PL 163:1073–1414 and consist primarily of 282 letters from him (columns 1093–1338) and six letters to him (columns 1338–60). Among the letters, there are several sent to Cluny and several to Gelmírez; the opening letter of the CC is not among them. There is also other biographical and bibliographical information as well as a discussion of Calixtus relative to the LSJ at columns 1365–68. Among the dubious works at the end of the PL section, there are four sermons and the miracles as recorded by Vincent of Beauvais. For detailed information on Calixtus, see Ulysse Robert, *Bullaire du Pape Calixte II* (Paris: Imprimerie Nationale, 1891; rpt. Hildesheim: G. Olms, 1979) and his *Histoire du pape Calixte II* (Paris: Alphonse Picard, 1891). The collection of bulls contained in the *Bullaire* exceeds 500 letters.

60. See Díaz y Díaz et al., *El Códice Calixtino de la Catedral,* 81–86.

INTRODUCTION

link to Spanish–French relations than to the actual battles between the Moorish and Christian kingdoms on the Iberian Peninsula. The importance of feast days and concern for the proper liturgy provide yet another possible purpose.

THE *CODEX CALIXTINUS* AND SALAMANCA MS 2631

The twelfth-century *Codex Calixtinus* (CC) has apparently been at the Compostela Cathedral since its compilation. It was "discovered" in the cathedral archives in 1879 by Fidel Fita y Colomé during a period of renewed international interest in Santiago de Compostela and the art and architecture of the pilgrimage route.[61] It apparently has never left Compostela.[62] It is made up of 225 folios. There are 184 folios of text for Books I, II, III, and V, plus 29 folios of the Pseudo-Turpin in Book IV, which is numbered separately, plus eleven folios of a miscellany contained in an appendix following Book V which ends on folio 184v. These eleven folios of additional material include liturgical materials, several hymns, five additional miracle tales, and the famous hymn "Dum pater familias." The colophon, found on folio 184v reveals the French monastic

---

61. Sasha Pack, "Revival of the Pilgrimage to Santiago de Compostela: The Politics of Religious, National, and European Patrimony, 1879–1988," *The Journal of Modern History* 82 (June 2010): 335–67 at 355. Fita, with Julien Vinson, published the first Latin edition of the Book V Guide: *Le codex de Saint-Jacques de Compostelle (Liber de miraculis S. Jacobi): Livre IV* (Paris: Maisonneuve, 1882). At that point it was called "Book Four" because the *Pseudo-Turpin* had been removed in the seventeenth century. This was the era of the creation of the castings replica of the Portico de la Gloria for the Victoria and Albert Museum and the initial study of the Compostela Cathedral by José Villa-Amil y Castro, *Descripción histórico-artístico-arqueológica de la Catedral de Santiago* (Lugo: Soto Freire, 1866); as well as Lopez Ferreiro's eleven-volume church history, *Historia de la Santa A.M. Iglesia de Santiago de Compostela* (Santiago: Seminario Conciliar Central, 1898–1910).

62. It did, however, go missing from the Cathedral archives for a year (July 2011–July 2012) when it was stolen by, and later recovered from a disgruntled cathedral employee.

influence on the compilation: "The Church of Rome first took up this codex. It was composed in fact in many places; namely, in Rome, at the shores of Jerusalem, in France, in Italy, in Germany, and in Frisia, and especially at Cluny."

The Salamanca manuscript of the LSJ, known as MS S (Universidad de Salamanca, MS 2631) was copied around 1325 in Compostela and is one of the four complete (long) versions of the LSJ, containing all five books found in the CC.[63] Salamanca MS 2631 has five illuminations, marginal decorations, and decorated capitals; it has a very compact two-column layout.[64]

Twentieth-century Editions and Translations of the *Liber Sancti Jacobi*

In the early 1920s, an American, Walter Muir Whitehill, spent several summers transcribing the Compostela manuscript. The publication of the transcription was a monumental aid to scholars of the medieval pilgrimage and of the stories surrounding it. The transcription process was fraught with problems, and the Spanish Civil War interrupted the work leading to its printing.[65] Despite its errors, some quite serious, it was the only printed version of the entire Latin manuscript until the 1998 publication of *Liber Sancti*

---

63. The other three are MS A (London, BL Add 12213), MS VA (Vatican, BAV Arch. Cap. S. Pietro C. 128), and MS P (Pistoia, Arch. di Stato, Documenti vari 27). Descriptions of these manuscripts as well as page photos may be found in Stones et al., *The Pilgrim's Guide*, 1:109–13, 114–16, 153–68.

64. Díaz y Díaz et al, *El Códice Calixtino de la Catedral* is the best source of information about the different manuscripts and has a thorough listing and discussion of the various complete and partial copies of the LSJ, including a sixteenth-century copy on paper by Juan de Azcona. Appendix 1 (pp. 327–34) contains a succinct and clear chart showing the disposition of the folios of the LSJ as they are found in 12 manuscript copies.

65. Díaz y Díaz, "El *Codice Calixtino*: Volviendo" recounts the story and some of the problems of Whitehill's work (126–28), as does Adalbert Hämel *Uberlieferung und Bedeutung des Liber Sancti Jacobi und des Pseudo-Turpin* (Munich: Bayerischen Akademie der Wissenschaften, 1950), 8–9.

INTRODUCTION

Jacobi: Codex Calixtinus, an edition by Klaus Herbers and Manuel Santos-Noya.[66] A 1951 Spanish translation, revised and corrected in 2004, and revised again in 2014[67] based primarily on the Whitehill transcription has been consulted by many scholars.[68]

Another important boon to scholarly work on the LSJ came in 1993 when, to celebrate the Holy Year, a facsimile edition of the *Codex Calixtinus* appeared.[69] With its publication, scholars everywhere could more readily consult and work with the text of this twelfth-century manuscript in a useful and faithfully reproduced format. More recently, in 2011, another facsimile, this time of the University of Salamanca manuscript 2631, was published under the technical and artistic direction of Juan José García Gil and Pablo Molinero Hernando.[70] While the only complete editions of the entire manuscript are Whitehill's and Herbers', and the only complete translation is Moralejo's, by 2018, based on the work of a group of American editors and translators, the entire codex will be available in English translation.[71]

66. Santiago de Compostela: Xunta de Galicia, 1998.
67. *Liber Sancti Jacobi: Codex Calixtinus,* trans. Abelardo Moralejo, Casimiro Torres, and Julio Feo (Santiago: Consejo Superior de Investigaciones Cientificas, Instituto Padre Sarmiento de Estudios Gallegos, 1951; Rev. ed with new notes, Juan José Moralejo and María José García Blanco, 2004; Rev. ed. María José García Blanco, Santiago de Compostela: Xunta de Galicia, 2014).
68. According to the introduction, only for the difficult passages or obvious errors did the translators try to consult the CC and use it as a basis (xv). They try to indicate this in their footnotes, but it is not always clear where they have relied on other sources. Their translation was also the first attempt to identify citations and sources, but there are enough errors to require a double check of the supplemental information.
69. Madrid: Kaydeda Ed, 1993.
70. Codex Calixtinus *de la Universidad de Salamanca MS. 2631* (Burgos: Siloé, arte y bibliofilia, 2011).
71. All volumes published by Italica Press, (New York): Book V, *The Pilgrim's Guide* by William Melczer in 1993; Book II, *The Miracles of Saint James* (plus the "Veneranda Dies" sermon and introductory letter) by Coffey, Davidson and Dunn in 1996; Book IV, the *Chronicle of Pseudo-Turpin*

The Miracles of Saint James: Book II of the *Liber Sancti Jacobi*

The introductory letter of Pope Calixtus to the entire *Liber Sancti Jacobi* notes that the miracle tales of Book II should be considered important edifying stories: "what is contained in the first two books is quite sufficient for reading at matins. And if all the sermons and miracles of Blessed James that are contained in this book cannot be read in church on his feast days because of their volume, they may at least be read afterwards throughout each week in the refectory."[72] This collection of miracles is quite distinct when compared to other miracle collections.

Although Saint James's cult had been in existence, centered in and around Santiago de Compostela, since about 900 CE, most of the Book II miracles occur between 1100 and 1135, and they represent a rather limited period, albeit a wide geographic distribution. Book II's twenty-two chapters, telling of twenty-five separate miracles represent a paltry number when compared to the more than 200 miracles that Gregory of Tours collected about Martin of Tours, for example.[73] The monk Benedict collected more than 250 miracles attributed to Saint Thomas Becket between 1171 and 1177 at his tomb or around Canterbury.[74]

---

by Kevin Poole in 2014; this present volume which includes an updated translation of Book II and a new translation of Book III, the *Translatio*; and finally, Book I, the sermons and liturgy, to be translated and edited by Coffey and Dunn and published in 2019.

72. Coffey et al., *Miracles*, 5–6.

73. These miracles, collected in four books include 60 that Gregory collected from other sources. The other 127 took place between c. 571 (the first year Gregory was bishop) and 592 and were narrated chronologically. See Raymond Van Dam, *Saints and Their Miracles in Late Antique Gaul* (Princeton: Princeton University Press, 1993) for a study and translation. Saint Martin proves himself to be a thaumaturgic saint in these narrations.

74. Benedicta Ward, *Miracles and the Medieval Mind: Theory, Record and Event, 1000–1215* (Philadelphia: University of Pennsylvania Press, 1982), 90.

INTRODUCTION

As with the entire LSJ, the compiler of the miracles is said to be Pope Calixtus, who explains how and why the miracles recounted in Book II are so diverse geographically: "...while wandering through barbarous lands, I found various writings in various places: some of these miracles in Galicia, others in France, others in Germany, others in Italy, others in Hungary, others in Dacia, others beyond the three seas, and yet others on barbarian shores."[75] He also accounts for the paltry number of miracles: "For if I had written down all the miracles that I had heard about him in the many places and in the accounts of many people, my strength, my supply of parchment, and my hand would have given out long before the stories had run out."[76] Indeed, the twenty-two chapters of miracles contained in Book II do not constitute the entire corpus of the LSJ manuscript's miracles. There are, in addition, several miracles mentioned in its other books: in the introductory letter to the LSJ, the author recounts many miraculous events that occurred to him and the manuscript while he was compiling it[77]; in Book I, chapter 2, the sermon for 24 July, the author recounts five miracles of vengeance that befell people who did not properly celebrate the saint's feast day[78]; in chapter 2 of Book IV (the Pseudo-Turpin) the walls of Pamplona fall before Charlemagne's siege through Saint James's miraculous help[79]; and finally, at the end of the Book V (the Guide), three miracles of vengeance occur to those who did not help pilgrims along their

---

75. Below, 1.
76. Below, 2.
77. Coffey et al., *Miracles*, 3–4.
78. Of these miracles one occurred in Navarre and another in Gascony, which was the scene of another, happier, miracle in Book II; two happened in Besançon, where Master Hubert, author of the Book II, chapter IV miracle was a canon; the last took place in Montpellier. These five miracles were included in the AASS and in Vincent de Beauvais without indication of their location in the sources of the respective works. Later in Book I, chapter XVII the sermon's author gives permission to future writers to record "those miracles he is yet to have performed as long as they have been testified by two or three witnesses" (Coffey et al., *Miracles*, 13).
79. Poole, *Pseudo-Turpin*, 8.

way.[80] The miracle of the castrated pilgrim (17) is also mentioned in the sermon for the Feast of the Miracles (October 3) in Book I and is ascribed to Anselm there, as it is in Book II.

The extreme geographic diversity of Saint James's miracles is explained in the "Veneranda dies" ("A Day to be Honored") sermon: "Why does he perform miracles in places where he does not lie bodily, as he does in Galicia? However if a sense of discretion looks into it, it is quite quickly apparent. For he is always and everywhere at hand, without delay, for helping those at risk and those in tribulation calling to him whether on sea or on land."[81] Only miracle 14 fails to identify the miracle site in any way. Most of the miracles takes place along the pilgrimage route either going to or returning from either Compostela (2–6, 16–19, 21–22) or Jerusalem (the "sea" miracles, 7–10). Of the seven miracles that occur to non-pilgrims (1, 11–15, 20), at least one recipient vows to make a pilgrimage to Compostela. In 13, the recipient is called "pilgrim of Saint James," implying he has been a pilgrim previously, and in 12 an ailing man asks for a shell from a Compostela pilgrimage to save him.

The broad geographic distribution of the miracles in this collection is in direct contrast to another set of miracles associated with Saint James, those wrought by the relic of his hand housed in Reading Abbey in England.[82] This collection of twenty-eight miracles, datable between 1127 and 1189, compares favorably in number and chronology with the miracles of the LSJ, but twenty-seven of these miracles occur only when the recipient is either in the presence of the relic or drinks or washes in the water into which the hand has been dipped.[83] Twenty-six of the Reading relic

---

80. Book V, chapter XI. One miracle deals with fire, two with bread. See Melczer, *Pilgrim's Guide*, 132–33.

81. Coffey et al., *Miracles*, 21.

82. See Brian Kemp, "The Miracles of the Hand of St. James," *Berkshire Archaeological Journal* 65 (1970): 1–19, for an English translation of these miracles.

83. Miracle 25 of this collection relates how Matthew, count of Boulogne stormed the castle of Driencourt on Saint James's day, against the wishes

INTRODUCTION

miracles are cures from various maladies,[84] whereas in the LSJ Book II collection only three of the twenty-two can properly be called miracles of healing (9, 12, 21), and only the last of these occurs at the shrine in Compostela.

THE AUTHORS OF THE MIRACLES

Unlike reports of miracles wrought by a particular relic at a specific saint's shrine — like Saint James's hand relic at Reading — the LSJ compilation is both more panoramic and more spiritual: "For when the stories of the saints are told by experts, the hearts of listeners are moved piously toward the sweetness and love of the heavenly realm."[85] The compiler of the LSJ miracles was not just a parochial priest or scribe who recorded thaumaturgic healings, but someone who has created a compendium of great miracles — resurrections, astonishing travels, extraordinary escapes, inexplicable protection against overwhelming odds — which are affirmed and confirmed by reliable witnesses: "I have written down…only those that I have judged to be true, based on the truest assertions of the most truthful people."[86] This opening implies that Pope Calixtus collected these reports of miracles from writings found across Europe and "beyond the three seas."[87]

Calixtus is directly credited with recording eighteen of the twenty-two miracles: "A story [miracle] of Saint James written down by his Excellency Pope Calixtus" (1, 3, 5–15, 18–22). Four

---

of King Henry III. During the battle, the count was hit by a small arrow under his kneecap and eventually died a painful death, "in this way a fitting death punished the shameful audacity of his arrogance." No miracle occurs in this tale, and Kemp (17) speculates that it is included to show an act of divine vengeance, as Matthew had previously sworn fealty to Henry in the presence of the relic and had broken this oath and was in rebellion against him.

84. Kemp, 4.
85. Below, 1.
86. Below, 2.
87. Below, 1–2.

miracles are attributed to someone other than Calixtus: 2: Venerable Bede (673–735); 4: Master Hubert, canon of the Church of Mary Magdalene at Besançon; and 16–17: Saint Anselm, archbishop of Canterbury. Calixtus does not give any indication of the source of the miracles. The attributions of these four chapters to three authors other than Calixtus are of varying accuracy.

Although Miracle 2 is ascribed to Bede internal evidence contradicts this assertion. The chapter begins "During the time of Blessed Teodomiro, bishop of Compostela"; Bede (673–735) lived a century before Bishop Teodomiro (c. 819–47) The miracle tale is similar to one told in the *Vita sancti Aegidii* (*Life of Saint Gilles,* 10th c) in which a king "Carolus" — possibly Charles Martel (686–741) or Charles the Bald (823–77) but traditionally assumed to be Charlemagne (742–814) — seeks out the abbot to ask forgiveness for a sin so terrible he cannot name it. While Saint Gilles is performing mass (and Charles is praying) an angel delivers a scroll with the unspeakable sin written down. The scroll also gives assurance that the sin will be forgiven through the intercession of Saint Gilles, with penance, and through the future avoidance of such a sin.

Hubert is named as the recorder of the chapter 4 miracle. A reference to an Humbertus, archbishop of Besançon, appears in a letter dated 1155 in the *Patrologia latina* (PL)[88]; later Vincent of Beauvais attributes this miracle to Hubertus Sibuntinus; and Voragine attributes it to Ubertus Bysuntinus.[89] No written text or miracle collection by Hubert survives outside the example in the LSJ.

The recognized work of Anselm (c. 1033–1109) does not include a miracle collection. R.W. Southern puts forward that a *Miracula*

---

88. There is also a copy of a letter sent by him that forms chapter 90 of the *Porbationes* appendix to the *De illustri genere Sancti Bernardi* (PL 185:1465). It begins "Humbertus, by the grace of God archbishop of Besançon...set down at Besançon in the year 1155, in the second indiction."

89. Johann Georg Theodor Graesse, trans., *Jacobi a Voragine Legenda Aurea: Vulgo Historia Lombardica Dicta* (Osnabrück: Otto Zeller, 1969), 426; in his later translation Ryan, *Golden Legend,* II: 6, ascribes the miracle to Hubert of Besançon.

INTRODUCTION

composed by Anselm's secretary Alexander is a report of tales that Anselm had recited.[90] Miracles 16 and 17 of the LSJ's Book II repeat, at times verbatim, the first two miracles of this *Miracula*; 18, although attributed to Calixtus, is actually the third miracle of this Alexander collection.[91] Although 18 is not attributed to Anselm, the provenance of these three miracles seems to confirm Southern's proposal that Alexander's *Miracula* were considered to be Anselm's.

CHRONOLOGY AND DATES OF THE MIRACLES

The opening to the first chapter proclaims that the tales will occur in "properly accounted place," but this does not necessarily mean in straightforward, chronological order. The earliest miracle in this collection is 2 (c. 830). The latest year in which a miracle was explicitly said to have occurred is 1135 (13). Of the twenty-two chapters, fifteen are specifically dated in the opening lines, with only three appearing out of order (3, 18, and 22).

While the dated chapters are not strictly chronological, they appear in an explicable order. Miracles 1–3 establish Saint James's patronage, reputation, and power. Miracle 1 confirms a relationship between Saint James and the Spanish monarchy when he frees Christian soldiers taken captive in their skirmish against Moslem-held Zaragoza. This miracle is related by one of the soldiers within the cathedral on December 30, the feast of the *Translatio*. The next chapter confirms the supremacy of the see of Compostela. An Italian man sent to Compostela, rather than to Rome, to confess his unspeakable sin substantiates Bishop Teodomiro's role as intercessor of Saint James. This miracle occurs on July 25, the feast day of his Passion, introducing his second major observance in the liturgical year. Finally, Miracle 3 provides proof of Saint James's great spiritual dominion and his supremacy over other saints (most notably over

---

90. R.W. Southern, and F. S. Schmitt, eds., *Memorials of St. Anselm*, (London: The British Academy and Oxford University Press, 1969) 1–2.
91. For a Latin edition of these three miracles, see Southern and Schmitt, *Memorials*, 196–209.

MIRACLES AND TRANSLATIO OF SAINT JAMES

Chronology of Dated Miracles

Chapter	Date
4	1080
5	1090
6	1100
22*	1100
7	1101
8	1102
9	1103
10	1104
11	1105
12	1106
14	1107
3*	1108†
15	1110
3*	1123‡
13*	1135

* Chronological order does not follow chapter order.
† First miracle, first pilgrimage.
‡ Second miracle, second pilgrimage.

Saint Martin) as it tells of two miracles: the miraculous pregnancy and birth of a son to a barren woman and, some years later, the resurrection of that same son who dies while on pilgrimage to Compostela. After these three introductory chapters, the following eleven miracles (4–15) occur in chronological order only breaking down with the placement of Miracle 13, which should be the last miracle in Book II. Although its heading says that it is written down by Calixtus (d. 1124), its internal date (1135) places it nine years after Calixtus's death.

There is a marked change in dating of the miracles beginning with Miracle 16. None of them — with the exception of Miracle

INTRODUCTION

22 — begins with a specific date. Most of them may be roughly dated through internal references or by external events:

Undated or Internally Dated Miracles

Chapter	Date	Internal Reference
2	c. 830	"in the time of Teodomiro, bishop of Compostela"
1	c. 1093 / pre–1118 (fall of Zaragoza to Christians)	"at the time of Alfonso, king over the regions of Spain" [Alfonso VI of Castille and Leon 1065–1109] "A certain count named Ermengotus" [Count of Urgel, Ermengol IV (1065–92) or V (1092–1102)]
16	post–1097	Girinus Calvus (living c. 1080) [Anselm's first visit to Lyon]
17	post–1097 / pre–1109	"Saint Hugh, (d. 1109) the most reverend abbot of Cluny, along with many others saw this man...."
18	"not long ago" / post–1097	[Anselm's first visit to Lyon]
19	post–1064 (fall of Coimbra)	"I will open the gates of the city of Coimbra with these keys.... At the third hour tomorrow I will hand over the city, which has been held under siege for seven years by King Ferdinand, to the power of the Christians who will then have entered there."
20	"still in our own times"	William III of Forcalquier (d. 1129), the son of Ermengol IV of Urgel, and William IV of Forcalquier (1130–1209), son of Bertrand II of Forcalquier
21	"in our time"	
22		"I met this man myself between Estella and Logroño"

LI

As noted above, Miracles 16, 17, and 18 are copied from the *Miracula* composed by Anselm's secretary Alexander. Miracles 16 and 17 are connected to the diocese of Lyon and to Saint Hugh, abbot of Cluny (d. 1109). While traveling to Rome, Anselm met Hugh at Lyon during the winter of 1097–98. Anselm perhaps learned of these miracles during this visit or during a second visit in 1103. Since Miracle 18 occurs at Compostela to a count of Saint-Gilles, it is probably not attributable to Anselm, but instead serves as a transition to the last four chapters, which are not only attributed to Calixtus, but mimic the style of the first chapter using oral markers in the first person plural: "we will tell straightforwardly a certain miracle that we heard" (Miracle 1); "not long ago" (18); "it is known to everyone" (19); "over the course of much time passing by and still in our own times" (20); "In our time" (21); "I met this man myself between Estella and Logroño" (22). If we consider "our time" to be "Calixtus's time," the period 1065–1124 — Calixtus being pope from 1119 to 1124 — would fit well within the chronology of the miracles.

Just as the miracles in the opening chapters of Book II seem to have been carefully chosen to frame the power and importance of Saint James and of his relationship with ecclesiastical and political leaders, the final miracle (22) appears to sum up his peripatetic nature and the extension of his supremacy as it relates multiple miracles that take place in a variety of places across the Mediterranean many years apart. A merchant from Barcelona makes a pilgrimage to Compostela in 1100 to ask Saint James that he be freed from his enemies should he be made captive. During his travels he is captured and bought and sold thirteen times in cities throughout the Mediterranean and as far away as India. The thirteenth time he prays for freedom, Saint James appears to tell him to pray for his soul, not just his body. The man is liberated from his chains but carries them with him when he returns to Compostela, since they continue to save him from both man and beast. Many years would have passed between the initial prayer and the man's second pilgrimage to Compostela, allowing this theoretically to be the latest miracle of the collection, belying its initial 1100 date. As the only miracle that "Calixtus" claims to witness — "I met this man myself" — it is a fitting final chapter of Book II.

Despite inconsistencies in dating style, chronological order, and attribution, the compiler consistently used the formulaic phrase: *A Domino factum est et mirabile in occulis nostris* ("This was accomplished by the Lord and it is miraculous in our eyes"),[92] intended to give papal weight and importance to the account. The only exceptions occur in Miracles 16–18 — the miracles copied from Anselm. In eleven chapters this phrase appears at the end of the miracle immediately prior to a prayer-like closure ("May glory and honor be to the King of kings for ever and ever. Amen"). In eight chapters the phrase is followed by an explanation of the significance of the tale (2, 3, and 6), an exhortation to follow the lesson of the tale (4 and 22), or even an additional resolution to the tale (5, 8, and 9). The formulaic closing of each miracle tale, with or without these mini-sermons, gives a sense that these tales belong to an oral tradition. The absence of this formulaic closing, however, in 16 and 17 (ascribed to Anselm) and 18 (ascribed to Calixtus, but clearly from the same source as 16 and 17) provides additional evidence that these three miracles were intercalated from a written source.

Five additional miracles, not included in the Salamanca manuscript, are included after the colophon of Book V in the CC. Only the first is in prose and follows the literary style of the Book II miracles. It was reportedly written by Alberic (1080–1148), abbot of Vezeley and bishop of Ostia, about a starving pilgrim for whom bread appears twice daily on his return trip from Compostela in 1139. This is the latest of the miracles with a recorded date in the CC manuscript.[93]

---

92. See Ps 117:23, Mt 21:42, Mk 12:11.
93. We have included this miracle separately at the end of the Book II in this translation.

Geographic and Regional Distribution of the Miracles

Miracle 22 confirms that there is no limit to where Saint James may work his miracles as he frees the captive in thirteen locations around the Mediterranean. Six other chapters occur in other specific places along the traditional Camino de Santiago. Nine of the miracles occur either along the route — not in a specific town or in multiple towns — or within the basilica in Compostela to French or German pilgrims. Four miracles occur on the Mediterranean to pilgrims either going to or returning from Jerusalem. Saint James does not limit his work to his shrine, nor to people of any specific region, although twelve of twenty-two miracle recipients are French and four are Italian. In only two are the recipients clearly residents or natives of the Iberian Peninsula: the twenty soldiers in the first miracle were probably from Urgel (Lérida) and the Barcelona merchant of the last miracle, giving symmetry to the collection. The origin of five miracle recipients is not mentioned. Since four of these are on the Mediterranean when they receive the saint's help — pilgrims to or from the Holy Land — they could be from anywhere.

Aspects of Saint James in the Miracles

Today, due to the popularity of pilgrimage along the many Caminos to Compostela, Saint James is most widely known in his appearance as a pilgrim (Fig. 3). This was not always the case. From a very early date, the cult of Saint James in Spain developed three distinct iconographies: as "Matamoros" (Moorslayer), as pilgrim, and as generic saintly apostle.[94] The LSJ in general, features all three representations. His most famous depiction is included in chapter 1 of

---

94. For a detailed analysis of the development of the dual nature of Saint James's pilgrim versus military aspect and history, see Márquez Villanueva, *Santiago: Trayectoria* and Javier Domínguez García, *Memorias del futuro: Ideología y ficción en el símbolo de Santiago Apóstol* (Madrid: Iberoamericana, 2008).

INTRODUCTION

the LSJ Book IV (the Pseudo-Turpin) where he appeared in a dream to Charlemagne as "a knight of splendid appearance"[95] encouraging the king's military incursion into Spain, an event that occurred in 778. Later, in chapter 2 of Book IV, through Charlemagne's prayers to Saint James, the walls to Pamplona crumble, engendering Charlemagne's grateful pilgrimage to the saint's tomb in Compostela, despite the fact that it had yet to be rediscovered. This dichotomy of aspect — intercessor or warrior — is seen throughout the miracles of Book II, but Saint James is never portrayed in the full image of "Matamoros" — astride his white charger and brandishing his sword — although he does appear on horseback in Miracle 4.

Saint James appears physically in sixteen of the twenty-two chapters of Book II. In most of these he is simply introduced as "the (glorious) apostle," or the narrator merely announces that he appeared without further description. In several chapters his actions are described: "he held me up with his hands" (5); "taking him by the hand, brought him back safely to the ship" (7); or "Saint James had guided him...by holding his head with his hand" (10). The two longest descriptions are found in Miracle 9: "His face appeared in this way: decent, and, if you will, elegant, and of such a type as none of them had occasion to see either before or after"[96]; and in 17: "James appeared to me to be young with a handsome face, lean and of that moderate color which people call brown."[97] In 20 not only does Saint James appear, but the whole house is "filled with a most serene light and with such a fragrance that all the soldiers and all the others who were there thought that they had been transported to the delight of paradise."[98] This is the only instance of an aroma of any sort in the Miracles.

Although in nine chapters the miracle recipients are soldiers, Saint James does not grant any of them success on the battlefield — nor did they request it — he saves them personally from death,

---

95. Poole, *Pseudo-Turpin*, 5.
96. Below, 33.
97. Below, 49.
98. Below, 58.

captivity, or prison. There is no strong correlation between Saint James's appearance as a warrior and the recipients being soldiers. In 4, when helping the loyal soldier to transport a dead pilgrim, he came "sitting on a horse like a soldier" and is called "the soldier of God." James miraculously transports both the dead man and the soldier to Compostela in one night on his horse.[99] Miracle 15 describes his actions in military fashion, but he is not described as a knight: "James freed the soldier from his pursuing enemies by protecting him with his shield."[100] Miracle 16 combines both the pilgrims' symbols of staff and satchel with the military symbols of lance and shield. In this story, a soldier–pilgrim first helps a female pilgrim by carrying her satchel and then an ill beggar by placing the poor man on his own horse and walking alongside using the beggar's staff. Later, when the soldier–pilgrim is at the point of death, Saint James appears to fight for his soul: "holding in his left hand the woman's little sack…in his right hand he was holding the beggar's staff.… He held the staff as a lance and the little sack as a shield."[101]

In 19 Saint James is rendered in his most warlike image in the Miracles: "adorned in the whitest clothing, bearing military arms, surpassing the rays of Titan, as if transformed into a soldier and also holding two keys in his hand."[102] He then utters his longest speech of any in the Miracles: "Stephen, servant of God, you who ordered me to be called not a soldier but a fisherman, I am appearing to you in this fashion, so that you no longer doubt that I am a fighter for God and His champion, that I precede the Christians in the fight against the Saracens, and that I arise a victor for them.… So that you might believe this, I will open the gates of the city of Coimbra with these keys that I am holding in my hand.… I will hand over the city, which has been held under siege for seven years by King

99. Below, 20.
100. Below, 40.
101. Below, 43; this sentence has been corrected by a new reading of the manuscript from our previous edition (Coffey, et al. *Miracles,* 83). This story evokes Mt 25:40.
102. Below, 56.

INTRODUCTION

Ferdinand, to the power of the Christians."[103] James promises to free Coimbra from Moslem control, not with a flaming sword, but with the keys to the city. The miracle here is not a description of the battle, but the confidence of James's prediction of the success of the Christians with his help. Saint James shows his "Son of Thunder" boldness in the fight for Christian control of the peninsula.

Feast Days and the Miracles

According to the introductory letter to the LSJ, the miracles of Book II are authentic and of sufficient authority that they be read in church, at matins or at mass. They should be read "at least on the day on which his feast occurred."[104] The author carefully arranged the stories so that the two major feast days associated with Saint James are observed in the first two miracle tales. In Miracle 1 the pilgrim reaches Compostela for the feast of the *Translatio* on December 30 (the third calends of January). The "Veneranda dies" sermon names this date as the double feast of both Saint James's calling to be an apostle as well as his *translation*.[105] The pilgrim in Miracle 2 reaches the apostle's tomb for the feast of his Passion or martyrdom on July 25, (the eighth calends of August). The only other mention in Book II of these feasts occurs in Miracle 20, when a soldier, grateful for rescue from execution and captivity, traveled and "came immediately to the saint's body and church on the feast of his *translation*."[106] Chapter 3 of the *Translatio* describes these feasts in greater detail.

---

103. Below, 56.
104. Coffey et al., *Miracles*, 6.
105. "A double solemn feast is celebrated by the faithful today: namely, the choosing of this very Saint James, or how he was chosen by the Lord into the apostolic order along with John, Peter and Andrew near the shores of Galilee; and his *translation*, that is to say, how his most precious body was moved from Jerusalem to the city of Compostela." Coffey et al., *Miracles*, 8.
106. Below, 58.

In addition to these two major feasts, there is a third, less commonly known or celebrated, the Feast of the Miracles. The miracle of the resuscitated pilgrim (17) — or the castrated pilgrim as it is more commonly known today — concludes with an exhortation to celebrate this and other miracles by Saint James on October 3: "And we give the order to all that every year on the fifth day of the nones of October a feast should be celebrated in all churches with worthy ceremony for this miracle and for the other miracles of Saint James."[107] Although this exhortation appears as a marginal note in the CC, it is fully incorporated into the Salamanca text. It was not simply an afterthought, as this feast day is mentioned again in Books I (the Liturgy) and III (the *Translatio*), both times specifically related to Miracle 17. In Book I, chapter 28, an introduction to the Mass for October 3: "Pope Calixtus about the Feast of the Miracles of Saint James that is celebrated on the fifth nones of October," describes several miracles:

> For the fifth of the nones of October [October 3], Anselm of Canterbury in past times ordered that one celebrate a feast for the miracles of Saint James; for how he, with the help of the Virgin Mary, raised from the dead a man who had committed suicide at the instigation of the devil; for how he tore away twenty men from the captivity of the Moors through the powerful force of God; for how he transported a dead man on the twelve-day trip from the Port of Cize to the city of Compostela in one night in order to bury him; and for the other miracles that he performed; and we confirm this very order.[108]

All three miracles in this introduction appear in Book II (17, 1 and 4 respectively). The third chapter of the *Translatio* reiterates this information: "Saint Anselm previously ordered the Feast of the Miracles of Saint James to be celebrated on the fifth nones of October, as it celebrates how the holy apostle raised from the dead a man who, on the advice of the devil, had killed himself and how the apostle

---

107. Below, 51.
108. Translated from Book I, fol. 128r of the CC.

INTRODUCTION

performed other miracles, and we affirm this order."[109] While the shocking self-castration of the young pilgrim grabs our attention and has given fame to the miracle, clearly for a medieval audience its importance was the ability of Saint James to wrest from the devil the young man's soul and bring him back to life. Saint James was also said to have restored to life another young boy who died of illness while on pilgrimage to Compostela (3); this chapter ended with a lengthy explanation of the greatness of saints who bring the dead back to life, making Saint James greater even than Saint Martin.[110]

The miracle stories of Book II illustrate the sanctity and the power of Saint James and present proof that Saint James is living with God and is able to help any who earnestly request his help. While his authority has no geographic limitations, clearly his shrine in Compostela is key to receiving his divine intervention. But of all the miracles associated with Saint James, the greatest is how he came to be buried in the farthest reaches of the Iberian Peninsula — the story of his *Translatio*.

THE *TRANSLATIO* OF SAINT JAMES: BOOK III OF THE *LIBER SANCTI JACOBI*

The Latin term *translatio* has clearly entered common English vocabulary as "translation" — meaning the rendering of something into another language. The historical use of *translatio* has not spread much beyond the Church, where it refers specifically to the transfer of a saint's remains (body or part thereof) from its initial resting place to another, as well as to the narrations that describe these transfers. Unlike a collection of miracle tales, there is no uniform or standard narrative for describing this transfer, miraculous or not. Various types of hagiographical works may report a *translatio* as a simple statement, or may, as we see in Book III of the CC, develop a long and complex account.

---

109. Below, 92.
110. Saint Martin of Tours (316–97). See p. 16, n. 49.

Patrick Geary, in his work *Furta Sacra*, points out that *translationes* were often composed long after the transfer took place, perhaps to explain the acquisition of, or establish a claim to, a specific relic. During the ninth to eleventh centuries, "[the] development of the *translation* as a substantial hagiographic subgenre was the result of...the growing importance of liturgical celebration of the anniversaries of *translations*— celebrations which required new liturgical readings."[111] In the hagiographical writings about Saint James, we see this evolution from brief references in martyrologies to the expanded *vitae* of early Eastern texts such as the pseudo-Abdias, to their inclusion in the Mozarabic liturgy, to the development of the *Pasionario Hispánico* as well as the early *Letter of Pope Saint Leo*. By the time the CC was assembled in the mid-twelfth century, the stories of the *Translatio* of Saint James existed in many documents, traditions, formats, and recensions.

The *Translatio* in Book III of the CC is the shortest but most complex of the five books making up the CC (fols. 156r–162r), as it gathers elements from a variety of sources and weaves them together into a seemingly disjointed prologue and four chapters. After the list of contents, the long prologue, ostensibly written by Pope Saint Calixtus, sets forth the purpose for including this book: "I did not want to leave out the *Translatio* of Saint James from our codex, as such wonders and treasures are written down in it to the honor of our Lord Jesus Christ and of the apostle...." [112] These "wonders and treasures" confirm the sanctity of Saint James's tomb and relics at Compostela, but they do not provide a history of the miraculous discovery of the physical site, nor in fact, does any part of the CC include the *inventio* or discovery story of the tomb by the hermit Pelayo.

Unlike the Book II miracles, the story of the *Translatio* was not required, nor even suggested as liturgical or refectory reading. Book

---

111. Patrick J. Geary, *Furta Sacra: Thefts of Relics in the Central Middle Ages* (Princeton: Princeton University Press, rev. ed. 1990), 11.
112. Below, 70.

INTRODUCTION

III supports December 30 as a double feast day,[113] and it also explains why the feast of James's Passion (July 25) does not occur during March or April, as expected, since he was beheaded during Passover.

At the time of its inclusion in the LSJ, the story of the *translation* of Saint James's body from Jerusalem — the site of his beheading — to Iria Flavia — where his boat reached shore — was not a single, straightforward narrative, as mentioned multiple times in the LSJ itself. In Book I, the chapter 17 sermon for the December 30 Feast of the *Translation* ("Veneranda dies"), includes not only its own account of the transfer of the body but also an enumeration of all of the false reports about it, for example, the story that the body sailed across the seas in a stone boat. The refutation of some versions of the *Translatio* suggests that these other stories were in circulation and common enough to warrant attention.[114]

Although Book III is called "the" *Translatio* of Saint James, the story of the transfer of his body from Jerusalem to Galicia is told three separate times in Book III, first in the prologue, in a slightly garbled manner with a passing mention of the transport of his body, but with specific information about his disciples from the *Passio Iacobi*; once in the incorporation and conflation of the stories of the Seven Apostolic Men from the *Pasionario Hispánico* in chapter 1 (called the *translatio magna*, the "great *translation*"); and yet again in the letter ostensibly written by "Pope Saint Leo" in chapter 2.

Book III evokes the four Gospels of the New Testament. Although each chapter speaks of the same topic — the Passion and

---

113. "A double solemn feast is celebrated by the faithful today: namely, the Choosing of this very Saint James, or how he was chosen by the Lord into the apostolic order along with John, Peter and Andrew near the shores of Galilee; and his *translation,* [f.74v] that is to say, how his most precious body was moved from Jerusalem to the city of Compostela." Translated from fols. 73r–74v of the CC. A double feast day does not mean that two separate events in the life of a Saint are being celebrated on a specific date, which one might expect since the December feast is said to celebrate the *translatio* and calling (*vocatio*) of Saint James, but refers to repeated or doubled elements of the day's liturgy.

114. See Appendix 8.

Translation of Saint James — each offers a different perspective and is included for a different purpose. Like the Synoptic Gospels — Matthew, Mark, Luke — the prologue and chapters 1 and 2 have many similarities, while chapters 3 and 4 — like John — are distinct in their purpose and scope. The prologue summarizes some parts of chapters 1, 2, and 3, but also supplies information not found in the other chapters. Some wording in chapters 1 and 2 is nearly identical, and they share elements within their stories, but chapter 1 provides greater detail and more specific information about the events leading to the construction of Saint James's tomb, and it also creates a firm link to Saint James's preaching in Galicia. Chapter 3 says little about Saint James's martyrdom and the physical *translation* of his body; it clarifies the liturgical issues surrounding the dates of Saint James's three feast days that celebrated not only his *Translation*, but also his Passion and his Miracles. It concludes with a long and detailed description of the pageantry and the magnificence of the clothing and accoutrements of Emperor Alfonso and his court in the celebration of the Feast of the *Translation*. Chapter 4, "Concerning the Trumpets of Saint James," is a very short, very specific, and very curious one-paragraph conclusion to the book, which has no relationship to any aspect of James's preaching, Passion, or passage from Jerusalem to Galicia.

The prologue, which is not listed in the chapter incipits at the beginning of Book III, is attributed to Pope Calixtus and is written in clear, straightforward Latin, using the first person singular, as is chapter 2, known as the *Letter of Pope Saint Leo*,[115] the stated source of the *Translatio* story: "these things in no way differ from the letter that bears the title of Saint Leo."[116] The compiler of the *Translatio*, however, was forced to grapple with and make sense of multiple sources, legends, tales, and manuscripts. Immediately after associating the *Translatio* with the *Letter of Pope Saint Leo*,

---

115. The clarity of the Latin of the prologue and chapter II is in stark contrast to that of chapter I, which is so dense and convoluted that it might be called the "Rubik's cube" of medieval Latin.

116. Below, 70.

INTRODUCTION

the author–compiler introduces Hermogenes and Philetus,[117] who are only named in the prologue and designated as bishop and archdeacon respectively among Saint James's disciples, roles which are not commonly assigned to them in earlier works. In the prologue, the number of disciples and the time and place of their "Calling" is bewildering, but the compiler has tried to reconcile this information. The prologue mentions "twelve special ones"[118] — three chosen in Jerusalem (perhaps implying Hermogenes, Philetus, and Josias) and nine in Galicia "while he still lived there"[119] — but of these nine, seven traveled with James to Jerusalem[120] and then carried his body back after his martyrdom, while the other two remained behind to preach. After Saint James was buried, seven of them went to Rome to be ordained by Peter and Paul and then returned to Spain. These seven, along with the places of their preaching, are then listed with names taken directly from the *Pasionario Hispánico*, concluding with the names of the last two — Athanasius and Theodorus — left behind to preach and ultimately buried alongside their teacher. With this explanation, the compiler has managed to account for all the followers, implicit or explicit, in all of the accounts that follow.

The prologue concludes with a contemporary miracle ("and happens in our time") told in a style similar to the miracles of

---

117. These two characters come, not from the letter, but from the *Pseudo Abdias*, *Passio Iacobi*, and *Pasionario Hispánico* traditions. See above, XXVII–XXVIII, XXXV–XXXVI.

118. A specific number is not given in any of the *Translatio* chapters. Chapter 1 names nine followers from the Iberian Peninsula including two who remained in Spain as "attendants" to the body; chapter 2 names Josias as a co-martyr and Theodore and Athanasius as two followers who kept vigil at James's tomb. Twelve seems the logical choice, as it was the number of Jesus's apostles.

119. Below, 71. Whether Saint James actually preached in Spain after Pentecost or whether he stayed in Jerusalem is resolved in all versions of the *Translatio* in the CC, clearly stating that James had traveled and spread the Gospel there.

120. This is in contrast to the report in chapter 1 that implies that James returned alone to Jerusalem.

Book II, in which "a certain cleric, who is known to me" pays for a copy of the book of the *Translatio* and several miracles to be made for him. Later while sitting in the basilica reading his copy, the twenty coins he had paid for it miraculously are returned to him. The miracle tale helps to integrate this book into the larger scope of the LSJ: by rewarding the cleric who has purchased a copy of this *Translatio*, Saint James shows not only his love and generosity, but also confirms that he approves of the story it tells.

Chapters 1 and 2 of Book III both narrate the same basic story: James in Jerusalem at the time of Passover is apprehended by Herod and beheaded. His disciples gather his body and steal it away to Joppa where a boat appears, outfitted for their needs. They sail across the Mediterranean and come ashore in Iria. (Fig. 4) After some trials they find a small pagan structure, destroy the idol within it, and rebuild it into the tomb for Saint James. Two attendants remain with his body until they too die and are buried at his side. Although nearly identical, each chapter has a distinct focus. Chapter 1 focuses on James as a favored apostle of Christ and fashions parallels between James's and Christ's life and passion. Its planting and harvesting imagery recalls the Parable of the Sower (Mt 13:1–9, 18–23) and the Parable of the Wheat and the Tare (Mt 13:24–30). The Sadducees and the Pharisees challenge James about his belief in Christ, and in their anger they give James over to Herod, who sentences him to death. From that point the narrative expands into the fanciful story of the Queen Lupa (Luparia): the wild cattle made tame, the dragon on the mountain, and the multiple miraculous events that occur before the disciples are allowed to consecrate the small shrine that Luparia finally gives them where they inter Saint James. The prologue's author may have implied that the *Translatio* story was the same as the *Letter of Pope Saint Leo*, but this chapter offers a much more fantastic, more expressly Spanish version, incorporating elements from the *Pasionario Hispánico* through the appropriation of the lives of Saint Torquatus and his followers as the named disciples of Saint James in Spain.

The heading of chapter 2 clearly states that it is the *Letter of Pope Saint Leo*, and it opens by addressing the "dearest rectors of

INTRODUCTION

all of Christendom" in order to tell them about the transfer of Saint James's body to Galicia. Half the length of chapter 1, this recounting of the miraculous journey is more reverent, with the disciples rejoicing and singing Psalms of thanksgiving for their safe passage. There are no evil kings, no devious women, no wild beasts to overcome; the disciples carry the body to an estate, "Liberum Donum," where they appropriate and rebuild a deserted crypt into a small church. Two faithful followers, Theodore and Athanasius, live out their lives caring for the sepulcher and are buried alongside Saint James at their death. This rendering of the *Translatio*, while not as colorful as chapter 1, does not contradict or differ from it to any great degree.

Chapter 3, however, takes an abrupt turn from James's *Translatio* story, opening instead with a discussion of Peter's imprisonment by Herod. This clarifies exactly when James's martyrdom took place and explains the liturgical issues surrounding the celebration of Saint James's Passion (and *Translatio*) in conjunction with or in apposition to other more important (i.e. higher-ranking) feast days. The author tells of James's arrest, trial, and condemnation, adding a new detail — that James was led outside the city in chains to be killed — couching all of it in Christ-like terms. At this point, the author refers to Saint Jerome's authority and asserts that Jerome (347–420) instructed that Saint James's Passion should be celebrated on July 25 (eighth calends of August), and that later Pope Saint Alexander (c.106–115) confirmed that date when he instituted the Feast of Peter's Chains on August first (calends of August). What follows is a justification for moving Saint James's feast day (as well as Saint Peter's) from Passover (March or April) when it would interfere with Lent, Easter, or the Annunciation of the Virgin, to another point in the liturgical calendar. The rationale for choosing December 30, rather than any other date, is to account for the time between the landing of the boat carrying James's body and the preparation of his tomb: "And so on the eighth calends of April, he suffered; and on the third calends of January he was carried from Iria to Compostela, and brought to the sepulcher. Procuring the material and doing the work on his sepulcher lasted from the month of August up to January."[121] This explanation provides ecclesiastical authority for celebrating the feast of his *Translation* on December 30, the date of the actual transfer of his remains to Compostela, as a separate feast from his Passion on July 25.

Next the author turns to validating the importance of the feast of the *Translation* to the people of Galicia through the political authority of King Alfonso, who shows his respect for the twelve apostles by offering twelve silver and twelve gold coins on the altar, as well as by providing food and drink for his soldiers and for the poor alike. The sumptuous attire of all of those attending, "famous people, governors, nobles, domestic and foreign counts...choirs of venerable women"[122] is described at length and in great detail. And then the chapter ends, abruptly. The account is written in a formal style fitting the regal nature of the feast with its noble participants. The nobility of the style is bolstered by the cataloguing of the richness of the materials described: furs, jewelry, and sumptuous clothing are listed in great detail in a crescendo-like ending to the chapter.

The last chapter (4) of the *Translatio* with the odd heading, "Concerning the Trumpets of Saint James," describes shells, but not the scallop shells (*pecten maximus*) found on Galicia's shores and insignia of pilgrims to Compostela, but conch shells (of a sea snail), often called shell trumpets. The chapter is only one sentence long and were the rubric for Book III not clearly placed directly below it, one would think that subsequent folios of the CC might have been lost. It is possible that the chapter was truncated abruptly to make room for the illustration, which takes up the bottom third of the folio, showing Saint James appearing to Charlemagne and pointing to the Milky Way, his way of the stars, the opening illustration of the Pseudo-Turpin.

---

121. Below, 91–92.
122. Below, 95.

INTRODUCTION

NOTES ON THE TRANSLATION

The *Codex Calixtinus* (CC) served as the base text for this translation. In addition, the CC text was compared word for word with University of Salamanca MS 2631 (S), which revealed an apparent dependency of MS S on MS CC in almost all cases. There were superior readings at times in Salamanca: *basilica* instead of *baselica, oblita* instead of *obutet, antequam* instead of *antique, funditus* instead of *fundit*; however, these and others fall into a category of easily corrected scribal errors. In addition, a passage of some twenty words that was marginal on folio 152v of the CC was copied into the main text of S. While not proof that S was a copy of CC, in conjunction with the corrections and the overall superiority of the readings of the CC, it is a good indication. Generally the CC was used as the authoritative text, and it was given preference in the translation where a distinction was required. Folio numbers for the CC are provided in brackets within the text.

There are relatively few peculiarities in the language of the CC or of the Salamanca manuscript, apart from a rather capricious use of *h*, both adding to it to words that do not have it, as with *hopus* for *opus* and dropping it from words that have it, as with *exalavit* for *exhalavit*. The text of chapter 3 of the *Translatio* contains a large number of words that were probably in flux: the names for the clothing, precious stones, and other cultural items vary somewhat from traditional Latin words. The author had a wide-ranging knowledge of people, places, moneys, and daily objects connected with Saint James's pilgrimage. While a few items were impossible to identify, and some items were difficult to explain to complete satisfaction, the notes identify a wide range of people, places, and things.

Comparisons to other popular saints, important persons, and mentions of certain specific geographical locations abound in the LSJ. For these, we have attempted specific identification in the notes and have tried to use modern equivalents where those are helpful.

The Miracles of Book II are written in a straightforward but animated style. However Book III, the *Translatio,* differs considerably based on its content and reliance on previous material and is written in a dated style. For that reason, an appendix was added with functional translations of texts that predated and formed part of the source material for the *Translatio*. The only exception to this is the entry on the feast of St. Luparia, which adds background information for this figure but which comes from a nineteenth-century French source. This appendix has no critical apparatus and minimal commentary, but it shows, especially in the case of the chapter 1 of Book III, the influences at work on its author. The style of the appendix is as varied as the different texts contained in it.

Neither the CC nor S manuscripts contain any indication of paragraph breaks; the separate chapters of both the *Miracles* and the *Translatio* begin with an illuminated capital and a rubricated heading and then continue unbroken until the end of the chapter. We have used modern punctuation and modern paragraphing to divide the text. Capitalization likewise reflects modern usage. Roman numbers were generally written as found. The historic present was found often in the Latin but could be used only rarely in the translation. In translating, nouns were often used in English where pronouns were found in Latin; commas or "and" or "but" and other transition words were used and modified so as to increase readability rather than preserve their exact usage in Latin; and longer sentences were broken into smaller segments to improve readability. Overall, in the present translation, we have endeavored to render the twelfth-century Latin text into clear, readable, modern English.

Within the *Miracles, Translatio,* and *Appendices*, we have placed references to the biblical citations in square brackets within the text. Throughout the Psalms are cited both with the numbering of the Vulgate and the King James translation, with a slash dividing them.

In general, the footnotes fall into five categories: 1) to note manuscript "errors" and peculiarities, which are relatively infrequent; 2) to identify Latin words not found in standard dictionaries; 3) to identify sources for quotations, allusions, and materials; 4) to identify specific saints and placenames; and 5) to note significant variations between the CC and the Salamanca manuscript.

INTRODUCTION

In all instances, the guiding principle has been to increase readability and understanding for the general reader and scholar alike.

3. Saint James as Pilgrim. Church of Santa Marta de Tera, Camarzana de Tera, Zamora, Spain. 12th century.

THE MIRACLES
OF SAINT JAMES

4. Martín Bernat. The *Translation* of the Body of Saint James the Greater at the Palace of Queen Lupa. (1480–90). Prado Museum.

THE MIRACLES OF SAINT JAMES

Here Begins the Second Book of Saint James of Zebedee, Patron of Galicia, about His 22 Miracles.

The Attestation of Pope Calixtus[1]

[f.140r] [2] Above all, it is worthwhile to commit to writing and to consign eternally to memory the miracles of Saint James for the glory of our Lord Jesus Christ. For when the stories of the saints are told by experts, the hearts of the listeners are moved piously toward the sweetness and love of the heavenly realm.

Turning my attention to this while wandering through barbarous lands,[3] I found various writings in various places: some of these miracles in Galicia, others in France, others in Germany, others in Italy, others in Hungary, others in Dacia,[4] others beyond the three

---

1. In this introduction to the miracle collection, "Pope Calixtus" claims their veracity as their compiler. For information on Calixtus and authorship of the Miracles, see the Introduction, XLVII–XLVIII.
2. The folio change [f.140r] occurs before the word *Summopere* or "above all"; the heading is found on [f.139v], where Book I ends. Folio indications are from the CC.
3. The author, ostensibly Pope Calixtus, uses the first-person singular rather than the more usual first-person plural that is the norm for popes and emperors. In the next paragraph, he will use the "we" form that is traditionally known as "the royal we." This kind of vacillation is not new, having occurred in the opening letter to the LSJ and in the "Veneranda dies" sermon in Book I.
4. This could refer to the ancient Roman province that corresponds roughly to modern Romania or could possibly even be a reference to the Scandinavian countries. Dacia was used as an example in the "Veneranda

seas[5] and yet others on barbarian shores.[6] I learned some from those for whom the blessed apostle deigned to work them, hearing about them from those who had seen or heard them. I saw others with my own eyes, and I have diligently committed them to writing for the glory of God and the apostle.[7] The more beautiful they are, the more precious they are.

Let no one think that I have written down all the miracles and stories that I have heard about him, but only those that I have judged to be true, based on the truest assertions of the most truthful people.[8] For if I had written down all the miracles that I had heard about him in the many places and in the accounts of many people, my strength, my supply of parchment, and my hand would have given out long before the stories had run out. Because of this we have ordered that this manuscript be considered among the true and authentic manuscripts, and that it be read diligently both in

---

dies" sermon of Book I in a list of pilgrim nationalities as well as to refer to one of the various routes to the saint's tomb. Coffey et al., *Miracles*, 18, 55.

5. The Mediterranean (*mare nostrum*) and its two gulfs, generally also called seas: the Tyrrhenian or Etruscan (*mare inferum*), and the Adriatic (*mare superum*).

6. The narrator is concerned with the geographical sphere of the saint. This reference to wandering in various lands repeats the opening letter of the LSJ and this relatively short list of countries echoes the much longer list of international pilgrims to the saint's tomb in the "Veneranda dies" sermon of Book I. Coffey et al., *Miracles*, 3, 18. See the Introduction, LVI.

7. The narrator relies on oral tradition rather than *auctoritas* (the use of written documents as a base for his own writing). Of the following twenty-two miracles, only four are attributed to written sources (chapters 2, 4, 16, 17). Of the eighteen others, all with Calixtus's name as author, only three indicate reliability of the information (chapters 1, 19, 20), in the last the author says, "I met this man myself...and he told me all these things."

8. The flavor of the Latin is retained here, where the word *true* is repeated three times: miracles are true (*vera*), assertions are most true (*verissimis*), and people asserting are most truthful (*verissimorum*).

THE MIRACLES

churches and refectories on the feast days of this apostle and on other days if it be pleasing. Here ends the attestation.[9]

Here begin the titles of the second book of Saint James about his twenty-two miracles.[10]

Chapter 1   About twenty men whom the apostle freed from the captivity of the Moabites.

Chapter 2   About a man whose handwritten note with his sin was erased through divine intervention on the altar of Saint James. [f.140v]

Chapter 3   About a boy whom the apostle raised from the dead in the grove of Oca.

Chapter 4   About thirty Lotharingians and about a dead man whom the apostle carried in one night from the Pass of Cize up to his monastery.

Chapter 5   About the hanged pilgrim, suspended on the gallows for thirty-six days, whom the blessed apostle preserved from death.

Chapter 6   About the man from Poitiers to whom the apostle sent an angel in the form of a donkey for assistance.

---

9. The material of Books I and II is considered appropriate for reading in church, although it may be read at refectory if time does not permit its reading at services. The elaborate Chi-Rho in which one can discern the X or CH (chi), the R (rho), possibly the I (iota) the S (sigma) and the T (tau) to denote the word *Christus* (Greek Χριστός) to show the beginning of suitably liturgical material appears in the introductory letter of the CC, as well as at the end of Book II's miracles in the CC, but only in the letter in the Salamanca manuscript. (Fig. 5)

10. A later hand has inserted the corresponding folio number for each miracle after its title in the CC manuscript. We have not reproduced that information. These titles are more like plot summaries, especially when compared to the actual title heading each miracle, which gives only authorship.

5. "Whatever is written in the first two books up to the sign that is similar to this, which denotes Jesus Christ, may be sung or read in churches." The Chi Rho, Book I of the *Codex Calixtinus*. Archivo-biblioteca de la Catedral de Santiago de Compostela. Folio 2r.

Chapter 7	About Frisonus, the sailor, dressed in helmet and shield, whom the apostle rescued from the depths of the sea.
Chapter 8	About the bishop who, after being liberated from the dangers of the sea, composed a responsorial verse for Saint James.
Chapter 9	About the soldier from Tiberias to whom the apostle gave the power of overcoming the Turks and whom he freed from sickness and from the dangers of the sea.
Chapter 10	About the pilgrim who fell into the sea and whom the apostle brought back to port in the space of three days by holding him by the head.

THE MIRACLES

Chapter 11   About Bernard whom the apostle miraculously rescued from prison.

Chapter 12   About the soldier whom the apostle freed from sickness by the touch of his shell.

Chapter 13   About Dalmatius, the soldier, whom the apostle brought to justice for the sake of Raimbert, his pilgrim.

Chapter 14   About the merchant whom the apostle freed from prison.

Chapter 15   About the soldier whom the blessed apostle rescued in a war, after his comrades had already been killed or captured.

Chapter 16   About the soldier who, in the agony of death, was oppressed by demons, and whom the blessed apostle freed with the staff of a beggar and the little sack of a small woman.

Chapter 17   About the pilgrim who, for love of the apostle and at the instigation of the devil, killed himself and whom Saint James led from death back to life with the help of Mary, the Mother of God.

Chapter 18   About the Count of Saint-Gilles for whom the apostle [f.141r] opened the iron gates of his oratory.

Chapter 19   About Stephen, the Greek bishop, to whom the blessed apostle appeared and to whom he revealed unknown things to come.

Chapter 20   About William, the captured soldier, whom a count struck on his bared neck with a sword, but whom he could not wound.[11]

---

11. This is the only title in which the apostle is not mentioned.

Chapter 21 About the crippled man to whom the blessed apostle appeared in his basilica and whom he caringly restored to health.

Chapter 22 About the man who was sold thirteen times and who was freed by the apostle the same number of times.

THE MIRACLES

Chapter I[12]

A Miracle of Saint James
Written Down by His Excellency Pope Calixtus[13]

Saint James the Apostle, who in the fervor of obedience was the first of the apostles to suffer the pain of martyrdom,[14] undertook, through countless signs of his powers, to remove the peoples' roughness, saturating it with the doctrine of his holy preaching.[15] Saint James, who arose by divine influence as the worker of such power, after he wiped away the sweat of his labor with the cloth of reward, now pours a display of his powers abundantly over those who tirelessly and unceasingly petition him. Therefore we will tell straightforwardly a certain miracle that we heard and recognized as true, in its properly accounted place among the other miracles.[16]

---

12. The chapter designations appear to have been added later in the margin of the CC manuscript by a different hand from that of the main text; these designations do not appear in the Salamanca manuscript.

13. The Latin consistently refers to Pope Calixtus with the Latin Dominus "Lord" whenever a miracle is attributed to him. The modern form of reference is "His Holiness" for a pope, but we have settled on "Excellency" as a compromise between "Holiness" and "Lord."

14. The Latin is simply *passionis*, "suffering." However, the context indicates and history confirms that this refers to his martyrdom inflicted by Herod Agrippa in Jerusalem. See Acts 12:2.

15. This begins a water image that continues in the next sentence with allusions to, perhaps, the legend about the cloth that Veronica gave to Jesus Christ to wipe his brow. It is followed by a "pouring" of powers, reminiscent of baptismal cleansing.

16. This paragraph, with its reference to Saint James's martyrdom and affirmation of his holy powers is unique and clearly sets this miracle as the first of the collection. The Latin *rationi* can be interpreted in several ways. Here, "in its properly accounted place among the other miracles" fits most appropriately. The AASS has the reading *notitiae* here, which would indicate the idea that it was told "for the knowledge of his followers." *Notitia* might well represent a *lectio facilior* (when the scribe chose an easier word) for the more ambiguous Latin *ratio*.

At the time of Alfonso, king over the regions of Spain,[17] the fury of the Saracens burned violently.[18] A certain count named Ermengotus[19] saw the Christian religion oppressed by an attack of the Moabites.[20] Encompassed with the support of his army for the purpose of overcoming their ferocity and based on indications of

17. Alfonso VI of Castille and León (1065–1109) was the strongest of the Peninsula's Christian rulers at that time, and he named himself "imperator totius Hispaniae," ("emperor of all Spain") probably to free himself from the efforts of Pope Gregory VII (1073–85) to gain control in the Peninsula, including some power over the efforts of the Reconquest. Another aspect of the struggles between King Alfonso and Pope Gregory revolved around the substitution of the Roman liturgy for the Mozarabic. During the conflict the pope managed to make Bernard de Sauvetot, a Cluniac, the abbot in Sahagún (León) on the French road to Santiago. For more of the history of this epoch, see Joseph O'Callaghan, *A History of Medieval Spain*, 200–15.

18. The burning fury may refer to the fact that Alfonso VI was so successful in his reconquest efforts that the Moors in Seville, Granada, and Badajoz realized that they needed help to maintain control of the southern part of the Peninsula. They called on a faction in North Africa, the Almoravids. This group was an ascetic warring dynasty which, when it arrived in Spain, dampened severely the successes of the Christians. It took about eight years, but by 1094, "the Almoravids had restored the unity of al-Andalus and confronted Christian Spain with the most serious threat since the days of Almanzor." O'Callaghan, *A History of Medieval Spain*, 211.

19. Moralejo (*Liber*, 338 n. 17) identifies him as the count of Urgel, Ermengol IV (1065–92) or V (1092–1102). Urgel is a province in northeast Spain in Lérida, part of Cataluña. It was recaptured from the Moors in the eighth century. The reconquest of the area of Lérida is credited to Ramón Berenguer, the count of Barcelona, in 1149; Berenguer also played a role in the reconquest of Almería.

20. This term is also used in Book IV, (the Pseudo-Turpin) along with many others, to refer to various Moslem groups: "Saracens, Moors, Moabites, mountain people, Parthians, Africans, and Persians." See Poole, *Pseudo-Turpin*, 22; also see p. 6 n. 6 regarding the use of the term Moabite to refer specifically to the land of the Almoravids. Moab, in the area of Jordan, was the site of the ancestry of Ruth in the Old Testament.

certain victory, he attacked. However, despite the merits of our side, with his stronghold overcome, he ran into the contrary of triumph.[21] As a result, the savage enemy, filled with a pride of elation bordering on arrogance, led the twenty men — among whom one held the priestly office — encouraged by a wave of faith into captivity in the city [f.141v] of Zaragoza as a sign of victory.[22] Here, in the semblance of the perpetual blindness of hell, in the intolerable darkness of prison, the prisoners, chained together and bound with restraints of various types, with divine inspiration and with the priest's advice,[23] began to call upon Saint James in this way, "James, precious apostle of God, you who piously come out of mercy in aid to those in distress from their oppressors and who offer your hand of consolation toward those wailing from unspeakable captivity, hasten to free those of us who are crushed so inhumanely."

21. This is an interesting variant of litotes: the author says, "he did not triumph" to indicate "he was defeated." It was because of the Almoravid invasion that Alfonso VI had to leave his siege of Zaragoza and go south to fight the new group. The reconquest of Zaragoza was thus delayed for about 20 years.

22. Zaragoza (Aragón) in the northeast Spain is approximately 150 km from Lérida. There were probably several Moorish prisons there. One possible candidate that remains is the famous "Aljafería," founded by Aben-Aljafe (864–89) in the western part of the city. It was the castle–palace of the Moorish rulers until 1118 when Alfonso *el Batallador* "the Battler" of Aragón (1073/74–1134), who had reconquered the city, gave it to a religious order. Zaragoza has long identified itself with the cult of Santiago. Part of the saint's legend relates that, as he was returning to Jerusalem, the Virgin Mary appeared to him in the year 40CE in what is now Zaragoza, asking him to build a church there. To prove that it was she and that her request was important, she brought the pillar on which Jesus had been flagellated. Thus the name of the church: La Virgen del Pilar and, subsequently, the popularity of the feminine name "Pilar" in Spain. See Ana Isabel Martín and José Carlos Martín, "La leyenda de la venida de la Virgen a Zaragoza (BHL 5388): Edición crítica y estudio," *Hagiographica* 21 (2014): 53–84 for a critical edition and study of this legend.

23. In this collection of miracles, this is the only time a priest must encourage the petitioners to call to Saint James.

Saint James, hearing their voices of inconsolable pain, appeared in brightness in the darkness of the prison, saying, "Behold, here am I, whom you have called."

The prisoners, whose heads were bent over onto their knees because of the magnitude of their pain, were strengthened by the clarity of this sound, and they threw themselves at the feet of the saint. Saint James, who viscerally felt their pain and poured the salve of his power on them, broke through their chains. Then with his potent right hand joined to the hands of the captives, the saint, with divine approbation, released them from this perilous prison and, leading the way, took them to the city's gates. When the saint had made the sign of the cross with apostolic reverence, the gates willingly granted exit,[24] and once the prisoners had exited, the gates returned to their former closed state. Saint James the Apostle, quite some time after the cock's crow and with the first ray of light almost shining on them, led them to a certain castle held in safety by the Christians. Then, after telling them that he could be called on by them, he rose toward heaven. After that, calling on him with a loud voice, as he had just told them to do, the gates opened, and the former captives were taken inside.

On the next day they left the castle and started to head back home. After some time one of them, seeking the threshold of Saint James,[25] told everyone on the feast day of the saint's *translation,* which in our time is celebrated annually on the third calends of January,[26] that all these things had happened in the way in which we have written down here.

---

24. See chapter 18 where the basilica's gates also open because of the apostle's aid.
25. That is, going on pilgrimage to the Saint's tomb in Compostela. The word *limina,* "threshold," or *ad limina,* literally "to the thresholds" are recurring synecdoche for the basilica of Saint James at Compostela and for making the pilgrimage.
26. December 30. See XXIX, n. 25.

This was accomplished by the Lord, and it is miraculous in our eyes. Therefore, let there be honor and glory to the supreme King for ever and ever. Amen.[27]

Chapter 2

A Story of Saint James Written Down by Venerable Bede, the Priest and Doctor[28][F.142R]

During the time of Blessed Teodomiro, bishop of Compostela,[29] there was a certain Italian man who scarcely dared to confess to his

---

27. See the Introduction, LIII, for information about this formulaic closure of the miracles. The common Latin prayer ending *per omnia saecula saeculorum*, literally "through all the ages of ages," alternates in the CC with *infinita saecula saeculorum*. We render these phrases into English with "world without end." A third, simpler, form in *saecula saeculorum*, is also used, and we translate it with the familiar English "for ever and ever."

28. The Venerable Bede (c. 673–735) was an English monk, historian, and saint. He was translating the *Etymologies* of Isidore of Seville (560–636) into the vernacular when he died. His feast day is May 29. See BHL 1067–76; PL 90–95. This particular miracle is not known to exist among the extant writings of Bede; this text would be inconsistent with his biographical dates and the date of discovery of Saint James's tomb in Compostela. It is possible that he believed that Saint James preached in Spain, for Isidore (or perhaps an eighth-century interpolation in Isidore's works) mentions this aspect of the saint's legend, and Aldhelm of Malmesbury (d. 709) attributes to Saint James the conversion of people in Spain. See the Introduction, XXX–XXXI. That the compiler of the CC knew at least some of Bede's writings is supported by the inclusion of two of Bede's sermons in Book I's liturgies: the first opens Book I with a sermon for July 24; the other is chapter 8, a homily for July 25. In the latter piece, Bede speaks about the saint's life and martyrdom, but does not refer to Spain. Pierre David ("Etudes sur le Livre de Saint-Jacques attribué au pape Calixte II," *Bulletin des études portugaises et l'Institut français au Portugal* 10 (1945): 1–41; 11(1947): 113–85; 12 (1948): 70–223; 13 (1949): 52–104) indicates that, given the faulty dating, the mention of Bede may be symbolic for "in ancient times" (II:161).

29. Teodomiro (d. 847) was the bishop at Iria Flavia at the time of the discovery of the saint's burial place in Compostela, c. 830. His tomb, or at least a sepulcher cover with his name on it, was found under the Compostela Cathedral during the 1955 excavations. The story of Teodomiro's involvement with the discovery of Saint James's tomb in Galicia is first

priest or bishop a great sin that he had once iniquitously committed. When finally the sin was heard, his bishop, who was horrified by such a great offense, did not dare to give the sinner a penance. Instead, moved by piety, the bishop directed the sinner to write down this sin in a note and to go to the threshold of Saint James for the sake of penance. He also ordered the man to implore the blessed apostle's help with all his heart and to submit to the judgment of the bishop of the apostle's basilica.

The man went without delay to Saint James in Galicia[30] and, repenting of committing such a crime and begging forgiveness from God and the apostle with tearful sobs, he placed the note[31] with his crime on it upon[32] the saint's venerable altar at the first hour[33] of the saint's feast day, which is on the eighth calends of August.[34]

When Blessed Teodomiro, bishop of the See of Compostela, had dressed in his episcopal garments[35] and had gone up to the

---

narrated in the *Concordia de Antealtares* as well as in the HC, chapter 2. See Appendices 6 and 7.

30. The first of several references in the miracles to Galicia as a specific geographical place. It is mentioned additionally once in miracles 4, 7–9, 11–12, 14, 16–17, and 22. All of these references use "Galicia" as a point of reference for the pilgrimage goal.

31. Latin: *cyrographum*, a particular kind of note where the same message is written several times.

32. This passage indicates that the basilica of Saint James allowed the pilgrims access to the altar.

33. The Latin *hora prima* could be taken literally to mean the first hour of daylight or as at or near the time of the prime service. It is unlikely that the pilgrim approached the altar during a ceremony, especially since the bishop wondered how the note had been placed there when he found it.

34. July 25. This feast celebrates Saint James's martyrdom. In the first two miracles, the author has referred to both important feast day celebrations of the saint. See the Introduction, LVII–LIX for information about the saint's feast days.

35. Teodomiro was actually the bishop of Iria Flavia (now a settlement of Padrón, Galicia). It was only after the discovery of Saint James's tomb that the bishopric became that of Iria Flavia and Compostela and was finally transferred to Compostela by Alfonso II.

altar on that day at the third hour[36] in order to sing mass, he found the sinner's note under the altar cloth, and he wondered why and by whom it might have been placed there. The penitent ran up to the bishop on the spot and sorrowfully and on bended knees told him, not without tears and with everyone listening, about his sin and about the command of his own bishop to whom he had gone. However, when the holy bishop opened the note, he found nothing written on it, as if no letters had ever been written down at all.[37]

This is a miraculous occurrence and a great joy. May great praise and glory to be sung for God and the apostle forever. It was accomplished by the Lord, and it is miraculous in our eyes.[38]

This holy bishop, believing that the sinner was obtaining forgiveness from God through the merits of the apostle, did not wish to give him any penance for the already-forgiven crime. He merely prescribed that the sinner fast on the sixth day after that[39] and sent him, absolved from all sins, back to his own country.

It is to be understood from this that whosoever is truly penitent and is from faraway shores, and has sought to request with all his heart forgiveness from the Lord and help from Saint James in Galicia, without doubt will have the slate of his sins wiped clean in eternity.

---

36. Simply "at the third hour" or a reference to terce and the morning mass, which generally occurred at about 8:00 a.m. Either way, two hours would have passed between the sinner's leaving the note and the bishop's finding it.

37. There is a curious marginal notation in the CC at this point reading *Non Dei miraculum,* or "Not a miracle of God." This miracle is similar to one attributed to Saint Gilles (c.650–c.710). According to one legend, Charlemagne could only confess his most heinous sin by writing it down on paper. The information — in some versions concerning Roland's parentage and in some versions delivered by an angel to the altar — magically disappeared at the behest of Saint Gilles.

38. The first example of how the formulaic ending is divided, with a moralistic warning inserted between the two phrases.

39. There is some ambiguity here: it could be on the "sixth day (Saturday) following that" or on simply whatever day happened to be the sixth after the day on which he gave the order to fast.

MIRACLES AND TRANSLATIO OF SAINT JAMES

May Jesus Christ our Lord deign to be our guarantor of this, who lives with the Father and the Holy Spirit [f.142v] and who reigns as God. World without end. Amen.

Chapter 3

A Miracle of Saint James[40]
Written Down by His Excellency Pope Calixtus

In the year of the Incarnation of our Lord[41] one thousand one hundred eight, on the shores of France, a certain man, desiring to have progeny, as is the custom, married a woman in legitimate fashion. Although he remained with her for a long time, he was frustrated in his hope for children because his sins weighed down upon him. Suffering painfully from this since he lacked an heir, he decided that he would go to Saint James and that he would appeal to the saint for a son. What more can one say?[42] There was no delay: he went to the saint's threshold. Standing there in the saint's presence, weeping and crying and entreating him with all of his heart, he managed to obtain what he forcefully solicited[43] from the apostle of God. According to the normal custom, when his prayer was ended,

---

40. This chapter narrates two miracles that happen to the same man and his family, the first through petition of the man and the second some years later through the petition of the mother.

41. In each of the chapters that begin with a specific year the author uses the phrase, "In the year of our Lord's Incarnation." See the Introduction, XLIX–LIV for dating of the miracles.

42. This is the first instance of this rhetorical question by the author. This phrase will appear once more in this chapter and again in chapters 11 and 22. It will also appear once in chapter 3 of the *Translatio*. This type of short, leading rhetorical question is typical of the era and used commonly in Cluniac and Beneventan texts.

43. The first verb for "entreating" is *deprecans*; the second reference to his requests is expressed with *inperpellavit* or "annoyed, disturbed, molested, seduced"; use of the literal meanings in English would not produce the desired effect here; the translation attempts to express the implied persistence without the potential negative connotations of the Latin.

he returned safely to his country, after having sought permission from Saint James. After resting for three days and after having said a prayer, he approached his wife. From that union, his wife became pregnant, and after the requisite number of months had passed, she bore a son, to whom they, out of joy, gave the name of the apostle.

When the son had nearly reached his fifteenth year, he undertook the pilgrimage to the blessed apostle together with his father and mother and some other relatives. While the boy arrived at the Montes de Oca[44] in good health, he was struck by a serious disease and breathed his last.[45] His parents lamented his death, filling the whole grove and the nearby dwellings with screams and wailing in the manner of those who are delirious.

His mother, almost out of her mind with grief and crying out in great pain, spoke with these words to the Blessed James: "Saint James, to whom such great power was given by God as to grant me a son, give him back to me now. Give him back, I beg, because you are able to do so. For, if you do not do this for me, I will kill myself at once or have myself buried alive with him."[46] With all the people present and attending to the funeral service of the boy and fashioning the tomb, the boy awoke almost as if from a deep sleep through the mercy of God and the prayer of Saint James.

All those present rejoiced and praised God for such a great miracle. Then the boy who was restored to life began to tell all those present how Saint James had kept his soul warm after it had left his body, [f.143r] from the third hour of the sixth day until the

---

44. The Montes de Oca are located east of Burgos between Villafranca and Atapuerca. See the Guide, chapters 3 and 7. Although the Latin text here terms them *montem*, "mountains," this area is really a forest, and as such it is called *nemore*, "grove" in this book's title index and in the Guide, chapter 7.

45. The Latin is *animam exhalavit* or literally "he breathed out his soul."

46. This is an impressive threat to a saint. Although in a plea to a saint there may be quite strong demands for action, we are unaware of any other miracle that has threat of suicide as a part of the supplication.

ninth hour of the Sabbath,[47] in eternal sleep in his bosom, and how at the Lord's command he restored it back to his body, raised him by the right hand from death, and commanded him to walk the path of the Saint James's pilgrims with his parents without delay. The young man also said that being in that heavenly life then was sweeter for him than being in this present miserable life now. Then he went forth with his parents to the threshold of Saint James. What more can one say?[48] He was offered up at the venerable altar of the saint at whose prayers he was created.

This was accomplished by the Lord, and it is miraculous in our eyes.

It is a revolutionary and thus far unheard-of event for a dead person to bring a dead person back to life. Saint Martin did so[49]

---

47. That is, from the third hour on Saturday until the ninth hour on Sunday.
48. The second occurrence of this rhetorical question. See n. 42 above.
49. The first mention of Martin of Tours (316–97). He was born in Pannonia (Hungary) of pagan parents, converting to Christianity sometime during his teens. The act that has become his emblem occurred while he was a youth in the army: he cut his cloak in half to share it with a beggar. He became a disciple of Saint Hillary of Poitiers, spent time as a hermit, and was finally made bishop of Tours in 372. He became committed to the dissemination of the Catholic religion throughout the region and the eradication of cult and heretical practices. He founded several monasteries in Gaul. During his life he had a complicated relationship with Priscillianists, occasionally defending their view, especially as he worked with the bishops in Spain. In the Guide the author describes the saint's miracles and his tomb (Melczer, *Pilgrim's Guide,* 108–9). Sources for his life are the *Vita* by Sulpicius Severus (PL 20:159–74) and the various works of Gregory of Tours (PL 71). BHL entries for Martin of Tours are 5610–66.

The idea that Martin had raised three dead persons was widely held, although Melczer (*Pilgrim's Guide,* 176 n. 243) believes the number three is symbolic. The *Vita* by Sulpicius Severus recounts two resurrections (chapters 7 and 8) and a third is in Severus's *Second Dialogue* (chapter 4). In the first instance, the man revived two hours after Martin lay across his body. The second instance is the resuscitation of a slave who had hung himself. The last example occurred in Vendôme where Martin was preaching to pagans. A woman approached with her dead infant son in her

THE MIRACLES

while still living, and our Lord Jesus Christ raised three dead people.⁵⁰ However, Saint James, while dead, brought a dead person back to life. Now someone may say in objection, "If it is read that our Lord and Saint Martin have brought back to life as many as three dead people before their own deaths and no one after their own deaths, then it is asserted that a dead person is not able to bring a dead person back to life but that a living person can do so." Saying these things, it can be concluded that if a dead person is not able to bring another dead person back to life, but a living person is able to do so, then Saint James, who has brought a dead person back to life, is truly living with God. Thus it is agreed that both before and after death any saint can bring a dead person back to life with God's help. The Lord says: "Whosoever believes in me, will do the works which I myself do and will do the greater of these things." [Jn 14:12] "All things are possible for the believer," [Mk 9:23] says the Lord elsewhere, who lives with the Father and the Holy Spirit and who reigns as God. World without end. Amen.

---

arms. After Martin prayed over the body, the baby revived, and the town was converted to Christianity. This miracle is also mentioned in his "First Letter to Eusebius" (PL 20:175), and Bernard of Clairvaux also made note of this (PL 183:495). Gregory of Tours in his *Historia Francorum,* Book I chapter 36 (PL 71:180) asserts that Martin raised three people from the dead. In addition, Gregory tells the story of a small boy resuscitated in his *De Miraculis Sancti Martini,* Book II chapter 43 (PL 71:960–61), another small child in Book III chapter 8 (PL 71:972–3). There is also passing mention of a resuscitated monk in Book III chapter 50 (PL 71:970).

50. The three people raised from the dead by Jesus were Lazarus (Jn 11:1–44), the daughter of Jairus (Lk 8:49–56), and the son of the widow of Nain (Lk 7:11–15).

Chapter 4

A Story of Saint James Written Down by Master Hubert, a Most Pious Canon of the Church of Mary Magdalene at Besançon.[51]

May His Soul Rest in Eternal Peace. Amen.[52]

In this present miracle of Saint James of Zebedee, the apostle of Galicia, it is affirmed that what Scripture attests to is true: "It is better not to vow than to go back on it after having vowed."[53]

It is reported that in the year one thousand eighty, thirty heroes from the area of Lorraine[54] proposed to visit the threshold of Saint James in Galicia out of pious devotion. [f.143v] However, since the human mind sometimes is changed for many reasons, they undertook to make a pact, promising each other the assurance of mutual service and the common charge of keeping their resolution. However, one member of the group did not wish to involve himself in this oath.

---

51. Besançon lies about 380 kilometers southeast of Paris and was the birthplace of Guy of Burgundy (Pope Calixtus II). There is evidence of a Humbert, archbishop of Besançon in a letter in PL 180:1465, dated 1155. Vincent of Beauvais (*Speculum Historiale,* Book 36 chapter 32) attributes this miracle to Hubertus Sibuntinus, while Voragine (Johann Georg Theodor Graesse and Friedrich Benedict, *Orbis Latinus: Lexikon lateinischer geographischer Namen des Mittelalters und der Neuzeit* [Braunschweig: Klinkhardt & Biermann, 1972], 426) ascribes it to Ubertus Bysuntinus.

52. This is the only chapter heading that ends with the word "Amen," attributable to the add-on prayerful wish relative to the soul of the writer and in imitation of the *requiescat in pace* of the funeral liturgy.

53. Cf. Eccl 5:4, Nm 30:2, Dt 23:21.

54. The province in northeastern France, named after Lothaire, Charlemagne's grandson, who ruled over the central strip of land in the empire. By the eleventh century its rule had passed to Alsace.

THE MIRACLES

All of the men then set out on the planned journey and came safely to the city in Gascony called Porta Clusa.[55] There one of the men was afflicted with an illness and could not continue on. Because of the pact of keeping their resolution, his companions carried him by means of their horses and by hand and with great toil up to the Cize Pass[56] in fifteen days, a journey which normally was covered by foot soldiers in five days.

Then, finally, burdened and afflicted with excessive fatigue and disregarding their oath, they abandoned the sick man. However, the one who alone had not made a promise to him, did not abandon him, but offered to the sick man a work of faith and piety. During the following night he kept vigil over him in the town of Saint-Michel[57] at the foot of the previously-mentioned mountain. When the next day had dawned, the sick man said to his comrade that he would try to climb the mountain, if the healthy man would give help to him according to his strength. The healthy man answered that he would not desert him until death. As they ascended the slope of the mountain together, and as day was coming to an end,

---

55. Gascogne is a province in southwestern France. We have not located "Porta Clusa," but its name suggests a difficult or high place. It cannot be in the Pyrenees, since the men walk a five-day distance in fifteen days before reaching the Cize Pass at the border of Spain in the Pyrenees. Therefore, the difficult place is perhaps a forest in the vicinity of Mont-de-Narsan.
56. This is the mountain pass (1577 m.) in the Pyrenees between the French Saint-Michel and the Spanish Roncesvalles on what is today called the Napoleonic route. This is also the route used by Charlemagne and his army according to the Pseudo-Turpin, (chapter 21) where Roland and his men met their fate.
57. Saint-Michel and Saint-Jean-Pied-de-Port are French villages near each other along the Nive River, at the foot of Cize Pass. Saint-Michel is named in the Guide, chapter 2, as the beginning point for the northern route across the Pyrenees. Pilgrims starting along the three northern routes (Paris, Vézelay, and LePuy) would meet in Ostabat and proceed a few kilometers southwest to enter Saint-Jean-Pied-de-Port and then begin to climb the Pyrenees. See Melczer, *Pilgrim's Guide*, 85–86. The Guide's writer warns pilgrims that toll collectors at Ostabat, Saint-Jean, and Saint-Michel are evil and may beat and search pilgrims for their money.

the most blessed soul of the ailing man went out of this worthless world and settled worthily into the sleep of paradise because of his merits, with Saint James leading the way. When the surviving man saw this, he was greatly terrified, first by the loneliness of the site, then by the darkness of the night, then by the presence of the dead man's body, and, finally, by the horror of that barbarous people — the impious Basques[58] — who were lingering around the pass. He was afraid beyond measure.

Since he could find no help either from within himself or from anyone else, he set his thoughts on the Lord and asked help from Saint James with a supplicant heart. The Lord, as the font of piety who does not desert those who believe in Him, deigned to call on this desolate man through His apostle. Saint James, sitting on a horse like a soldier, came to this man who was placed in such difficulty.[59] He said to him, "What are you doing here, my brother?"

"Lord," the man answered, "I need very much to bury my companion here, but I do not have the wherewithal [f.144r] to bury him in this wasteland." The saint responded, "Hand me this dead man and sit behind me on this horse until we come to the burial place."

Thus it was done. The apostle held the dead man carefully in his arms, facing him, and he had the living man sit behind him on the horse. Blessed power of God! Blessed clemency of Christ! Blessed help of Saint James! During that night they crossed the distance of a twelve days' journey.[60] Before sunrise the next morning, the apostle set down from his horse those whom he had carried, about a mile on this side of the monastery[61] of the aforementioned apostle, on

---

58. The Latin is *Basclorum*. The Guide, chapter 7, singles out the Basques as particularly barbarous.

59. Here, as in chapter 19, the saint exhibits his militant image (Fig. 6).

60. Twelve days is the appropriate amount of time for travel between Cize and Compostela, according to the Guide.

61. The use of "on this side of the monastery" to refer to the area east of Santiago would support the authorship / narration of the miracle by someone from France, or at least not by someone within the city of Santiago de Compostela.

THE MIRACLES

Monte de Gozo.[62] He indicated to the living man that he should request the canons of the basilica of the aforementioned saint to bury this pilgrim of Saint James.

Then he went on to say, "After you have seen the burial ceremonies completed for your dead friend and after you have kept vigil in prayer for the accustomed length of time, you should start the return journey. You should meet up with your friends in the city named León.[63] Say to them, 'Since you acted unfaithfully toward your companion by deserting him, the blessed apostle is telling you through me that your prayers and your pilgrimage are displeasing to him until you have sincerely done fitting penance'." Having heard all these things, and realizing that the speaker was the apostle of Christ, the man wanted to fall down at his feet, but the soldier of God no longer was visible to him.

With all of this done, on his way back he found his friends in the town mentioned above, and he told them in order the things that had happened to him after they had abandoned him and how many and how great were the threats the apostle had made for their not keeping their word in its entirety to their companion. Having heard these things, they were dumbfounded beyond description. They received penance from the bishop of León on the spot, and they finished their pilgrimage journey.

This was accomplished by the Lord, and it is miraculous in our eyes.

These are, in fact, things that the Lord has done. Let us exult and rejoice in them. If there is something to be established by this miracle, it is that whatever is vowed to God must be fulfilled with joy, inasmuch someone fulfilling worthy vows obtains forgiveness from the Lord.

---

62. The mountain top called Monte de Gozo (*Monte Gaudii* "Mount Joy") is about five kilometers east of Compostela. From there, pilgrims could, and still can, see for the first time the cathedral of Compostela.
63. This is the correct city according to the number of days' journeys in the Guide.

MIRACLES AND TRANSLATIO OF SAINT JAMES

May Jesus Christ our Lord Himself deign to be our guarantor of this, who lives with the Father and the Holy Spirit and reigns as God. World without end. Amen.

CHAPTER 5[64]

A STORY OF SAINT JAMES
WRITTEN DOWN BY HIS EXCELLENCY POPE CALIXTUS [F.144V]

It is also worth remembering that in the year of the Incarnation of our Lord one thousand ninety, certain Germans, traveling as pilgrims to the threshold of Saint James, reached the city of Toulouse[65] with an abundance of their riches,[66] and they took lodging there with a certain rich but evil man who, as if hiding under a sheepskin, feigned the gentleness of a sheep. He received them properly but compelled them under the guise of hospitality to become inebriated with various drinks. Oh blind avarice! Oh worthless mind of man

---

64. This is one of the most popular and widely known of Saint James's miracles. Versions have been created in prose, poetry, sculpture, and painting through the nineteenth century, in England, France, Germany, Portugal, and Switzerland. Over time the site where the miracle takes place changes to Santo Domingo de la Calzada and, as proof of the son's innocence, two roasted chickens spring to life, complete with feathers, in the mayor's house. Two live chickens reside in the Santo Domingo church to commemorate the miracle. It also was said to have occurred (complete with chickens coming to life) in Barcelos, Portugal, giving rise to the famous colorful rooster used as a symbol of Portugal. The bibliography on this miracle is extensive. See Auriol, Boschung, Ciril, Ferreiro Alemparte, Gaiffier, Jacomet, Lima, *Ludus,* Piccat, and Southey. David ("Etudes" 10:17–18 and 11:159–85, especially 182) mentions similarities of this miracle with one attributed to Saint Gilles, written by Pierre Guillaume.

65. In the Guide Toulouse is named as a principal town on the Arles route (Saint-Gilles, Montpellier, Toulouse, and the Somport Pass), the southernmost of the four traditional routes across France. This route crossed the Pyrenees over the Somport Pass and united with the other three routes in Puente la Reina (Navarra) Spain.

66. In Book I, the "Veneranda dies" author speaks forcefully against pilgrims' carrying an abundance of riches on their pilgrimage unless it should be for distribution to the needy.

THE MIRACLES

6. Saint James Matamoros. Tympanum in the south transept. S.A.M.I. Cathedral of Santiago de Compostela. 13th century.

prone toward mischievous evil! Finally, with the pilgrims weighed down by their drunkenness more than by their usual tiredness, the cunning host, driven by a spirit of avarice, secretly concealed a silver cup in one of the sleeping pilgrim's knapsacks, so that he could have them convicted of theft and, once they were convicted, get their money for himself.[67]

After the cock crowed the next morning, the evil host, with an armed band, pursued them, shouting, "Give it back, give back the money stolen from me!"

The pilgrims said to him, "You may condemn at your will the one on whom you might find it."

When the search was carried out, the host brought the two — a father and a son in whose knapsack he found the cup — to court, and unjustly took away their goods. The judge, however, moved by pity, ordered that one of them be let go and the other condemned

---

67. The theme of the wicked innkeeper appears throughout the LSJ. See more cautions and curses in the "Veneranda dies" sermon, Coffey et al., *Miracles*, 35–39 and 44–48. Chapter 11 of the Guide lists several miracles that happened to those who offered hospitality to pilgrims as well as punishments that were inflicted upon those who took advantage of pilgrims.

23

to capital punishment. Oh depths of mercy! The father, wanting the son to be set free, indicated himself for the punishment.

The son, on the contrary said, "It is not just that a father be handed over to the peril of death instead of his son. It is the son that should receive the infliction of the announced penalty." Oh venerable contest of clemency! The son, at his own wish, was hanged for the freedom of his beloved father. The father, however, weeping and mourning, went on to Saint James. After he had visited the venerable apostolic altar, and after thirty-six days had passed, the father returned from Compostela and made a side-trip to the body of his son, still hanging.[68] He cried out amidst tearful sighs and pitiable exclamations, "Woe to me, my son, that I begot thee! Woe to me that I have lived to see you hanged!"

How magnificent are your works, O Lord! The hanged son, consoling his father, said, "Do not grieve, most loving father, about my pain, but [f.145r] rather rejoice, for it is sweeter for me now than it had ever been before in all my former life. For the most Blessed James held me up with his hands and revived me with all manner of sweetness." The father, hearing this, ran to the city, calling the people to witness such a great miracle of God. The people, coming and seeing that the one whom they had hanged long ago was still alive, understood that he had been accused by the insatiable avarice of the host but that he had been saved by the mercy of God.

This was accomplished by the Lord, and it is miraculous in our eyes.

Therefore, they took the son from the gallows with great honor, but they hanged the innkeeper then and there, as he very much deserved, after he had been condemned to death by common judgment. Therefore, those who are designated by the name "Christian" must watch with great care, lest they contrive to perpetrate against guests or any other acquaintances any fraud of this type or any similar to it. They should, rather, strive to impart mercy and benign piety toward the pilgrims, since it is thus that

---

68. It was customary to leave the bodies of convicted felons hanging on the gibbet so that passers-by could be reminded of the penalties of crime.

THE MIRACLES

they may deserve to receive the rewards of eternal glory from Him who lives and reigns as God. World without end. Amen.

Chapter 6

A Story of Saint James
Written Down by His Excellency Pope Calixtus

Around the beginning of the year of the Incarnation of our Lord one thousand one hundred, during the time of William, count of Poitiers,[69] when Louis, king of the French, was still a prince,[70] a deadly plague grievously assaulted the people of Poitiers, so much so that sometimes the father of a family went to the grave with all of his relations.

A certain hero of the time, frightened by such devastation and wishing to avoid this scourge, decided to go through the region of Spain to Saint James. With his wife and two small children seated on his horse, this pilgrim arrived at the city of Pamplona.[71] However, when his wife died there, the evil innkeeper nefariously took the

---

69. William IX, duke of Aquitaine and (as William VII) count of Poitiers (1071–1127), is best known as a troubadour, not a warrior. His work, written in Provençal, is the oldest known troubadour poetry to survive.

70. Louis VI the Fat was king of France c. 1108–37. Philip I was king in the year 1100. One solution to the contradiction is to assume this miracle was not written down until at least 1108, after Louis had become king.

71. This city is in northeast Spain on the St-Jean-Pied-de-Port to Roncesvalles pilgrim route across the Cize Pass. It is east of Puente la Reina in Navarra. The Guide mentions the town several times, but gives no details about it (Melczer, *Pilgrims Guide*, chapters 2, 3 and 7). According to the Pseudo-Turpin (chapter 2), it was the first city attacked by Charlemagne. After a three-month siege, Charlemagne finally called upon Saint James for help and "almost immediately" the foundation of the walls of the city crumbled, and Charlemagne captured the city from the Saracens. Poole, *Pseudo-Turpin*, 8.

goods that the man and wife had brought with them.⁷² The pilgrim, deprived of his wife and completely fleeced of his money and the horse on which he was transporting his children, began his journey again, bearing his children in his arms with great suffering.

Another man, wearing fine clothing and with a very strong donkey, met up on the road with this pilgrim who was fettered by anxiety and in great distress. When this compassionate stranger had grasped [f.145v] the type and extent of the adverse things that had happened to this poor man from this man's own recounting, he said to him, "Since I consider your anguish to be very great, I will supply you with my best donkey for transporting your little children to the city of Compostela, of which I am a citizen, provided that you return it to me there."⁷³

Thus the pilgrim accepted the donkey and placed his little children on it and arrived at the threshold of Saint James. When at last he was devoutly spending the night in a secluded corner of the venerable basilica,⁷⁴ the most glorious apostle, wearing very bright clothing, appeared to him, saying simply, "Don't you know me, brother?"

The pilgrim responded, "Not at all, my lord."

To this the other responded, "I am the apostle of Christ who in the region of Pamplona supplied you with my donkey when you were in such grief. Now, however, I am supplying you with the donkey from now until you have returned to your own area, and I am announcing to you that your wicked innkeeper in Pamplona is about to fall headfirst from his seat and die from this serious fall, because he took your goods unjustly. I also declare to you that all

---

72. The "Veneranda dies" sermon (Coffey et al., *Miracles*, 36) warns about this type of theft. See also p. 23, n. 67 about evil innkeepers.

73. The "Veneranda dies" sermon cautions pilgrims about accepting gifts from strangers to be returned upon arrival in Compostela (Coffey et al., *Miracles*, 37).

74. Here is the first of four references to the basilica being open at night (see also chapters 18, 19, and 21). The "Veneranda dies" also describes the church as being open, "the doors of this basilica are never closed day or night, and it is never dark at night within it." (Coffey et al., *Miracles*, 19.)

THE MIRACLES

evil innkeepers dwelling on my road who unjustly take as theirs the goods[75] from their guests, whether living or dead, which should be given to the church and to the poor for the redemption of souls of the dead — will be condemned for all eternity."[76]

As soon as the prostrate pilgrim tried to embrace the feet of the one speaking to him, the most reverend apostle disappeared from his worldly eyes.

Afterwards, the pilgrim, who was gladdened by the apostolic vision and so much consolation, started back from the city of Compostela together with the donkey and his little children as dawn was just glowing. Arriving in Pamplona, he found the innkeeper quite dead, having fallen from his seat in his house and having fractured his neck, just as the apostle had predicted. When he had arrived joyfully in his own country and had taken his little children off of the donkey at the entrance to his house, the donkey disappeared from sight. Many people marveled beyond description upon hearing this from the pilgrim, and they have said that it was either a real donkey or an angel that appeared in the form of a donkey such as the Lord often sends into the midst of those fearing Him so that it might rescue them.

This was accomplished by the Lord, and it is miraculous in our eyes.

Therefore, it is plainly shown in this miracle that all crafty innkeepers are condemned to eternal death [f.146r] if they unjustly take the goods of a guest — whether living or dead — which should be given to the churches and the poor of Christ as alms for the redemption of souls. Through the merits of Saint James the Apostle, may Jesus Christ our Lord deign to avert completely from all believers any crime or fraud, as He lives with the Father and the Holy Spirit and reigns as God. World without end. Amen.

---

75. The Latin *census* literally means "inventory." The word *census* seems to have a special meaning in these miracles: while this literally means the listing or inventory of goods, it appears to refer to the assets behind that inventory. Thus, it is translated as "goods" here and elsewhere.

76. See p. 23, n. 67 about curses.

MIRACLES AND TRANSLATIO OF SAINT JAMES

Chapter 7[77]

A Miracle of Saint James
Written Down by His Excellency Pope Calixtus

In the year of the Incarnation of our Lord one thousand one hundred one, a certain sailor named Frisonus[78] piloted a ship traveling over the sea and filled with pilgrims wishing to go to the Lord's sepulcher in the area of Jerusalem in order to pray there.[79] At a certain point a Saracen named Avitus Maimon,[80] wishing to take all the pilgrims away with him into the land of the Moabites,[81] approached Frisonus's ship for the purpose of doing combat. After the two boats — that of the Saracens and that of the Christians — had come together and after they had fought fiercely, Frisonus, outfitted with his metal breastplate and his helmet and his shield, fell

---

77. The first of four miracles that take place on the sea. See also chapters 8–10.

78. The name *Frisonus* is reminiscent of several references to Frisians throughout the LSJ. Here the word is clearly used as a proper name, possibly to imply a northern European.

79. The only specific geographical clue in this chapter is Jerusalem, the others are generic ("sea," "port"); we can only assume that this miracle occurred somewhere in the Mediterranean.

80. As both Moralejo (*Liber*, 351) and David ("Etudes," III:165) point out, the names "Avitus" and "Maimon" appear in the Pseudo-Turpin (Poole, *Pseudo-Turpin*, 22), but what they do not make clear is that they appear separately. "Avitus" is listed as the king of Bougie, and Maimon as the king of Mecca. Both of the names and kingdoms have multiple variant forms in the other manuscripts. Poole gives Avitus as "Abbâd, king of Bejaïa." See Poole, p. 93 for more detailed identification of Abbâd, and p. 106 for that of Maimon. Reinhart Dozy, *Recherches sur l'histoire et la littérature de l'Espagne pendant le Moyen Age* (Paris: Maisonneuve, 1881), 410, however, identifies a group, the Beni-Maimon, as admirals for the Almoravid invaders (end of the 11th c.) who plagued the Christian coast, even battling Compostela Archbishop Diego Gelmírez's ships off the northwest coast. Several historical texts, including the *Historia compostelana*, mention this group.

81. See p. 8, n. 20 for information about the Moabites.

THE MIRACLES

between the two ships into the depths of the sea. When, through the mercy of God, he had regained some strength, he began to call on Saint James within his heart, saying these words, "Great and most glorious James, the indescribably pious apostle, whose altar I once kissed with my unworthy mouth,[82] deign to free me together with all these Christians who are committed to you."

Thereupon the blessed apostle appeared to him in the depths of the sea, and taking him by the hand, brought him back safely to the ship. Immediately, with everyone listening, the apostle said to the Saracen, "Unless you let this boat of Christians go free, I will hand you and your galleon over to their power."[83]

Avitus responded to him, "Why, if you please, glorious hero, do you strive to take away my booty?[84] Would you, who would resist our people on the sea, be God[85] of the sea?"

The apostle said to him on the spot, "I am not the god of the sea, but I am the servant of the God of the sea, who comes in aid to those who are in danger and who cry out to me whether they be on land or sea, inasmuch as God wills it."

Through the power of God and [f.146v] the help of Saint James, the ship of the Saracens immediately began to be put to a dangerous test by a great storm. The Christians' vessel, with Saint James leading with divine approval, arrived at its destination. Then

---

82. Although Frisonus is not currently a pilgrim to Compostela with these words he indicates that in the past he has visited the saint's tomb.

83. This is the first occasion in which Saint James holds a conversation with someone other than the beneficiary of a miracle.

84. Travel to the Holy Land by sea was fraught with danger, including the possibility of being taken prisoner for ransom, since the area was held by the Moslems until the First Crusade and again after the fall of the Latin Kingdom in the late thirteenth century. See John Wilkinson, et al., *Jerusalem Pilgrimage, 1099–1185* (London: Hakluyt Society, 1988) for English translations of nineteen pilgrimage narratives between 1099 and 1185.

85. It is uncertain if this could be the "god of the sea" of mythology or a reference to the Christian or Saracen God, but it is clear in Saint James's answer that the Saint is referring to the Christian God.

Frisonus, after visiting the Lord's tomb, went to Saint James in Galicia that same year.

This was accomplished by the Lord, and it is miraculous in our eyes.

May honor and glory be to Jesus Christ our Lord, the King of kings, for ever and ever. Amen.

CHAPTER 8

A MIRACLE OF SAINT JAMES
WRITTEN DOWN BY HIS EXCELLENCY POPE CALIXTUS

In the year of the Incarnation of our Lord one thousand one hundred two, a certain bishop, returning from Jerusalem, was sitting at the edge[86] of the ship and singing from his open Psalter,[87] when a strong wave surged up and swept him, along with several others, into the sea. As they were floating away on the wave and already at a distance of 60 cubits,[88] they called in a loud voice to Saint James, who was there for them immediately. Standing on the waves of Thetis[89] with the soles of his feet still dry, he said to those in danger and calling on him, "Do not fear, my little children." Then he immediately ordered Thetis to return those to the ship whom she had wickedly taken from it, and he called out from afar and advised the sailors to halt the boat.[90]

---

86. The Latin is *borum,* a non-existent word used here and again in Chapter X in both the CC and the Salamanca manuscript. It should probably read *bordum* or "edge." Vincent of Beauvais (Book 36, chapter 34) has *oram* here while the AASS corrects this to *bordum.*

87. The Psalter is an alternative name for a book containing the Psalms.

88. Sixty cubits is approximately ninety feet. A cubit is an ancient measure equal to the length of a man's forearm, including the length of the hand, or rather approximately eighteen to twenty inches.

89. In Greek mythology Thetis is one of the Nereids and the goddess of the sea. She is also known as the mother of Achilles and wife of Peleus. Her name is used here as a metonym for the sea.

90. This is the second time the saint directs his words to someone other than the beneficiary of the miracle.

THE MIRACLES

Thus it occurred. The sailors halted the ship, and the wave of Thetis, with the saint's help, returned all those whom it had wickedly seized from the ship — including the bishop with the book from which he was reading still open — safely and completely unharmed. Then the apostle immediately disappeared.

This was accomplished by the Lord, and it is miraculous in our eyes.

Afterwards, this venerable bishop of the Lord, who had been rescued from the dangers of the sea through the help of Saint James, went to the most glorious apostle in the region of Galicia and composed the following responsory in the saint's honor in the first tone of the musical art.[91] He intoned it joyously singing in this way:

> *Oh help for all ages,*
> *Oh honor of the apostles,*
> *Oh bright light of the Galicians,*
> *Oh advocate of the pilgrims,*
> *James, supplanter of vices,*
> *Release the chains of our sins,*
> *And lead us to the port of safety.*

Afterwards he composed a versicle in this way: "You, who help those at sea or on land calling out to you in their peril, help us now and in the trial of our death." Then he repeated: "Lead us [f.147r] to the port of safety."[92]

May Jesus Christ our Lord himself deign to be our guarantor, who, with the Father and the Holy Spirit, lives and reigns as God. World without end. Amen.[93]

---

91. The first of the nine tones of Gregorian chant.
92. The text of this responsory is found in Book I, chapter 22, where it is noted that the author was a certain bishop returning from Jerusalem.
93. The usual concluding phrase, "And it is miraculous in our eyes," is separated from the closing prayer by the author's story of the composition

Chapter 9

A Miracle of Saint James[94]
Written Down by His Excellency Pope Calixtus

In the year of the Incarnation of our Lord one thousand one hundred three, a certain glorious and very noble soldier from the nation of France, near Tiberias[95] in the region of Jerusalem, vowed that if the apostle James would give him the power of conquering and destroying the Turks[96] in war, he would go to James's threshold. With the help of God, the apostle conferred on him such power that he overcame all the Saracens who did battle with him. However, just as every man is said to be false, this soldier consigned his vow to the apostle to oblivion. Because of this, he deservedly became weak to the point of dying. When he could no longer speak because of his excessive weakness, Saint James appeared to his shield bearer in a trance and told him that if his master would fulfill what he had promised the apostle, then he would be immediately cured. When the shield bearer informed his lord of this, the soldier understood. Then he indicated to the priests who were there that they should give him the pilgrim's staff and blessed purse.[97] When he had

---

of the responsory. The formulaic ending is interrupted in other miracles, but this is the longest separation of the phrases.

94. Like chapter 3, this miracle tells of multiple instances of Saint James's intervention, and of miracles happening to several people: the soldier's success on the battlefield, James's appearance to the shield-bearer, the soldier's recovery, and the calming of the storm.

95. Probably the modern Teverya, in ancient times Tiberias, on the western shore of the Sea of Galilee. The Latin is *Thabariam*. The Christian armies of the First Crusade arrived at Jerusalem in 1099. This French soldier had probably settled in the Latin Kingdom of Jerusalem, a crusading state that lasted until 1187.

96. Here "Turks" is a general name for the infidels.

97. The "Veneranda dies" sermon explains the ceremony for bestowal of these pilgrim items and the way they are to be blessed. Coffey et al., *Miracles*, 23–24.

THE MIRACLES

accepted these accouterments and had packed the necessary provisions, he recovered from the sickness by which he was plagued. He immediately began to travel toward Saint James.

While he was aboard ship, the boat began to be threatened by a savage storm, so great that, with the waves sweeping across the ship's deck, all the passengers who were on the ship might be drowned. Immediately, all of the pilgrims[98] exclaimed in unison, "Saint James, help us!" Some promised to make a pilgrimage to Saint James's threshold, while others pledged various sums for the work of his basilica there.[99]

This soldier collected sums of money on the spot, and immediately the blessed apostle appeared in human form to these people in difficulty on the ship, saying, "Do not be afraid, my children, because, behold, I on whom you have called am here with you. Be confident in Christ, and well-being shall come to you here and in the future."

He immediately bent the sails' ropes, cast the anchor, stabilized the vessel, and controlled the storm. Then, after bringing about great tranquility on the sea, the apostle disappeared.

His face appeared in this way: decent and, if you will, [f.147v] elegant and of such a type as none of them had occasion to see either before or after.[100]

This was accomplished by the Lord, and it is miraculous in our eyes.

After this, the ship and its pilgrims came to the desired port in Apulia with smooth passage.[101] Then this soldier happily went to

---

98. These apparently were Holy Land pilgrims returning to Europe.

99. According to the Guide (Melczer, *Pilgrim's Guide*, 130), work began on the present cathedral in Compostela in 1075, with the last stone laid in 1122, so donations of money would be appropriate pledges of faith.

100. The first of two physical descriptions of Saint James's face. See also chapter 17.

101. Apulia in southeast Italy includes the medieval ports of Bari and Brindisi, regularly used by pilgrims traveling to the Holy Land. Apulia is also the miracle location in chapter 12.

the basilica in the region of Galicia with the other pilgrims, and he placed the sum of money that he had collected in the coffer of Saint James for the work on the church.

May glory and honor be to the King of kings, for ever and ever. Amen.

Chapter 10

A Miracle of Saint James
Written Down by His Excellency Pope Calixtus

In the year of the Incarnation of our Lord one thousand one hundred four, while a certain pilgrim returning from Jerusalem was sitting on the edge of the ship for the sake of digestion, he fell from the ship into the open sea. While he was appealing to Saint James with great noise, one of his companions threw his shield[102] down from the ship to him in the sea, saying, "May the most glorious apostle James, whose help you invoke, assist you."

The drowning man grasped the shield and for three days and three nights, with Saint James leading with divine approbation, swam through the sea's waves, following the wake of the ship, until he came unharmed to the desired port together with the others. He then told everyone how Saint James had guided him from the moment when he had called to him by holding his head with his hand.

This was accomplished by the Lord, and it is miraculous in our eyes.

May glory and honor be to the King of kings, for ever and ever. Amen.

---

102. Probably a leather shield instead of metal, in which case there would be greater likelihood of its floating, although being a miracle, it probably did not matter.

THE MIRACLES

Chapter 11

A Miracle of Saint James Written Down by His Excellency Pope Calixtus

In the year of the Incarnation of our Lord one thousand one hundred five, there lived a man named Bernard who was captured near the castle of Corzanum[103] in Italy in the diocese of Modena and who was then bound in chains and thrown into the depths of a tower by his enemies.

As he implored the help of Saint James night and day with a continual cry, the most glorious apostle of Christ appeared to him, saying, "Come, follow me to Galicia." When this man's chains were broken, James disappeared.

Immediately the pilgrim, with his shackle around his neck, climbed to the top of the tower, supported by the help of Saint [f.148r] James but without the help of any human. What more can one say?[104] He made a single jump from the top of the tower to the ground outside without incurring any harm. The height of the tower was sixty cubits.[105] Thus it was a great wonder that someone who fell from such a height avoided death.

This was accomplished by the Lord, and it is miraculous in our eyes.

May glory and honor be to the King of kings, for ever and ever. Amen.[106]

---

103. The Latin is *Corzanum* and it is left as such. For what this might refer to, see Leardo Mascanzoni. "Un miracolo Emiliano-Romagnolo nel *Codice Callistino* di Compostela," *Studi Romagnoli* 63 (2012): 509–24.
104. This is the third instance of this rhetorical question. See chapters 3 and 22.
105. About 90 feet. See p. 30, n. 88.
106. A second "Amen" appears here in a marginal addition to the manuscript, as in miracles 11–14, 21 and 22

MIRACLES AND TRANSLATIO OF SAINT JAMES

Chapter 12

A Miracle of Saint James
Written Down by His Excellency Pope Calixtus

Around the beginning of the year of the Incarnation of our Lord one thousand one hundred six, a certain soldier in the region of Apulia[107] had his throat become swollen like a bag full of air. Since he could find no remedy for his health from any physician, he entrusted himself to Saint James who said that if he could find a shell,[108] such as pilgrims are accustomed to bring back with them on their return from Saint James, and if he could touch his ailing throat with it, he would immediately be cured.[109] When he had found one at the house of a certain pilgrim who happened to be his neighbor, he touched his throat with it, and he was cured. Then he set out from there toward the threshold of Saint James in Galicia.

This was accomplished by the Lord, and it is miraculous in our eyes.

May glory and honor be to the Lord himself, Father and Son and Holy Spirit, for ever and ever. Amen.[110]

---

107. For Apulia, see p. 33, n. 101.

108. This is the only mention of the shell (Latin: *crusillam*) in Book II. The "Veneranda dies" sermon (Coffey et al., *Miracles*, 25) talks about its importance, and the Guide (Melczer, *Pilgrim's Guide*, 22), refers to Compostela shell-vendors where the term is *crusillae piscium*. *Crusilla* was literally "small crosses," but it is clear that the medieval writer was referring to the scallop shell on which a cross was often painted. See Christopher Hohler, "The Badge of St. James," *The Scallop: Studies of a Shell and Its Influences on Humankind* (London: Shell Transport and Trading Co., 1957), 49–70, for the scallop as pilgrimage symbol. There is a curious discussion of shells in chapter 4 of Book III. See pp. 95–96.

109. This is the only miracle which mentions the use of a "touch relic," an item which has been touched against the relic and which then transferred the power of the relic to the item. See Brian Spencer, *Pilgrim Souvenirs and Secular Badges* (London: The Stationery Office, 1998), 16–20, about the use of pilgrim signs as touch relics.

110. See p. 35, n. 106.

THE MIRACLES

Chapter 13

A Miracle of Saint James
Written Down by His Excellency Pope Calixtus

In the year of the Incarnation of our Lord one thousand one hundred thirty-five, a certain Allobrogian soldier named Dalmatius from Chavannes,[111] unjustly struck Raimbert, who was one of his serfs and a pilgrim to Saint James, on the cheek with his fist when he quarreled with him. While Raimbert was being struck by the soldier, he said, "God and Saint James, help!" Immediately, with divine wrath at work, the soldier was felled to the ground as if knocked unconscious, with his arm twisted and broken.

After being absolved by priests,[112] he asked forgiveness from his serf. "Oh Raimbert," he said, "pilgrim of Saint James, pray to the apostle, in whom you confide, for my well-being."

After being asked by Raimbert to do this, Saint James restored the soldier to his original condition [f.148v] through divine mercy.

This was accomplished by the Lord, and it is miraculous in our eyes.

May glory and honor be to the King of kings, for ever and ever. Amen.[113]

---

111. Chavannes is in the French department of Drôme, south of Vienne, formerly in the province of Dauphiné. The Latin *Allobrox* or *Allobros* represents roughly the modern areas of Savoy and Dauphiné, the area between the Rhône and Isère Rivers, in the province of Vienne, where Calixtus had been archbishop. This group of people is one of several mentioned in the "Veneranda dies" sermon. Coffey et al., *Miracles*, 18.

112. It is unclear in the Latin how much time has passed. It is unusual to be absolved by more than one priest.

113. See p. 5, n. 11. The chapter list at the beginning of Book II says of chapter 13 only that the apostle brings Dalmatius "to justice," but there is a second miracle, the physical healing of Dalmatius after he asks for and receives forgiveness from Raimbert.

MIRACLES AND TRANSLATIO OF SAINT JAMES

Chapter 14

A Story of Saint James
Written Down by His Excellency Pope Calixtus

In the year of the Incarnation of our Lord one thousand one hundred seven, a certain merchant, wishing to go to a market fair with his goods, approached the lord of that land where he wished to go. This lord had, by chance, come to the city in which the merchant was staying. The merchant asked and implored the lord to conduct him safely to the festival and then to conduct him back to his home. The lord agreed to his request, promised that he would do so, and gave the merchant his guarantee.

The merchant, believing the words of such a great man, set out with his goods toward the region where the fair was taking place. Afterwards, however, the lord, who had given his guarantee that he would protect the merchant and his goods and conduct him to and from his destination, was moved by the instigation of the devil. He went to see the merchant, took his goods, threw him into jail, and held him fast.

The merchant, however, remembered the countless miracles of Saint James that he had heard from many people. Then he called on the saint to come to him in aid, saying, "Saint James, free me from this jail and I promise to give myself and my belongings to you."

Saint James indeed heard the merchant's sighs and prayers. One night, with the guards still on watch, he appeared to the merchant in the jail, ordered the merchant to get up and led him to the top of the tower, which bent itself so much that it appeared to place its top on the ground. The merchant stepped off of the tower without jumping and without injury, and, freed from his chains, he walked away. The guards went after him and came up next to him, and, finding nothing, went back from there blinded.

The merchant took the chains by which he had been held along with him to the basilica of the blessed apostle in Galicia, and they hang there today in front of the altar of the most glorious James in testimony of such a deed."[114]

This was accomplished by the Lord, and it is miraculous in our eyes.

For this may honor and glory be to the supreme King, for ever and ever. Amen."[115]

Chapter 15

A Story of Saint James
Written Down by His Excellency Pope Calixtus [F.149R]

Around the beginning of the year of the Incarnation of our Lord one thousand one hundred ten, soldiers from two cities in Italy that were feuding with each other, gathered for battle. One group, overcome by the other group, turned their backs and began to flee in confusion.

Within this group was a certain soldier who was accustomed to seek the threshold of Saint James. While he was fleeing, he saw one group of his fleeing comrades already captured and another group killed, and he despaired of his life. He began to call out to Saint James to aid him hardly as a cry but merely as a groan. Finally he said with a loud voice, "Saint James, if you will deign to free me from this imminent danger, I shall dispatch myself and my horse to your court without delay. I hold nothing more precious. I shall hasten to your presence."

When this prayer was completed, this most blessed James, who does not deny himself to those asking with a proper heart, but who is, on the contrary, ready to help in all things, hastened to appear between the soldier and his enemies who were savagely pursuing him, eagerly desiring to capture him and who had already taken by the sword or by captivity all the others who were fleeing. And

---

114. Compostela scholars and custodians of the cathedral treasury assert that there are no extant chains anywhere in the Compostela cathedral.
115. See p. 35, n. 106.

James freed the soldier from his pursuing enemies by protecting him with his shield for a distance of six leagues.[116]

Lest this miracle be attributed to the power of the soldier's horse instead of to the glory of Saint James, as is customarily done by those who assail the Church and are envious of its goods, and so that any question of these envious people be answered, it was evident that this horse was not worth twenty *solidi* in terms of money.[117]

Lest his vow remain unfulfilled the soldier offered himself and his horse in the presence of the blessed apostle, and, so he might completely fulfill what he had vowed, he hastened to the gates of the altar, over the protests of the guards. Because of their joy over this miracle, both clerics and lay persons, as is the custom, ran to the church and gave thanks to God with hymns and psalms.

This was accomplished by the Lord, and it is miraculous in our eyes.

May honor and glory be to the Lord Himself, for ever and ever. Amen.

---

116. The "league" varies in its equivalents from country to country and from epoch to epoch, but may be from four to six and a half kilometers (between 3933 and 6620 meters). For a second time Saint James is described with a militant aspect as he covers the man with his shield.

117. The *solidus*, which gave us the English "soldier" and the Spanish *sueldo* "salary," was a coin authorized by Charlemagne to be worth 12 *denarii*. It has its origin in the idea of a solid or compact method of carrying coins. It was originally "solid gold" fit to be carried by a "soldier."

THE MIRACLES

CHAPTER 16

A MIRACLE OF SAINT JAMES
WRITTEN DOWN BY SAINT ANSELM, ARCHBISHOP OF CANTERBURY[118]

Three soldiers from the diocese of Lyon and from the church in the town of Donzy[119] agreed that they would go to the region of Galicia for the sake of praying to Saint James the Apostle, [f.149v] and so they set out.

While they were en route on this pilgrimage, they encountered a small woman who was carrying the things she needed in a little sack.[120] When she saw the horsemen, she asked that they have mercy on her and carry her little sack on their horses out of love for the blessed apostle and thus relieve her from the toil of such a great journey. One of them agreed to this pilgrim's request and took her bag and carried it. As evening was drawing near, the woman, who had followed the horsemen, took what she needed for herself from the little sack. At the first crowing of the cock, when pilgrims on

---

118. Anselm (c. 1033–1109) was born in Burgundy, became bishop of Caen in 1063 and became archbishop of Canterbury in 1093. This and the next miracle are chapters 21 and 22 of Anselm's *De miraculis* (R.W. Southern and F. S. Schmitt, eds., *Memorials of Saint Anselm* [Oxford: Oxford University Press, 1969], pp. 196–207), but the PL places them in his *Spuria* (PL 159:335–38) and signaled them as being from a *Codex Sangermanensis*. See Southern "The English Origins of the Miracles of the Virgin," *Medieval and Renaissance Studies* 4 (1958): 188–90, 205–8, about the provenance of Anselm's *De miraculis*. See BHL 525–25 and PL 158–59. This is the third of the four miracles ascribed to an author other than Calixtus.

119. Latin: *Dumzeii*. In conjunction with the diocese of Lyon — some 470 kilometers southeast of Paris — two possibilities arise: Donzy-le-National and Donzy-le-Pertuis, both north of Lyon in the department of Saône-et-Loire. See also miracle 17 below.

120. Latin: *saculo*. Both the woman and the sack are consistently described here with diminutive endings. The "Veneranda dies" sermon gives a fairly elaborate description of the bag that the pilgrim should carry, giving the term in Provençal (*sporta*), French (*ysquirpa*) and Italian (*scarsella*) as well. (Coffey et al., *Miracles*, 24.)

41

foot typically set out, she gave the little sack back to the horseman. Thus unimpeded, she made the journey a happier person. In this way, the soldier was helping the woman out of love for the apostle as he was hastening toward the desired place of prayer.

When they were twelve days[121] away from the city of Saint James, this soldier came across a poor sick person on the road. He began to beg the soldier to give him his animal to ride on until he could arrive at Saint James, otherwise, the sick man would die on the road, since he was unable to walk any further. The soldier agreed, dismounted, placed the beggar on the horse and took the beggar's staff[122] in his hand, still carrying around his neck the little bag that he had accepted from the woman.

As he traveled along in this way, and as he was afflicted by the heat of the sun and by the weariness from such a long journey, he began to grow sick. When he sensed this, he took into account that he had often offended a great deal in many ways, and he endured his discomfort calmly out of the love for the apostle, going all the way to the threshold on foot. There, after he had prayed to the apostle and found lodging, he lay down in a small bed and remained there for several days with increasing weariness from the malady that had begun on the road. When the other soldiers, who had been his friends, saw this, they went to him and counseled him to confess his sins, to seek the other things that are appropriate for Christians, and to prepare for his impending death.

When he heard this, the sick pilgrim turned his face away and could not answer. He lay this way for three days without uttering a single word. Because of this, his friends were afflicted with a heavy grief, partly because they were distressed about his health, but especially because [f.150r] he could not ensure the health of his soul. One day, however, when those sitting around him and awaiting his death thought that was he would soon breathe his last breath, he

---

121. According to the Guide, this would put the soldiers in Viscarret (Navarra).

122. Latin: *baculum*. The "Veneranda dies" describes the type and uses of the pilgrim's staff. (Coffey et al., *Miracles*, 23–24.)

THE MIRACLES

said to them with a great sigh, "I give thanks to God and to Saint James, my lord, because I have been freed."

When those present asked what this might mean, he said, "From the moment I felt myself growing worse from my weakness, I silently began thinking to myself that I might want to confess my sins, to be anointed with holy oil, and to be fortified by receiving the Body of the Lord. But while I dealt with these thoughts in silence, a band of dark spirits suddenly came toward me, which oppressed me to such a degree that from that hour forth I could not indicate either with word or sign anything that might pertain to my well-being. I understood well what you were saying, but I could not respond with any speech. For the demons flocked together, some plucking at my tongue, others closing my eyes, still others turning my head and body first this way and then that, according to their desires and against my will.

"However, just a little while before I began to speak to you, Saint James entered here, holding in his left hand the woman's little sack, which I had borne on the road. In his right hand he was holding the beggar's staff that I had carried while he had ridden my horse on the day when my illness began. He held the staff as a lance and the little sack as a shield.[123] He immediately came toward me in a kind of indignant fury, raised the staff and tried to strike the demons who had held me.[124] Terrified, they fled immediately and he followed them, forcing them to leave here through that corner. Behold, after being liberated from those who were harassing and tormenting me, I am able to speak through the grace of God and Saint James. Send quickly and get a priest who can give me the viaticum of Holy

---

123. This was originally translated as "weapon" based on the Whitehill edition; we subsequently determined, using Kaydeda and Salamanca facsimile versions that it should not have been transcribed as *arma* or "weapon" but rather as *parma* or "shield."

124. An interesting use of the typical pilgrim symbols (the scrip and staff) as weapons, given the duality of Saint James's depiction as either a pilgrim or a warrior (Santiago Peregrino or Santiago Matamoros). This is the third time Saint James appears with military or knightly attributes.

Communion.¹²⁵ For in fact I do not have permission to remain in this life any longer."

After they had sent for the priest and during his delay in coming, the dying man admonished one of his companions publicly, saying, "Friend, do not fight for your former lord, Girin, le Chauve,¹²⁶ to whom you have until now owed allegiance, for he has truly been damned and is about to die an evil death in the near future."

The matter proved true in just this way, [f.150v] for afterwards the pilgrim came to rest with a good conclusion to his life, and he was given burial. When his companions returned home and told what had occurred, Girin, surnamed "le Chauve," who had been a rich man, considered their story a dream, and he did not correct his depravity in the least. For this reason, not many days later, it happened that while he was killing a soldier in an armed invasion, he also died, run through with the soldier's lance.

Therefore, may honor and glory be to the King of kings, our Lord Jesus Christ, for ever and ever. Amen.¹²⁷

---

125. Latin: *sanctae communionis viaticum*. Viaticum is the Eucharist administered during the last rites.

126. David ("Etudes," 11:169) suggests that Girinus Calvus is known through several cartularies of Savigny, and he was, in effect, the lord of Donzy, son of Girin de Sail and of Gothelande. David also suggests "it would not be impossible" for this to have been recorded by Anselm who was in Lyon during the winter of 1097–98, again in the fall of 1100 and yet again in 1104–1105. Here we have translated Calvus as "le Chauve" as it seems to be used as a family name (similar to a French family name like "Lebrun").

127. This miracle does not end with the formulaic statement "It is miraculous in our eyes."

THE MIRACLES

Chapter 17

A Great Miracle of Saint James Written Down
by Saint Anselm, Archbishop of Canterbury[128]

Near the city of Lyon is a village in which a certain young man named Gerald dwelled. He was instructed in the art of tanning and lived from the just labor of his hands, supporting his mother, when his father had died. He ardently loved Saint James and was accustomed to travel to the saint's threshold every year to make an offering. He had no wife but lived a chaste life alone with his old mother. While he could contain himself for a fairly long time, finally on one occasion, he was overcome by the voluptuousness of the flesh and fornicated with a certain maiden.

When the next morning arrived, since he had previously arranged it, he set out on his pilgrimage to Saint James in Galicia with two of his neighbors and brought a donkey with him. While they were on the road, they met a beggar going to Saint James and took up with him for the sake of company and even more so out of love for the apostle, sharing with him the necessities of life.

Continuing their travels, they spent several days together happily. The devil, however, who envied their peaceful and charitable company, approached in charming human guise the young man who had secretly fornicated back home and said to him, "Do you know who I am?"

---

128. See p. 41, n. 118. This miracle is not original to Anselm. John Benton, ed. *Self and Society in Medieval France. The Memoirs of Abbot Guibert of Nogent* (Toronto: U of Toronto P, 1984) points to an eleventh-century poem by Guaiferius of Salerno, *De miraculo illius qui seipsum occidit* (PL 147:1285–88), whose conclusion cites the miraculous cure "near Cluny in the time of Abbot Hugues" <sic>. What is most interesting is that "the theme of sexual mutilation is absent from the poem..." (218 n. 2). Another early eleventh century version of this miracle, in prose and with castration as part of the story, is recounted by Guibert of Nogent in his *Monodiae* (*Memoirs*), chapter 19, written c. 1125. This miracle is found in Anselm's *Spuria* (PL 159:337–40), also in Southern and Schmidt, *Memorials*, 200–207.

The young man answered, "Not at all."

The demon said, "I am James the Apostle, whom you have been accustomed to visit every year for a long time now and to honor with your offerings. May you know that I took great joy from you and that I had hoped that great good would come from you. However, just before you left your home you fornicated with [f.151r] a woman, and between then and now you have done no penance, nor have you wanted to confess this act. Thus you have set out for a foreign land with your sin, as if your pilgrimage would be acceptable to God and to me. It must not occur in this way. For whoever wishes to make a pilgrimage out of love for me, must first disclose his sins through a humble confession, and afterwards wipe out those acts through making a pilgrimage. Whoever does otherwise will have his pilgrimage go unheeded."[129]

Having said this, the devil vanished from the young man's sight. After hearing these things, the man began to grow sad, thinking in his mind that he should return home to confess to his priest and then return to the journey that he had started.

While he was running this course of action through his mind, the demon came to him in the same form in which he had previously appeared and said to him, "What is this that you are thinking in your heart about wanting to go back home to do penance, so that you might be able to return to me more worthily afterwards? Do you think you can erase such a great crime with your fasting or tears? You are acting very foolishly. Believe my advice, and you will be saved. Otherwise you will not be saved. Although you may have sinned, I still love you, and because of this, I have come to you, so that I might give you counsel by which you can be saved, if you should wish to believe me."

---

129. This type of moral sermon is not typical in this collection of miracles. It is ironic that such sound advice should come from the mouth of the devil, who is busily deceiving the pilgrim. The devil's speech does, however, confirm the "Veneranda dies" warning about preparing oneself physically, spiritually, and morally before leaving on a pilgrimage (Coffey et al., *Miracles*, 26–34).

THE MIRACLES

The pilgrim said to him, "I was just thinking along the same lines as you are saying, but now that you assert that this course of action is not beneficial for my salvation, tell me what action is pleasing to you by which I may be saved, and I will willingly carry it out."

The devil then said, "If you wish to be completely cleansed from sin, cut off very quickly the manly parts with which you have sinned."

After hearing this advice, the terrified man said, "If I do to myself what you are advising, I will not be able to live, and I will be my own murderer, which I have often heard is damnable in the eyes of God."

The demon, laughing, said, "Oh, you fool, how little you understand the things that could be a benefit for your salvation. If you die in this way, you will, without doubt, come to me, since, in effacing your sin, you will be a martyr. Oh, if you were so prudent that you would not hesitate to kill yourself, I would certainly come to you immediately with a multitude of my followers and would gladly accept your soul to remain with me." Then he affirmed, "I am James the Apostle who advises you. Do as I have said if you wish to come into my company and find [f.151v] a solution to your sin."

After hearing these things, the simple pilgrim turned his mind toward his crime and while his companions were sleeping at night, he took out a knife and cut off his manly parts. Then, turning his hand, he raised the knife, thrust its sharp point into his stomach and pierced himself through.

As the blood flowed freely and as the man was causing a commotion by thrashing about, his companions were awakened, and they called to him, asking what was the matter. When he did not give them any answer, as he was anxiously drawing his last breath, they became alarmed, got up quickly,[130] lit their lamps, and found their half-dead companion unable to respond to them. They were stupefied by this and stricken with great terror, lest his death be blamed on them if they should be found in that place in the morning. They took flight and left him behind, rolling in his blood, leaving as well the donkey and the beggar whom they had begun to feed.

---

130. Latin: *concite*. the word is not found, but the meaning is clear.

The next morning, when the family of the house arose, they found the slain man. As they were uncertain whom they might blame for this murder, they called their neighbors and carried the dead man to church for burial. There, because of the flow of blood, they placed him in front of the doors while the grave was being prepared. After a short delay, the man who had been dead came to and sat upright on the funeral bier on which he was placed. When those who were present saw this, they fled and cried out in terror. Alarmed by their cry, people ran up and asked what had happened, and heard that a dead man had returned to life.[131]

When they came closer and began to speak to him, he told all of them freely what had happened to him. He said, "I, whom you see raised from the dead, have loved Saint James since childhood, and I have been accustomed to serve him as much as I could. However, a short while ago, I decided to make a pilgrimage to his tomb, and as I was approaching this village, the devil deceived me, saying that *he* was Saint James...." Then he told the whole series of events, just as it is set forth above, and added, "After I took my life and after my soul was taken from my body, that same malignant spirit who had deceived me came to me, leading a great hoard of demons. [f.152r] Without mercy, they immediately grabbed me and took me, weeping and uttering miserable cries, to their torments.

"They directed their course toward Rome. When we had to come to the forest situated between the city of Rome and the town called Labicum,[132] Saint James, who had followed behind us, flew up to us and said to the whole group of demons, 'Where do you come from and where are you going?' They said, 'Oh James, certainly this is none of your business. For this man believed us to such an

---

131. This is the second pilgrim resurrected from the dead by Saint James in this collection. Cf. chapter 3.

132. About fifteen miles southeast of Rome near Valmontone. The *Via Labicana,* ran between the town, which is no longer extant, and the Coliseum in Rome. The present town of Labico, probably named for it, is not on the same site. The trial would have taken place somewhere along the *Via.* It is interesting to note that the demons take the pilgrim to a specific and real location near Rome, the seat of the Church.

THE MIRACLES

extent that he killed himself. We persuaded him. We deceived him. We must have him.' James said to them, 'You have not answered my questions, but you rejoice by boasting that you have deceived a Christian. For this may you receive ill thanks. This is my pilgrim whom you boast of possessing. You will not bear him off with impunity.' James appeared to me to be young with a handsome face, lean and of that moderate color that people call brown.[133]

"With him coercing us, we turned toward Rome. Near the Church of Saint Peter the Apostle,[134] there was a green and spacious place on an airy plain, to which an immeasurable crowd had come for a council, over which Our Lady Mary, the venerable Mother of God and perpetual virgin, presided, with many admirable nobles sitting at her right and left. I began to contemplate her with a great affection in my heart, for never in my life have I seen such a beautiful creature. She was not of a large, but rather moderate, stature, and pleasing in appearance with a most beautiful face. The blessed apostle, my most pious advocate,[135] sat in front of her and before all of the others and he publicly made complaint concerning the treachery of Satan with which he had deceived me. She immediately turned to the demons and said, 'Oh you miserable creatures! What do you seek in a pilgrim of my Lord and Son, and of James, His faithful one? Your pain should be enough for you. There should be no need for you to increase your pain through this depraved act of yours.'

"After this most blessed lady had spoken, she compassionately turned her gaze on me. The demons, however, were beset by great

---

133. The second physical description of the saint's face. See chapter 9.

134. The author could be referring to one of two Roman churches dedicated to Saint Peter: Old St. Peter's Basilica on the site where St. Peter's Basilica sits today in Vatican City or St. Peter in Vincoli that houses the relic of the chains that bound Saint Peter in Jerusalem and is only a short distance from the Coliseum. The chains and this church are discussed at length in the *Translatio*, chapter 3.

135. See Francisco Puy Múñoz, "Santiago abogado en el 'Calixtino' (1160)" in *Pistoia e il Cammino di Santiago* (Perugia: Edizione scientifiche italiane, 1984): 57–92 for a study of the theme of Saint James as advocate and lawyer in the LSJ.

fear, as all those sitting in council were saying that the demons had acted unjustly against the apostle by deceiving me, and the lady ordered that I be returned to my body. Saint James immediately picked me up [f.152v] and brought me back to this place. That is how I died and was restored to life."

Upon hearing this, the inhabitants of the place rejoiced enthusiastically and took him directly to their house. They kept him with them for three days, telling everyone about him and exhibiting him as the one on whom God through Saint James had worked such an unusual and miraculous thing. His lesions were healed immediately with only scars remaining in the place of his wounds. In place of his genitals there grew a sort of wart through which he could discharge urine.

When the days during which the residents of the place had kept him with them out of joy came to an end, he prepared his donkey and set out on his journey along with his beggar friend who had joined him on the road. As he was approaching the threshold of the blessed apostle, lo and behold, he met his friends who had abandoned him and who were making the return journey. While they were still at a distance, and when they saw the two men goading the donkey, they said to each other, "These men are similar to our companions whom we left behind, the one dead, the other alive, and the animal that they are goading is not much different, as far as can be seen, from the one that was left behind with them." Then, as they were approaching the two men, and as each group began to recognize the other, they learned what had occurred, and they exulted fervently.

When they returned home, they told everything just as it had happened. Furthermore, the man who had been raised from the dead confirmed in substance what his friends had earlier said when he returned from Saint James. As the story spread far and wide, he retold the story, showed his scars and even showed what had been in his most private place to the many people wanting to see it. Saint Hugh, the most reverend abbot of Cluny,[136] along with many

---

136. Saint Hugh, abbot of Cluny (1024–1109), feast day April 29, canonized in 1120 by Pope Calixtus II (BHL 4007–15). For his works, see PL 159.

THE MIRACLES

others, saw this man and all the signs of his death, and it is said that he was accustomed to assert rather often, out of admiration, that he had seen it.

We have also consigned this miracle to writing out of love for the apostle, lest it be dropped from memory. And we give the order to all that every year on the fifth day of the nones of October,[137] a feast should be celebrated in all churches with worthy ceremony for this miracle and for the other miracles of Saint James.[138]

Therefore, may honor and glory be to the King of kings, who has deigned to work so many and such great miracles for His beloved James, for ever and ever.[139] Amen.

See p. LII and p. 45, n. 128. Hugh had a great interest in the pilgrimage to Compostela, and Cluny reached its maximum influence under his leadership.

137. October 3. See the Introduction, pp. LVII–LVIX, for a discussion of the saint's feast days.

138. "And we give the order...miracles of Saint James" is found in the margin of the manuscript in the *Codex* but is integrated fully into the text of the Salamanca manuscript.

139. This miracle does not end with the formulaic "and it is miraculous in our eyes."

MIRACLES AND TRANSLATIO OF SAINT JAMES

Chapter 18

A Miracle of Saint James
Written Down By His Excellency Pope Calixtus[140]

Not long ago a count of Saint-Gilles[141] named Pontius[142] came to Saint James with his brother in order to pray to the saint. [f.153f] When they had entered the church and were unable to enter the oratory in which the apostle's body lay,[143] as they wished to do, they asked the guard to open the oratory for them so that they could spend the night keeping vigil in front of the saint's body.[144]

---

140. This miracle, like the previous two, is found in Anselm's *De miraculis*. It forms chapter 23 of Anselm's collection. The first sentence is a direct quote, which accounts for the lack of the formulaic opening sentence typical to the other miracles ascribed to Calixtus. See Southern, "The English Origins," pp. 188–90, 205–13.

141. Saint-Gilles is in the department of Gard in France. Saint Gilles is a favorite saint of the author. Chapters 3 and 5 of this book tell miracles similar to those attributed to Saint Gilles. See p. 13, n. 37 and p. 22, n. 64. The saint and the town bearing his name are cited several times in the "Veneranda dies" sermon as well as an extended description of both saint and church in the Guide, chapter 8 (Melczer, *Pilgrim's Guide*, 98–102).

142. "Pontius, count of St. Gilles, was count of Toulouse from c. 1037 till his death in 1061." Southern and Schmidt, *Memorials*, 208 n. 3. His son Raymond IV (c. 1041–1105), originally just count of Saint-Gilles, succeeded him and became one of the leaders of the First Crusade. Pontius's younger son Hugh became abbot of Saint-Gilles. Pontius died in Toulouse and was buried in Saint-Sernin. For more detailed information, see the website by Charles Cawley on the rulers of Toulouse: http://fmg.ac/Projects/MedLands/TOULOUSE.htm (accessed July 2018).

143. See Kenneth Conant, *The Early Architectural History of the Cathedral of Santiago* (Cambridge: Harvard University Press, 1926) and the annotated edition of Conant by Serafín Moralejo Álvarez, *Arquitectura románica de la Catedral de Santiago de Compostela. Notas para una revisión crítica de la obra de K.J. Conant* (Santiago: Colexio de Arquitectos de Galicia, 1983) for detailed descriptions of the architecture of the twelfth century cathedral.

144. The main area of the basilica, as established in the "Veneranda dies" and in chapters 6, 18 and 19 was open day and night. See p. 26, n. 74.

THE MIRACLES

When they saw that their request had no effect, since it was the custom there that the gates of this oratory remain closed from the sun's setting until it shone again the next day, they departed sadly toward their lodging.

When they arrived there, they ordered all the pilgrims of their group[145] to come together. The count said to all those present that he wanted to go to Saint James, with those of a similar mind accompanying him, if, by chance, the place should deign to open for them all by itself.

Since they all accepted this idea harmoniously and freely, they prepared lamps, which they held in their hands while keeping watch. With the evening thus spent, they lit their lamps and went to the church with about two hundred in their number. As they approached the front of the blessed apostle's oratory, they prayed in a loud voice and said, "Most blessed James, apostle of God, if it pleases you that we might come to you, open your oratory for us so that we may keep vigil before you."[146]

What a miraculous event! Hardly had they finished these words when lo and behold, the oratory's gates made such a noise that all who were there thought that the gates would break into small pieces. When they inspected these things, the bolt, bars, and chains with which the gates were locked were found unfastened and shattered. Thus the gates were opened by an invisible power and not by human hands and offered entry to the pilgrims.

They rejoiced enthusiastically and entered, and they exulted all the more over this miracle in as much as they saw that they had demonstrated that this blessed apostle, who is a soldier of the Invincible Emperor, most truly lives, as they saw him attend to their

---

145. Traveling in groups was necessary and typical. Noble pilgrims often had a retinue with them.

146. See Humbert Jacomet, "Santiago: En busca del gran perdón" in *Santiago, Camino de Europa: Culto y Cultura en la Peregrinación a Compostela* (Madrid: Fundación Caja de Madrid, 1993), 77 for a miniature from a fifteenth-century manuscript of Vincent de Beauvais' *Speculum historiale*, which shows this scene.

petition so quickly.[147] In this event, one can examine how attentive the saint is to a pious petition, since he was so gracious in attending to this petition from his servants.

May your clemency, most gracious James, apostle of God, come to our aid, so that we might thus avoid the deceits of Satan in the course of this present life and inherit the heavenly kingdom through our good efforts [f.153v] and be able to arrive in this kingdom with your help, through Christ our Lord, who lives and reigns as God. World without end. Amen.[148]

Chapter 19

A Miracle of Saint James
Written Down by His Excellency Pope Calixtus[149]

It is known to everyone, both cleric and lay, dwelling in Compostela, that a certain man named Stephen, who was endowed with divine

---

147. The third time Saint James is specifically called a soldier.

148. The closing sentence is only part of the formulaic termination of these miracles, omitting the phrase "and it is miraculous in our eyes." The narrator takes advantage of the moral lesson just taught by adding his own brief prayer addressed to Saint James, asking for guidance in this life. Reminders of more abstract and heavenly goals appear a few times in these miracles. Compare chapters 2–6, 17, and 22.

149. This miracle is connected to a specific historical event, the conquest of Coimbra (1064) and the saint's part in it, first related in the *Historia silense*. See Manuel Díaz y Díaz, *Visiones del más allá en Galicia durante la alta edad media* (Santiago de Compostela: Xunta de Galicia, 1985) for a comparison and transcription of the two narrations. See Francisco Santos Coco, *Historia silense* (Madrid: Sucesores de Rivadeneyra, 1921). For the development of Saint James's military imagery from *caballero* to "Matamoros," see Angel Sicart Giménez, "La figura de Santiago en los textos medievales" in *Il Pellegrinaggio a Santiago de Compostela e la Letteratura Jacopea* (Perugia: Università degli studi di Perugia, 1985), 271–86; and Javier Domínguez García, *De Apóstol Matamoros a Yllapa Mataindios: Dogmas e ideologías medievales en el (des)cubrimiento de América* (Salamanca: Ediciones Universidad de Salamanca, 2008) for additional political and ideological observations through the eighteenth century.

THE MIRACLES

powers, had set aside the episcopal dignity and the pontifical office out of love for Saint James and set out from the region of Greece for the threshold of the apostle. He renounced the enticements of this world so that he might adhere to the divine dictates. Therefore, he refused to return to his own area, and he approached the guards of the building in which the most precious treasure and honor of Spain, namely, the body of Saint James, is located. He cast himself at their feet and begged them to grant him an out-of-the-way place in the church where he might be permitted to devote himself to continuous prayer. He asked this out of love for the most precious apostle, out of love for whom he had rejected worldly delights and earthly pleasures. Although he was wearing poor clothing and conducting himself not as a bishop but as a poor pilgrim, they did not hold him in contempt, but agreed to his just request. They prepared a sort of dwelling for him that was constructed out of rushes in the manner of a cell and located inside the basilica of the blessed apostle and from its right front he could look at the altar. In this place Stephen spent his celibate and most blessed life in fasts, vigils, and prayers, both day and night.

One day, however, while he was engaged in his customary prayer, a crowd of peasants who were gathering for a special feast for the most precious James and were standing next to this most holy man's cell near the altar, began to appeal to the apostle of God with these words, "Saint James, good soldier, remove us from current and future evils."[150]

This most holy man of God reacted indignantly to this word, and because the peasants had called James a *soldier*, he said to them angrily, "You stupid peasants! You foolish people! It is not proper to call Saint James a *soldier*, but rather a *fisherman*, in remembrance of the time when, at the Lord's calling, he left the fishing profession, followed the Lord and after that was made a fisher of men."[151]

On the night following the very day [f.154r] in which the most holy man had said this about Saint James, Saint James appeared,

---

150. The fourth time Saint James is specifically called a soldier.
151. Mt 4:18–22, Mk 1:19–20.

adorned in the whitest clothing, bearing military arms surpassing the rays of Titan,[152] as if transformed into a soldier, and also holding two keys in his hand.[153] After calling to the holy man three times, James spoke in this way, "Stephen, servant of God, you who ordered me to be called not a soldier but a fisherman, I am appearing to you in this fashion, so that you no longer doubt that I am a fighter for God and His champion, that I precede the Christians in the fight against the Saracens, and that I arise as victor for them.

"I have sought something, in fact, from the Lord, as I am a protector of those loving me and calling on me with a proper heart and as I am a support against all dangers. So that you might believe this, I will open the gates of the city of Coimbra with these keys that I am holding in my hand. At the third hour tomorrow, I will hand over the city, which has been held under siege for seven years by the King Ferdinand[154] to the power of the Christians who will then have entered there." After saying this James disappeared from sight.

On the following day, when matins were finished, Stephen called on a great number of clerics and lay people and told them in proper order what he had seen with his eyes and heard with his ears. Afterwards, this was shown to be true for many reasons. In fact, they had written down the day and hour that Stephen had told them, and messengers sent by the king after the city's capture offered a confirmation of their accuracy, as they asserted that the city had been captured on just that day and just that hour. When he recognized the truth of this, Stephen, the servant of God, asserted that Saint James was stronger than all others for those calling out

---

152. The reference is to Titan's embodiment as the sun-god from Greco-Roman mythology. His clothing thus shone brighter than the sun.

153. This is the most detailed physical description of a military Saint James. Although the saint has appeared in most of the miracles, he is described in few beyond a simple mention of the brightness of his clothing. The narrator has already called him a soldier of God twice previously (in chapters 4 and 18) as well as in Book I, chapter 7, a sermon for his feast day on July 25, referring to 2 Tm 2:4.

154. Coimbra, Portugal was captured by Ferdinand I of León, also known as *el Magno* "the Great" (c. 1015–65) on July 25, 1064.

THE MIRACLES

to him in battle, and he preached that he should be called upon by those fighting for truth.[155] So that he himself might merit the saint's protection, he increased his penance, kept vigil more efficaciously with prayers, spent the rest of his life there in the service of God, and finally received burial in the basilica of the blessed apostle.

This was accomplished by the Lord, and it is miraculous in our eyes.

Therefore, may honor and glory be to the King of kings for ever and ever. Amen.

Chapter 20

A Miracle of Saint James
Written Down by His Excellency Pope Calixtus

As, over the course of much time passing by, and still in our own times, the most blessed apostle James has enriched the whole [f.154v] world both far and wide with many signs of miracles, it happened that a very great war arose between the count of Forcalquier[156] and one of his soldiers by the name of William.[157] As the soldier resolutely rode into battle against this count, they both came together in battle along with their soldiers. However, since the soldier's army was weak and turned tail, the soldier was captured in the war and brought into the count's presence.

When the count himself ordered him to be decapitated, the soldier called out in a loud voice, "James, apostle of God, whom

---

155. This is a brief attempt to broaden the meaning of this miracle to encompass not only physical battle but the spiritual battle as well.
156. The town of Forcalquier, located in the department of Alpes-de-Haute-Provence, formerly Basses-Alpes, in the former province of Provence and Burgundy.
157. The name of William could apply to the count rather than the soldier, and there could exist a relationship between this miracle and chapter 1. William III of Forcalquier (d. 1129) was the son of Ermengol IV of Urgel who, along with his soldiers, was miraculously freed from captivity after losing a battle near Zaragoza. See p. 8, n. 19.

Herod killed with a sword in Jerusalem,[158] help me and free me from the sword of the executioner." With his hands raised toward heaven, he withstood the blow on his lowered neck three times, and no trace of injury appeared on it.

When the executioner saw that he could not harm the soldier with the sword's blade, he directed its point at his stomach, so that he might run him through. However, Saint James dulled the sword so that the soldier did not even feel the blow. When the count as well as all the others who were there together marveled at these events, the count ordered the soldier to be bound and locked up in his castle.

As the next morning was just dawning and as the soldier was calling on Saint James between his sobs, lo and behold, the apostle himself was standing before him, saying, "Behold, I whom you have called, am here." Then, the whole house was filled with a most serene light and with such a fragrance that all the soldiers and all the others who were there thought that they had been transported to the delight of paradise.[159] In this gleam, with Saint James leading and holding his hand, the soldier arrived at the outermost castle gate in full view of everyone, but with the guards almost blinded. After the gates had opened both went together for a mile beyond the walls.[160]

Because of this, it happened that the soldier, who was burning with love for Saint James, came immediately to the saint's body and church on the feast of his *translation*[161] and recounted all these things in the same order as we related them here.

---

158. Acts 12:1–2.

159. The fragrant scent and the "magical" light surrounding a saint's appearance are typical in medieval hagiographic and other tales. In other descriptions of Saint James in Book II, light or brightness is a factor (e.g., chapter 1), but this is the only mention of a fragrant scent surrounding James in this miracle collection.

160. This second miracle within chapter 20 is reminiscent of the miracle of chapter 1, both in the use of light and gate imagery, as well as the interesting coincidence of familial connection.

161. December 30. See the Introduction, LVII–LIX, for Saint James's feast days.

THE MIRACLES

This was accomplished by the Lord, and it is miraculous in our eyes.

Therefore, may honor and glory be to the highest King, for ever and ever. Amen.

Chapter 21

A Miracle of Saint James Written Down by His Excellency Pope Calixtus

In our time[162] a certain famous man named Guibert from Burgundy had been suffering for fourteen years a loss of the use of his legs, such that he could not take a step. The man set out for Saint James, together with his wife and his servants, mounted on two [f.155r] horses.

While he was in the hospital of the apostle, near the church,[163] not wanting to be lodged anywhere else, he was admonished in a dream to devote himself to continuous prayer in the saint's church until the saint extended his constricted legs. After he had kept vigil in this way in the apostolic basilica for two nights and while he was keeping vigil with prayer on the third night,[164] Saint James came and took his hand and raised him up. When the man asked who he was, he said, "I am James, the apostle of God."

The man, who was restored to health, kept vigil for thirteen days in the saint's church and revealed these things to everyone with his own tongue.

162. Unlike most of the others in the collection, this one has no specific date. "In our time," just as chapter 20's similar nonspecific phrasing, "still in our own times" brings the miracle closer to the audience's era.

163. Melczer describes the Hospital del Apóstol Santiago, "on the north side of the north parvis of the cathedral" (*Pilgrim's Guide*, 225 n. 587). Moralejo, *Liber*, 379, also gives similar information, including that it was designated for poor pilgrims. See Fernando López Alsina, *La ciudad de Santiago de Compostela en la alta edad media* (Santiago: Ayuntamiento de Santiago de Compostela, 1988) for maps and descriptions of the evolution of Santiago de Compostela's physical space.

164. The fourth reference within the Miracles to the basilica being open at night for vigil. See p. 26, n. 74.

This was accomplished by the Lord, and it is miraculous in our eyes.

Therefore may honor and glory be to the highest King for ever and ever. Amen.

Chapter 22

A Miracle of Saint James Written Down By His Excellency Pope Calixtus

It is said that in the year of the Incarnation of our Lord one thousand one hundred, a certain citizen of Barcelona[165] came on pilgrimage to the basilica of Saint James in the area of Galicia. However, he had asked only that the saint might free him from captivity by his enemies, if perchance he should fall into this predicament. Thus, after he had returned to his own area, he then set out for Sicily for the sake of business,[166] and he was captured at sea by the Saracens. What more can one say?[167] He was bought and sold thirteen times at markets and fairs.[168] However, those who bought him could not hold him, because each time Saint James destroyed

---

165. The second miracle for a resident of the Iberian Peninsula. Cf. chapter 1. The ancient port of Barcelona has long been the principal city of Cataluña, in the northeast portion of the Peninsula. It is mentioned in passing in the Guide (Chapter VII). During the twelfth century Barcelona and Cataluña were strongly expanding their roles and strength in resettling the reconquered lands to the south in the Peninsula, and in the Mediterranean, as part of growing sea power. It is quite in keeping with the commercial role that Barcelona was beginning to play that this citizen should travel to Sicily.

166. Sicily, an island at the southernmost tip of Italy, was part of Moslem-controlled lands from the early ninth century until c. 1061 when the island fell to the Normans under the leadership of the Guiscards. Although the Norman groups conquered much of the Italian Peninsula, the power of the Saracens in the Mediterranean Sea was not completely quashed.

167. The fourth appearance of this rhetorical question. See chapters 3 and 11.

168. The number thirteen generally implies disaster or bad luck, as is certainly the case in this miracle.

his bonds and chains. The first time he was sold in Corociana,[169] the second in the city of Zadar in Slovenia,[170] the third in Blasia,[171] the fourth in Turkey,[172] the fifth in Persia,[173] the sixth in India,[174] the seventh in Ethiopia,[175] the eighth in Alexandria,[176] the ninth in Africa[177] the tenth in Berber Africa,[178] the eleventh in Biskra,[179] the twelfth in Bougie,[180] and the thirteenth time in Almeria,[181]

169. Latin: *Corociana*. Possibly Corsica. This list of thirteen sites circumscribes a nearly perfect circle around the Mediterranean from the east to west and back again to Spain.

170. Latin: *apud urbem Iazeram in Esclavonia*. Probably the town of Zadar, a port on the Adriatic Sea in modern Croatia. Slavic pilgrims to Compostela were not unknown in the Middle Ages. See Mejac Ciril, "Galicia en los romances eslovenos," *Cuadernos de estudios gallegos* 3.9 (1948): 81–92; and Zoran Ladić, "Some Remarks on Medieval Croatian Pilgrimages," presented at the international conference on Christian civilization in Lublin (Poland), 1996. https://hrcak.srce.hr/file/120800 (accessed July 2018).

171. Latin: *Blasia*. Not located.

172. Latin: *Turcoplia*. Not located, but it likely has some relationship to Turkey.

173. Latin: *Perside*. Persia was under Arab control from the seventh century to the thirteenth century.

174. Latin: *India*. The general eastward journey ends here.

175. Latin: *Aethiopia*, south of Egypt on the east coast of Africa.

176. Latin: *Alexandria*, in the north of Egypt.

177. Latin: *Africa*. While Africa, as a broad designation, may signify land under Saracen control, this may well represent the area to the west of Egypt on the North African Mediterranean coast. The likely area given the directions here is Libya.

178. Latin: *Barbaria*, could refer to the Barbary Coast or to the Berber area of the African coast, in the area of Libya.

179. Latin: *Beserto*, probably *Bescera* or *Bescerensis*, the modern Biskra in Algeria.

180. Latin: *Bugia*, for Bougie or for Bugeaud in Algeria. The twelfth-century Arabic geographer al–Idrisi mentions a town named Bugia as a four-day sea trip due south from Barcelona on the central coast of Africa. He defines a day's sea trip as 100 miles. See *Geografía de España* (Valencia: Anubar, 1974), 206. In Rosamund Allen, ed., *Eastward Bound: Travel and Travellers 1050–1550*, p. 22, the map would seem to confirm that Bugia is the modern Béjaïa, Algeria on the north coast of Africa. Bugia is linked with Avitus and Maimon. See p. 28, n. 80.

181. Latin: *Almaria*, a port city and capital of a province of the same name in the extreme southeast of the Iberian Peninsula. It was held by the

where he was firmly tied by a Saracen with double bonds around his thighs.

As the captive implored Saint James with loud noise, the apostle himself appeared and said, "Because, when you were in my basilica, you asked me only for deliverance of your body and not the salvation of your soul, you have fallen into these dangers. However, since the Lord has had mercy on you, He has sent me to you so that I might remove you from this slavery."

The blessed apostle immediately broke his chains through the middle and then disappeared from sight. [f.155v] The man, thus freed from his bonds, began to go back openly to the land of the Christians, through the cities and the strongholds of the Saracens with the Saracens looking on, and he carried a section of the chain as witness to the miracle.[182] When a pagan happened on him and tried to capture him, the man showed him the section of chain and his adversary immediately fled. Hordes of lions, bears, leopards, and dragons[183] attacked him in order to devour him as he walked through the wild places, but once they saw the chain, which the apostle had touched, they retreated far from him.[184]

Saracens until 1147, when Alfonso VII and other Christians, including Ramón Berenguer of Barcelona, reconquered it. The Christians held the area only ten years. The Moors reconquered the land in 1157 and held it until 1310. Almería is a fitting site to close these twenty-two miracles that opened with the saint's freeing captives after a battle against the Moors in the northern part of the same peninsula.

182. The freeing of the captive from his chains is also reminiscent of the miracles in chapters 1 and 11, as well as in chapter 14 where the prisoner also carries his chains as proof of his liberation, leaving them as testimony of the miracle at the basilica.

183. The dragon is often a symbol of demonic power or of frightening things one cannot see or touch. There is also a mention of a dragon in chapter 2 of the *Translatio*, where the holy men are attacked by a dragon who had threatened the neighboring towns for years. See below p. 81.

184. This is the only thing that the apostle has touched that a miracle recipient has kept. The chains then served him as a third-class relic — something that the saint has touched, although not owned — to which his power is transferred. (A second-class relic is an article used or owned

THE MIRACLES

I met this man myself between Estella and Logroño, as he was walking back toward the threshold of Saint James with the chain in his hands, both feet bare and lacerated, and he told me all of these things.[185]

This was accomplished by the Lord, and it is miraculous in our eyes.

In this story[186] those people are to be rebuked who seek from the Lord or from the saints a wife or earthly happiness or honors or goods or the death of their enemies or other things similar to these, which pertain only to the benefit of the body and not to the salvation of the soul. If the necessities of the body are to be sought, then the requirements of the soul are to be more sought, namely good virtues, such as faith, hope, charity, chastity, patience, temperance, hospitality, generosity, humility, obedience, peace, perseverance, and others similar to these, through which the soul may be crowned on thrones amongst the stars. May He deign to be our guarantor of this, whose kingdom and empire remains without end, for ever and ever. Amen.

HERE ENDS THE SECOND BOOK.
MAY GLORY BE TO THE ONE WRITING
AND TO THE ONE READING THIS.[187]

---

by a saint, and a first-class relic is an actual body part.) This is also the only mention of Saint James protecting a pilgrim against wild beasts.

185. This is the only miracle in which the narrator personally attests to having met and talked with the beneficiary. The miracle recipient is walking "back" (or toward) Compostela, suggesting he is on his way to give thanks for his freedom, similar to the pilgrim in chapter 14.

186. The Latin is *exempla*, clearly meaning just this chapter and miracle, but the moral is applicable to almost all of the miracles in the book.

187. The Chi-Rho sign appears in this place in the CC but not in the Salamanca manuscript at this point.

Another Miracle[188]

[F.192V] A MIRACLE OF SAINT JAMES WRITTEN DOWN
BY ALBERIC,[189] ABBOT OF VÉZELAY,[190]
BISHOP OF OSTIA AND LEGATE IN ROME

In the year of our Lord's Incarnation 1139, while Louis[191] reigned as king of France and Innocent[192] presided as pope, a certain man by the name of Bruno of Vézelay — the town of Mary Magdalene[193] — was coming back from Saint James, and lacking money, he began to beg. Since he did not have anything with which he might buy a penny's worth of bread, on a certain day he was still hungry at about the ninth hour, and he was ashamed to beg. He was very distressed, and he implored with all his heart the help of Saint James and rested alone under a certain tree. While there, he slept a short time and dreamt that Saint James fed him some food. In fact, when he woke up, he found ash cake[194] bread near his head, on which he lived

---

188. This miracle is found in the additional material at the end of the codex on f.192v of the CC. It is not included in the Salamanca manuscript.

189. Alberic of Ostia (1080–1148), abbot 1131–38. He was also a cardinal of Ostia and was sent as a legate from Rome on various missions.

190. Vézeley is in the department of Yonne, in the region of Burgundy–Franche–Compté.

191. Louis VI, the Fat (1081–1137; reigned 1108–37).

192. Innocent II, born Gregorio Papareschi (d. 1143; pope 1130–43).

193. From the eleventh century it has been claimed that Mary Magdalene's relics were housed there. See Susan Haskins, *Mary Magdalen: Myth and Metaphor* (New York: Harcourt, Brace & Company, 1993), 98–100.

194. Latin: *subcinericium panem* certainly refers to a low-quality bread, baked in ashes rather than an oven as evidenced by the base *cinericius* or "ash-like." Bread baked in this way (*khubz malla*) is mentioned in a tenth-century Arabic cookbook. Nawal Nasrallah, *Annals of the Caliphs' Kitchens: Ibn Sayyār al-Warrāq's Tenth-Century Baghdadi Cookbook.* (Leiden: Brill, 2010), 567, describes it as "a simple bread of humble origin. It is baked in *malla*, a pit in which bread is baked in hot ashes and stones.... It is mostly baked by Bedouins and travelers.... This bread is a premonition of hard

THE MIRACLES

for fifteen days until he came to his own region. On each day he would eat sufficiently from it twice, and every other day, he would find a full loaf of bread in his small bag. O wondrous renewed deed of Elias the Prophet![195]

This was done by the Lord, and it is miraculous in our eyes.

Therefore let there be honor and glory to the King of kings. World without end. Amen.

---

times to come, financially, because it is bread to eat only when pressed by necessity."

195. In 1 Kgs 17:8–16, the prophet Elijah asks a poor woman to feed him. She has only a small jar of meal but is able to make a cake to feed Elijah for many days without the meal running out.

THE TRANSLATIO
OF SAINT JAMES

THE TRANSLATIO OF SAINT JAMES

Here Begins the Third Book of Saint James

Chapter 1   The Great *Translatio*[1] of Saint James, *After the Passion*[2] *of our Savior*...[3]

Chapter 2   A Letter of Pope Saint[4] Leo, [f.156r] *May your brotherhood know, dearest...*

1. The technical ecclesiastical use of *translatio* "translation" in reference to the transfer of relics has not spread much beyond the domain of the church. To avoid the confusion with the more common meaning of translation as moving from one language to another, we use the word *translation* (in italics) or transfer (no italics) to refer to the general relocation of a saint's remains. We have chosen to retain the word *Translatio* (Latin, capitalized and in italics) to refer to Saint James's story. This is the only place within Book III where the *Translatio* is referred to as the "Great *Translation*" (*translatio magna*).

2. The Latin *passio* is used here to mean "suffering," "enduring," and even "death"; the idea of "passion" to indicate extremes of emotion was a later development. The original Latin meaning is retained in expressions like *Passion Sunday*, which can indicate either Palm Sunday or the Sunday before Palm Sunday. When the word "passio" indicates "death" rather than "suffering" or "enduring," the English "*Passion*," capitalized and italicized, is used.

3. The author gives the initial words of each of the separate chapters. Since these represent cited text, they are set off here in italics.

4. The Latin *beatus* is a synonym for *sanctus*. It is not clear that the modern distinction between "blessed" for those who are candidates for canonization and "saint" for those who have been canonized was current in the period. For the sake of consistency, we have translated both as "saint" when used as an honorific before the name of an individual who was known to be a saint, and in cases where the person is known not to have been canonized, "blessed" is used. "Blessed" is also used in contexts where "saint" is inappropriate, such as "the very blessed."

Chapter 3 Concerning the Three Feasts of Saint James and the Procession of King Adefonsus, *Saint Luke the Evangelist in the Acts of the Apostles...*

Chapter 4 Concerning the Trumpets of Saint James, *It is reported that wherever....*

HERE BEGINS THE PROLOGUE[5] OF POPE SAINT CALIXTUS[6] TO THE *TRANSLATIO* OF SAINT JAMES THE GREATER

I did not want to leave out the *Translatio* of Saint James from our codex, as such wonders and treasures are written down in it to the honor of our Lord Jesus Christ and of the apostle, and these things in no way differ from the letter that bears the title of Saint Leo.[7] However, it should be noted that, while Saint James had many disciples, he had twelve special ones. One reads that he chose three in the region of Jerusalem, and Hermogenes[8] was made their bishop,

---

5. The Prologue gives information about Saint James not strictly related to the story of his *Translatio*, vaguely linking his post-Pentecostal preaching to the Iberian peninsula via the description of the calling of his disciples. It also adds details to Saint James's *Passion* that are not included in the following chapters. See the Introduction, LXII–LXIV.
6. See the Introduction, XLVII–XLIX, on the identity of Pope Calixtus.
7. The identity of this Pope Leo is unknown. Considering the presence of the Turpin material in the CC, one might be tempted to consider Pope Leo III, who crowned Charlemagne on Christmas Day in the year 800. However, this is not possible. See the Introduction, XXXIII–XXXIV, for the relationship of this letter to the legend of Saint James and the LSJ.
8. This story of Hermogenes is best known from Saint James's biography in Jacobus de Voragine's *Golden Legend*, (Ryan, 2:3–10), a collection of hagiographic stories from the mid-twelfth century. Hermogenes is mentioned once in the "Veneranda dies" See Coffey et al., *Miracles*, 56. The name Hermogenes appears once in the New Testament, when Paul writes, "You are aware of the fact that all who are in Asia turned away from me, among whom are Phygelus and Hermogenes." (2 Tm 1:15) There is no indication that Paul's Hermogenes and the Hermogenes of this story

THE TRANSLATIO

and Philetus[9] was made their archdeacon. After Hermogenes's martyrdom at Antioch, and after they were favored with many miracles, they took rest in the Lord from a holy life. Blessed Josias,[10] the servant of Herod, together with the apostle, was also crowned with martyrdom. The apostle is said to have chosen nine disciples in Galicia while he still lived there. Of these disciples, seven went with him to Jerusalem and carried his body over the sea to Galicia after his martyrdom, while the other two remained in Galicia for the purpose of preaching. Saint Jerome wrote about them in his

---

are related. In the second century, Tertullian wrote *Adversus Hermogenem* ("Against Hermogenes," PL 2:195–238) in his crusade against gnostic heresy. This is interesting considering the premise that the tomb in Compostela actually houses the bones of Priscillian, a gnostic heretic. See Chadwick, *Priscillian of Avila* for an overview of the Priscillian issue within Spain.

9. As an agent of Hermogenes, Philetus plays a role alongside him in the *Golden Legend* stories. He is mentioned eight times in Book One of the LSJ, always with an "F" rather than the "Ph" — the more learned transcription of the Greek Φ — while Hermogenes is mentioned seven times in Book One. Curiously, someone with the name Philetus is possibly considered a disciple of Hymenaeus in 2 Tm 2:16–18, where they are both held up as bad examples: "But avoid worldly and empty chatter, for it will lead to further ungodliness, and their talk will spread like gangrene. Among them are Hymenaeus and Philetus, men who have gone astray from the truth saying that the resurrection has already taken place, and they upset the faith of some...." As these names (Hermogenes and Philetus along with Hymenaeus and Phygelus) are found in the Christian New Testament they could represent a later conflation of minor disciples. As is evident with early martyrologies and florilegia, there is a desire to compile lists of who comprised various groups, such as the disciples, and this would inevitably lead to grasping at straws.

10. The Latin of the CC uses both *Iosias* and *Josias*. We have translated using the form with "J" (Josias) throughout.

Martyrology,[11] just as he had learned from Saint Chromatius[12]: after the body of James was buried in Galicia, they were ordained by the apostles Peter and Paul with episcopal vestments in Rome, and they were sent to Spain, which was still shrouded in pagan error.[13] Finally, however, countless people were instructed by their preaching,

11. The *Martyrologium Hieronymianum* is the oldest surviving list of martyred saints and their feast days, probably compiled in the sixth century and pseudo-epigraphically ascribed to Saint Jerome (347–420). This assertion is not contained in Jerome — at least not in surviving copies: (PL 30:449–50: *VII <Sic> Calends of August. Feast of the death of St. James the apostle and Brother of John the Evangelist*, and PL 30:482: *VIII Calends of August. Feast of the death of Saint James the Apostle*). Jerome had correspondence with Chromatius, and two letters between them (and Heliodorus) serve as a preface to the *Martyrology*. They are found in PL 30:449–50.

12. Chromatius of Aquileia (345–407), became bishop of Aquileia after the death of Valerianus in 388. These assertions about James and his disciples are not found among Chromatius's surviving works.

13. The following seven names were first gathered in the Mozarabic liturgical text of the *Pasionario hispánico* of the eighth century. See Appendix V. The *Pasionario* grew out of individual *libelli* ("little books") that recounted the accomplishments of local Christians. These small works often grew to include sermons, panegyrics, and hymns as elegies to these martyred saints. Some saints were recognized with an individual account, while others, such as the "seven apostolic men," were treated together. With the introduction of the Roman rite in Spain, the *Pasionario* was replaced by the missal and breviary and remained only as a monastic spiritual reading. (Riesco Chueca, xi–xiv.) Karl D. Uitti briefly identifies these seven men in his article "The *Codex Calixtinus* and the European St. James the Major: Some Contextual Issues" in *"De Sens rassis": Essays in Honor of Rupert T. Pickens* (Amsterdam: Rodopi, 2005) 654–5. A listing of these disciples is found again at the beginning of chapter 1 of the *Translatio*. See p. 76. The *Pasionario hispánico* exists as a separate text (in one tenth- and one eleventh-century manuscript) and tells that these men were named as priests in Rome and were sent to Spain to spread the Catholic faith. There is no mention of Saint James accompanying them or greeting them upon their arrival (Riesco Chueca, 130–33).

and Torquatus in Guadix,[14] Tissephons in Vera,[15] Secundus in Avila,[16] Endalecius in Urci,[17] Cecilius in Heliberri,[18] Esicius in Carcese[19] and Eufrasius in Eliturgi[20] entered into rest, undoubtedly on the Ides of May.[21] A very great miracle occurs even today as a witness to their worthy death. For it is said that every year on the previously-mentioned feast, namely on the vigil, in the city of Guadix at the sepulcher of Saint Torquatus, [f.156v] the olive tree behind the church by divine power flowers and is adorned with mature fruits from which oil is made right away. With this oil, the lamps are lit before his venerable altar. However, two other disciples, namely Athanasius and Theodorus, as is written in the *Letter of Pope Saint Leo*,[22] are buried next to the apostle's body, one on the right and the

14. Torquatus of Acci is patron saint of Guadix (Granada province). Torquatus's story is also briefly told in Book IV, the Pseudo-Turpin (Poole, *Pseudo-Turpin*, 11).
15. Tissephons of Vera: "at *Vergu* (Albuniel de Cami, in Jaen province, perhaps Verga, in Almeria province[?]" (Uitti, 655), while Riesca Chueco places Tisifone in Bergii (Berja), near Adra in the Alpujarras (*Pasionario*, 136–37).
16. Secundus of Avila: "at *Abula* (Avila, or, more likely, *Abla*, located between Guadix and Almería" (Uitti, 655).
17. Endalecius of Urci: "at *Urci* (a town close to Vera, province of Almería)" (Uitti, 655); Riesca Chueco notes that in the *Pasionario* it is given as Indalecius with Urci being near Torre de Villaricos in Campo de las Dalías, Almería (136–37).
18. Cecilius of Heliberri: "Elvira, near Granada" (Uitti, 655).
19. Escius of Carcese: "there exist various possibilities: Cazorla or Carchel, both in Jaén province, or perhaps Caravaca or Cieza, in the province of Murcia" (Uitti, 655); Riesca Chueco cites Flórez giving Carteya near Algeciras (*Pasionario*, 136–37).
20. Eufrasius of Eliturgi: "Cuevas de Lituergo, in Jaén province, between Bailén and Andújar" (Uitti, 655).
21. May 15. The *Pasionario Hispánico* (Riesco Chueca, 131) says that they were martyred on May 1; their festival week was from 27 April to 3 May.
22. See the Introduction, XXXIII–XXXIV.

other on the left. And it should not appear to anyone that Athanasius might be Esicius, as Esicius is one person and Athanasius is another.

But it remains for us to say something about the small book of this *Translatio*. It is related to a certain pilgrim and happens in our time. A certain cleric, who is known to me and who is devoted to and a pilgrim of Saint James, wanted to bring this *Translatio* and certain other miracles of the apostle[23] back with him to his own country. He had a certain writer named Fernando in the apostle's city copy it, and he paid him twenty Rouen coins[24] as the price. When he had received the small book at the given price and when he was reading alone secretly in a certain corner of the apostle's basilica, he found in his lap the same number of coins as he had given to the writer, and he believed they had not been placed there by any mortal but rather by the apostle through divine power. Because of this, the blessed apostle, who very quickly paid back his servant with earthly gifts, is believed to be a most generous disburser of heavenly gifts.[25]

HERE ENDS THE PROLOGUE.

23. This is almost certainly a reference to the present Book III and probably parts of Book II of the CC.
24. Rouen was one of several centers for minting coins from an early date.
25. This miracle is not found in other books of the LSJ, nor is it included in Voragine.

THE TRANSLATIO

Chapter 1

Here begins the *Translatio* of Saint James the Apostle and Brother of Saint John the Apostle and Evangelist.

This *Translatio* is Celebrated on the Third Calends of January.[26] Concerning How He Was Brought from Jerusalem to Galicia.

After the *Passion* of our Savior and after the most glorious triumph of His Resurrection and after His miraculous Ascension, in which He ascended to the seat of His Father, and also after the Holy Spirit's outpouring in bursts of flame[27] over the apostles whom He had chosen, they were enlightened by the ray of wisdom and illuminated by heavenly grace, and they disclosed the name of Christ with their preaching far and wide to peoples and to nations. Of these apostles, there stood out from the esteemed group of wondrous virtue, Saint James — blessed in life, admirable [f.157r] in virtue, bright in genius and splendid in speech — whose brother John is held as an evangelist and apostle. So much grace was given to James by divine power that the Lord of inestimable glory Himself did not fail to be transfigured with incomparable brightness before his eyes on Mount Tabor, as Peter and John stood with him as true witnesses.[28] While the others went to different regions of the world, James, by

---

26. December 30. See the Introduction, LVII–LIX, for more information on Saint James's feast days.
27. Latin: *flammivomam,* the spewing or "vomiting" of flame, as from a volcano. The image does not carry well into English, and more typical imagery is that of the tongues of flames above the apostles' heads in relation to these events from Pentecost prior to their dispersal into the world to preach. See Acts 2.
28. For the story of the Transfiguration, see. Mt 17:1–9, Mk 9:2–9, Lk 9:28–36.

the will of God, traveled on to the shores of the West[29] and there he eloquently and dauntlessly sowed[30] the word of God among the people living there and dwelling in their native land. There he remained a short time, while a wheat field that he wanted to have cultivated became fruitful among the thorns.[31] He was supported by Christ and is reported to have chosen seven followers, whose names are the following: Torquatus, Secundus, Endalecius, Tissephons, Eufrasius, Cecilius, and Yscius.[32] This group of men would wipe out the rye,[33] pulling it up by the roots, and would willingly commit the seeds of the Word to this persistently long-sterile ground.

And when his final day was imminent, James, from whose comrade-like solace not a single one of the followers is ever turned away, went quickly to Jerusalem.[34] A wicked band of Sadducee and Pharisee surrounded him and posed questions to him about Christ

29. *Hesperie* meaning the evening and where the sun sets. It was used to refer to Italy and to Spain. At times the word *ultima* was used with *Hesperia* to remove any ambiguity when referring specifically to the Iberian Peninsula.
30. The author uses the homonym *dissero* meaning "to speak eloquently" and "to sow," leading to the following metaphor on the wheat and the weeds. The word play with "sow" and "speak eloquently" cannot be captured by the English.
31. Allusion to the parable of the sower, cf. Mt 3:1–8, Mk 4:3–9, Lk 8:4–8.
32. This is the second listing of the names of these seven men, although with a slight variation of order, without their geographical origin, and with some slight variations in spelling, most notably "Escicius" / "Yscius." See p. 72.
33. Latin: *lolium* meaning "weed"; it is also the word for "rye" which is fast-growing and damaging to a wheat field.
34. The first clause of this sentence is clear: James heads straight to Jerusalem when he perceived it was time for his death. The second clause is thorny; the best solution, given the case endings, seems to be to treat *contubernali* or "comrade" as adjective and *solacio* or "solace" as a noun. The sense seems to be that somehow James never abandons people, and there is at least a hint that this refers to James as being there for those who entreat him, even in later times.

with the unimaginable and unlawful craftiness of the serpent,[35] but he was filled with the grace of the Holy Spirit, and his eloquence was truly surpassed by no one. Because of this, their roaring wrath was incited and raged more bitterly against him, and this wrath was ignited and grew wild, and the zeal of envy goaded them on so much so that he was seized and assaulted with savage brutality by these violent people and was handed over to the fierce sentence of death before Herod.[36]

After he had poured forth a wave of red blood, he was crowned with triumphant martyrdom, soared away to heaven, and was crowned with an everlasting laurel wreath. His disciples, however, furtively seized their master's dead body and with great labor and excited haste went off to the shores and found a ship ready for them. They climbed in, set out on the high sea, and on the seventh day[37] they arrived at the port of Iria,[38] which is in Galicia, and they approached their destination using their oars.

They did not hesitate at that time to give copious thanks and worthy praise to the author of these things, as much for such great favor [f.157v] granted to them by God, for they escaped at times the ambushes of pirates, at times collisions with projecting rocks, and at times the dark jaws of gaping whirlpools without harm to anyone. Therefore, supported by such a great a patron, they directed their minds to the remaining things beneficial for their needs, and they

35. An allusion to Gn 3:1.
36. Herod Agrippa (11–44CE; king of Judea 41–44CE). The martyrdom of James would have occurred during his last year. See Acts 12:1–2, 20–23.
37. The arrival on the seventh day may be understood, not as a literal passage of time, but as a symbol of completeness, the end of a cycle.
38. Iria (Flavia), an early settlement near the coast at the confluence of the Sar and Ulla rivers now in the municipality of Padrón, A Coruña, Galicia. The second name "Flavia" came in c. 70CE when the Roman emperor Vespasian granted its inhabitants Roman citizenship, and in his honor the town was called Iria Flavia. From the sixth century there are bishops associated with Iria. The See was transferred from Iria to Compostela in 860. See Antonio López Ferreiro, *Historia de la S.A.M. Iglesia de Santiago* (Santiago: Seminar Conciliar Central, 1898), 1:218–30.

tried to determine what place of rest the Lord might have chosen for His martyr. And so, they journeyed to the east, and they carried and then set down his sacred coffin at the estate of a certain woman by the name of Luparia[39] about five miles from the city.

They asked who was the owner of that place, and they found out from the statements of some inhabitants of the province, and these inhabitants eagerly and passionately wanted to become participants in their search. At last, as one might expect, they went to speak to the woman and told, in order, the events that had occurred. They requested a certain temple where she had placed a statue to be adored, which through the mistaken error of paganism was frequently visited as a shrine.

Although she was of most distinguished birth, and through the ultimate intervention of fate, was widowed from her husband, and although she was given over to profane superstition, she did not forget her nobility.[40] She would reject any union with both noble and lowborn men alike, lest she should defile her former marital bond as if she were a harlot.[41] Certainly, before she would give a response of any sort, she would reflect many times on their request and words, and she considered in the depth of her heart in what way she would hand them over to deadly destruction.

39. This is the only mention of Luparia by name in the LSJ. Luparia ("Luporia") appears in the *Pasionario Hispánico* much as she does in the CC, but in the *Pasionario* she begs to enter the holy men's presence. They will not admit her unless she constructs a basilica to be used as a baptistery. She agrees and as soon as it is done, she is baptized there, serving as an example followed by the entire town. Luparia is counted among the saints in at least one French collection of saints' lives: M.J. Collin de Plancy, *Grande Vie des Saints* (Paris: Librairie Louis Vivès, 1899), 4:414–15. See Appendices 5 and 9.

40. Latin *oblita* from S is followed here rater than the meaningless *obute* of CC.

41. The irony cannot have been lost on the writer between this stress on noble character while using the name "Luparia" as in Latin *lupa* means "prostitute" and *lupanar* a brothel.

THE TRANSLATIO

Finally she returned with her word, and raging with treachery, she said: "Go and ask the king who is staying in Dugium[42] and request a place from him where you might prepare a sepulcher for your dead person."

They obeyed her words. One group watched over the apostolic body in one place, in the ritual way for earthly remains, and the other group went speedily over a rugged mountain path and arrived quickly at the royal palace. There they were led into his presence, surely greeting him in a regal manner, and revealed in their tale who they were, where they were from, and why they had come there.

While in the beginning the king was attentive and benevolent about their plea, he was nevertheless struck by an incredible stupor, and he hesitated about what was to be done. After being stricken by a demoniacal dart, like a savage, he ordered that [f.158r] traps be set out secretly and the Christ-worshipers be killed. However they learned this privately by the will of God, so they departed fleeing hastily away.[43] When, however, their flight was reported to the king, he was aroused by a most bitter ire, and he took on the rage of a rabid lion. Then together with those who were in his court, he steadfastly pursued the tracks of the fleeing God-worshippers. And it had come almost to the point where the disciples were afraid that they would be abandoned to the hands of these cruel pursuers. So they were fearful while the pursuers were confident as they reached the bridge of a certain river at one and the same moment. Then, by the sudden judgment of God Almighty, the stonework of the bridge they were walking on was dissolved and completely destroyed from its top down to its foundation. And so the certain judgment of God, who is Eternal Judge and King, determined that, out of the entire crowd of those pursuing, not a single one should survive who could retell in the hall of the king the things that had happened.

---

42. According to López Ferreiro, *Historia*, 1:252–54, this probably refers to the Celtic town of Duyo of A Coruña, near Finisterre

43. This prophetic warning to flee is similar to that of the Wise Men's of Mt 2:12.

At the sound of the falling weapons and stones, the holy men turned their heads and proclaimed the mighty works of God as they gazed upon the bodies and horses and military weapons of the great men that were pathetically whirled about under the water of the river, just as[44] an army had suffered with the people of Canopus.[45] Therefore, helped by the right hand of God and animated and impassioned by this event, the disciples took a more favorable path to the woman's house and told her how the savage decision of the king demanded that they be killed and what God had done against him as revenge. Moreover, they stood firm in insisting that she give over the aforementioned house dedicated to demons to be dedicated to God. They urged and insisted that she reject the hand-made idols that can neither benefit her nor damage others nor see with their eyes nor hear a word with their ears nor smell with their noses nor use any of their members at all as functioning limbs.

Her mind was moved at the drowning of the king since she feared for death of her relatives and in-laws. Yet she was deaf of good counsel, as often happens in such matters, and so, just as if they were deemed frauds, she schemed with a frivolous and vain trick. While the disciples were rather strongly urging her with requests that she offer a small part of her estate for burying [f.158v] the remains[46] of the most holy man, she was considering new and unusual battle plans,[47] and she thought she might be able to kill them by some deception, so she began to speak with the following thought and said: "Since I see your purpose is so efficaciously focused on this

---

44. Latin *haud secus* of S is followed here, rather than *aut secus*, or "like" of CC, which does not offer a second alternative.

45. It is not certain which army, but the location is the city of Canopus in northern Egypt, named after Canopus, the pilot of Menelaus's ship, who died there from a snake bite. This story is reminiscent of that of Moses and the crossing of the Red Sea, Ex 14:21–28. A similar miracle is also told in the *Pasionario Hispánico* about Torcuato and several of his followers who went into Guadix to purchase food on a festival day for Jupiter, Mercury, and Juno. See Appendix 5.

46. The Latin *membra* is literally "members."

47. The Latin *prelia* for *proelia* is literally "battles."

and that you never want to be foolish about it, I have tame cattle on a certain mountain. Go there and take them and take whatever else might seem very useful to you along with them, and build. If you lack any provision, I will willingly undertake to give these things to you."

When the apostolic men[48] heard this, they did not weigh carefully womanly creatures, and went joyfully until they arrived at the mountain, and they saw something other than what they expected. While they were walking the boundaries of the mountain, unexpectedly a giant dragon, whose frequent attacks of the neighboring dwellings of the villages laid waste all around with the same misfortune, came out of its cave spewing flames and sending fire on the saints of God and sprang out as if in an attack and threatened destruction.

Then they recalled the teachings of the Faith and fearlessly wielded the Cross as a defense and drove him away with their resistance. As he was not worthy to bear the sign of the Lord, he burst open from the middle of his stomach. With the battle finished, they fixed their gaze on heaven and made vows from the depth of their hearts to the highest King. Finally, so that the throng of demons would be driven out of there, they exorcised the place with water that they sprinkled everywhere on the whole mountain. And this mountain, formerly called *Illicinus* — as if to say "misled," because many mortals were badly seduced before then and supported rituals for the demons — now was named *Mons Sacer*, that is, Mount Holy, by these men.[49]

---

48. The Latin *viri apostolici* ties this story to the Seven Apostolic Men of the *Pasionario hispánico*. See Appendix 5.
49. Situated 16 km southeast of Santiago de Compostela, this peak is now known as Pico Sacro (Sacred Peak). The name *Illicinus* may derive from Jove Illicinus or *Elicius*, "of the oak tree" suggesting a pre-Roman Celtic or Celtiberian sacred site. See Joaquín Caridad Arias, *La lengua romance Vasca: Vocabulario comparado* (Lugo: El Tablero de Piedra, 2012), and Antón Bouzas Sierra, "Aportaciones para una reinterpretación astronómica de Santiago de Compostela," *Anuario Brigantino* 32 (2009): 47–92. In folklore the deep crevice that cuts through the peak is called the "Rúa da Raíña" or

7. One of two cave entrances on the Pico Sacro, commonly known as the "Dragon's Lair." Boqueixón, Galicia, Spain. May 2016.

From there they also saw from afar the cattle deceitfully promised to them, which were wandering about, untamed and bellowing, tossing dirt into the air with their horns onto the top of their heads, and pawing the ground forcefully with the hooves of their feet. Immediately, a great gentle docility crept over these cattle who were facing each other across the slope of the mountain and with their dangerous running were threatening one another with the cruelty of death. Now those who were previously rushing headlong with savage ferocity, so as to bring disaster, lowered their necks to the hands of the holy men and pointed their horns away. And the holy bearers of the body actually petted the harsh animals made mild, and without delay quickly placed yokes [f.159r] on them, walked on a straight path, and with the yoked cattle entered the palace of the woman.

The woman was certainly stunned, and she recognized these wondrous miracles, and she was stirred by these three obvious signs[50] and she complied with their request. From an impudent person she was made into an obedient one. The small building was handed over to them, and she was reborn by the threefold name of faith.[51] She — along with her family — became a believer in the name of Christ. And so, with God inspiring her, after previously being deluded by senseless error, she was imbued with the dogma of faith, and she became humble and was bent rather than upright. She destroyed the idols, and she demolished whatever temples were under her control.

With these overthrown and minutely reduced to powder, the ground was excavated, and a great sepulcher was constructed with wondrous stone work where the apostolic body was buried with artful genius. A church of some size was built above on that spot,

---

"Queen's Street" and the cave entrance just beyond it, the "Dragon's Lair" in reference to this legend (Fig. 7).

50. The three obvious signs would be the miracle of the bridge collapsing on the king's soldiers, the dragon being vanquished, and the cattle being tamed and yoked.

51. A reference to the Trinity: Father, Son and Holy Spirit.

and it was adorned with a rich altar and affords a pleasing entrance to a devout people.[52]

In a short time, after the people had been instructed with the knowledge of faith by the disciples of this apostle, from the formerly squalid fields, after being sprinkled with heavenly dew, there was soon an abundant harvest that was increased and offered to God.[53] However, out of reverence for him, two attendants of this teacher constantly watched with the greatest love over this sepulcher. At the certain but unknown limit of life, they paid their debt to nature, breathed out their breath in a happy death, and gave up their souls to heaven rejoicing. Their illustrious teacher did not abandon them on earth or in heaven. On the contrary, he arranged through divine intervention for them to be gathered with him, as he, adorned[54] with a purple stole and wearing a crown, gleamed in the heavenly court, together with his followers, ready to protect the unfortunate who make requests of him with unfaltering voice.

With the help of our Lord and Savior, Jesus Christ, together with the Father and the Holy Spirit, whose kingdom and power remains, for ever and ever. Amen.[55]

---

52. For the early architecture of the Santiago Cathedral, see Conant and Moralejo Álvarez. For a dynamic visualization, watch The Met, "A Full-Scale 3D Computer Reconstruction of the Medieval Cathedral and Town of Santiago de Compostela." https://youtu.be/SmVJSmLA7BU (accessed July 2018.

53. The story returns to the field and harvest metaphor.

54. The Latin *purpurea purpuratus,* "purpled with purple," shows the significance of purple as the royal color.

55. Similar prayer-like closings are found throughout the various books of the CC, including chapters 1 and 2 of the *Translatio* and several of the chapters of Book II. See p. 11, n. 27.

THE TRANSLATIO

CHAPTER 2

HERE BEGINS THE LETTER OF POPE SAINT LEO[56]
ON THE *TRANSLATIO* OF SAINT JAMES THE APOSTLE
WHICH IS CELEBRATED ON THE THIRD CALENDS OF JANUARY.[57]

May your brotherhood know, dearest rectors of all of Christendom, how the complete body of the most blessed James the Apostle was transferred to the territory of Galicia in Spain. After the Ascension of our Savior to heaven,[58] [f.159v] and after the arrival of the Holy Spirit upon the disciples,[59] at the turn of the eleventh year from the Passion of Christ,[60] after the synagogues of the Jews were purified, the most blessed James the Apostle, together with Josias his disciple,[61] was captured by Abiathar the Priest[62] at the order of Herod, and he suffered the punishment of beheading.[63] The body of this most holy James the Apostle was taken up, however, by his disciples at night out of fear of the Jews. With an angel of the

---

56. For a history of the *Letter of Pope Saint Leo*, see Manuel Díaz y Díaz, "La *Epistola Leonis*," 133–81.
57. December 30.
58. Acts 1:1–12.
59. Acts 2:1–4.
60. The eleventh year of the *Passion* would be the year 44CE, based on Jesus's thirty years of private life, followed by three years of public life.
61. On Josias, see pp. XXIV–XXVI.
62. The author possibly takes the name Abiathar from Mk 2:25–27: "And he said to them, 'Have you never read what David did when he and his companions were hungry and in need of food? He entered the house of God, when Abiathar was high priest, and ate the bread of the Presence, which it is not lawful for any but the priests to eat, and he gave some to his companions." Mark's reference is incorrect; the priest's name was Ahimelech as originally narrated in 1 Sm 21:1–9, and his son was Abiathar. The other Synoptic Gospels leave out this reference. The name is anachronistic here.
63. The author uses the "punishment of the head"; the actual punishment was beheading by the sword.

MIRACLES AND TRANSLATIO OF SAINT JAMES

Lord accompanying them, they arrived at Joppa[64] on the seashore. There, however, they hesitated and discussed amongst themselves what they should do. Then, lo and behold, by the will of God, an outfitted boat appeared. They rejoiced and entered it bearing the disciple of our Redeemer. They raised the sails as soon as there were favorable winds, and they sailed on the waves of the sea with great tranquility. Together they praised the mercy of our Savior, and then they came to the port of Iria. There they sang for joy this verse of David: "On the sea are your ways and your paths are on many waters." [Ps 76:20 / 77:19] They got out of the boat, removed the most holy body, and deposited it at a certain estate, called by the name of *Liberum Donum*[65] where it is now venerated, about eight miles distant from the aforementioned city.

In this place they found an abandoned idol[66] built by pagans. However, as they looked around there, they found a crypt in which there were iron tools that stone artisans used to use in building homes. These poor followers, therefore, demolished this idol, and they rejoiced and reduced it little by little to powder. Then they dug down deeply, laid a very firm foundation and placed above there a small arched house where they constructed a sepulcher with stone work. There, with artistic genius, the body of the apostle was placed. The church, of a very small size, was built and adorned with an altar

---

64. Jaffa, the oldest section of the port city of Tel Aviv, Israel.

65. *Liberum Donum* is also known as Libredón, literally Free Gift. It is the mountain where the current Cathedral of Santiago de Compostela is built. The *Historia compostelana* says that "James body was taken from the port of Iria" to "the place that was called *Liberum donum* and that now is called Compostela, where they laid him, according to church custom, under some marble arches" (English translation ours from HC, 68). See appendix 7. Fernando López Alsina, *La Ciudad de Santiago,* 118–19, points out that this toponym only appears in narrative works and not in documents. He speculates that "Libredón" indicates that the space around Compostela was given to the apostle long prior to the ninth-century interest in the area by the Asturian kings.

66. The Latin is clearly *idolum* in both CC and S. Still the context more readily admits the concept of "temple," which is one letter off: *idolium* or *idoleum*.

that extends to a pleasant entrance for devout people.⁶⁷ After the burial of the most holy body, they celebrated lauds to the supreme King, singing these verses of David: "The just one shall rejoice in the Lord and will also hope in Him, and all with a proper heart will give praise" [Ps 63:11 / 64:10]. And again, "In eternal memory will the just one be, and he will not have fear of an evil hearing" [Ps 111:7 / 112:6–7].

After a short time, however, when the people had been instructed with the knowledge of the faith by the disciples of this apostle, there was soon an abundant and [f.160r] increased harvest offered to God. After considering good advice, two followers⁶⁸ remained there to watch over the most precious treasure⁶⁹ and, of course, to venerate the body of Saint James. Of these, one was called Theodorus, while the other was called Athanasius.

Other disciples, however, with God as a companion, went out preaching in Spain. As we said earlier, those two followers of the disciple, out of reverence for their teacher, constantly watched with greatest love over this sepulcher in ceaseless vigils. They ordered that after their death they be buried by Christians next to their teacher, one on his right side and the other on the left.⁷⁰

And so when the term of their life ended, they paid their debt to nature and exhaled their breath in a felicitous death, and they rejoiced and delivered their souls to heaven. The illustrious teacher did not abandon them on earth or in heaven. Adorned with a purple stole and a crown, he arranged by divine power for them to be lodged with him. He rejoices in the heavenly court with these

67. Several passages, such as this one, are identical or nearly identical in chapters 1 and 2, indicating that they perhaps came from a common source.
68. See the Introduction, LXIII and p. 72, n. 13 about the choosing of the seven holy men.
69. Latin *talentum*, literally a "talent" or coin, perhaps more broadly "something of value"; cf. the "Parable of the Talents" of Mt 25:14–30.
70. Their demand that they be buried on James's right and left, mirrors James's and John's demand that they be given seats at Christ's right and left in Heaven (Mk 10:36–38).

disciples, ready to protect the unfortunate who make requests of him with unfailing voice, with our Lord and Savior Jesus Christ as his Helper, whose kingdom and power remains forever, together with the Father and the Holy Spirit, forever and ever. Amen.[71]

Chapter 3

Pope Calixtus on the Three Feasts of Saint James

Saint Luke the Evangelist in the *Acts of the Apostles* declares that Saint Peter was thrust into prison by Herod in the days of the unleavened bread, where he says, "They were, however, the days of the unleavened bread" [Acts 12:3] and that Saint James was killed before Passover by this same Herod. This was without doubt at the time of famine predicted by Agabus the Prophet, which occurred under Claudius the Roman emperor.[72] He speaks thus: "At the same time, King Herod sent out his forces so that he might strike down some from the church. Moreover, he killed Saint James, the brother of John, with a sword" [Acts 12:1–2]. He points out the time of the suffering of Saint James and also the people at the time, but he is silent as to the exact day.

This day was certainly once unknown for a lengthy amount of time to all, but it was revealed in a spiritual vision to a certain faithful person who is known to me. For on the night of a vigil of the Annunciation of the Blessed Virgin Mary,[73] he saw that, while Saint James was led into a certain room to be judged at an assembly, [f.160v] a great debate occurred among the Jewish people and the Gentiles, with some saying that the pious apostle must not be

---

71. These last two sentences are nearly identical to the last two sentences of chapter 1.
72. Agabus the Prophet, a Christian in Antioch who predicted a famine across the Roman Empire (Acts 11:23–30). Claudius is Tiberius Claudius Caesar Augustus Germanicus (10BCE–54CE, Roman emperor from 41–54CE).
73. The Annunciation of the Virgin Mary is March 25, thus the vigil is March 24.

killed and others saying that he must be. At last, judged unjustly by Herod, he was led outside the city with chains tied to his neck to the place of his Passion by a band of the abominable adherents of Herod, and he was beheaded.

Immediately a certain illustrious man, who was like a prelate, lamenting him with tears and with sweetness, spoke about him to the people in the royal room in this way, saying:

> He was judged at about the third hour, and at about the ninth hour he suffered, like Christ. On the same day and at the same hour as the Teacher suffered, the disciple certainly did also. Some were going toward their business or doing work. He, however, was going to his worthy work, that is, toward acquiring the crown of martyrdom. Others were going to eat and drink, he was going to accept the blessed food and drink of suffering, by which he would deserve to acquire the continual drink of eternal life, promised to him earlier by the Lord: 'You shall drink from my chalice' [Mt 20:23].[74]

Saint Jerome, however, in the *Martyrology* that he wrote to the bishops Chromatius[75] and Heliodorus[76] said, rather early, that his Passion should be celebrated on the eighth calends of August.[77]

---

74. Mt 20:20–23 is the passage in which James's and John's mother ask that they be allowed to sit at Jesus's right and left hand in paradise. It begins with phrases reminiscent of the Crucifixion (cf. Mk 13:25, 15:33), emphasizing the parallels between Jesus's Passion and James's death "on the same day and the same hour." This would confirm that James was beheaded at Passover.

75. Possibly refers to correspondence of Jerome with Chromatius and Heliodorus found in PL 30:449–50, a sort of prologue to the *Martyrology*. Eusebius's book on martyrs survives only in part; his writing on James is from the *Ecclesiastical History*. Jerome gives the 8 calends of August (July 25) for the date of James's feast in his *Martyrology*, however, it is recorded as 7 calends or July 26 in the section on the apostles, probably a scribal or typographical error. See p. 72, nn. 11 and 12.

76. Saint Heliodorus (d.c. 390), first bishop of Altinus (Altina, Italy), disciple of Valerianus and traveling companion of Saint Jerome. See p. 72, n. 11.

77. July 25.

Afterwards,[78] Pope Saint Alexander[79] ordered it to be celebrated on that same day, when he instituted the celebration of the Chains of Saint Peter on the first day of the calends of August.[80] On this day — as it is written in the Roman histories — this same pope certainly deposited in a sanctuary the chains of Peter that had been moved from Jerusalem to Rome long before by the Empress Eudoxia[81] and had been bathed in holy water and holy oil.

Earlier the pagans had customarily celebrated festivals on this day in honor of Augustus Caesar, because Caesar had conquered Anthony and Cleopatra,[82] who was deceived by the serpent, on the calends of Sextil,[83] namely on the first day of August. Now in a turn

---

78. The word *deinde* would indicate after Jerome; if this refers to Alexander, it must mean "next" in his argumentation rather than "next" in chronological order of events.

79. The only pope named Alexander to enjoy sainthood is Pope Alexander I (c. 106–16). The story of Saints Quirinus and Balbina is often associated with him. The word *deinde* would usually indicate that he was subsequent to Jerome (but he was not); Pope Alexander II (1061–73) would be another possibility. For a clear, brief explanation of the changes in dates of the feast days of Saint James, and the relationship between Rome and Spain about the liturgy of the time, see Jan Van Herwaarden, "The Integrity of the Text of the *Liber Sancti Jacobi* in the *Codex Calixtinus*" in *Between Saint James and Erasmus* (Leiden: Brill, 2003) 371–74.

80. The Feast of Saint Peter's Chains (August 1) celebrates the liberation of Saint Peter by an angel from his imprisonment by Herod. See Acts 12:3–9. These chains are claimed as relics by the Church of San Pietro in Vincoli, Rome.

81. Licinia Eudoxia (422–62) was the wife of Valentinian III and also Petronius Maximus. Clearly there is a lack of sequencing in all these events. Various legends have been conflated.

82. This refers to Mark Antony (83–30BCE) and Cleopatra (69–30BCE). Mark Antony was killed on August 1; Cleopatra reportedly committed suicide about 11 days later through the bite of an asp.

83. *Sextilis* was the sixth month with a construction similar to April or *Aprilis*; likewise, September, October, November, and December were the seventh, eighth, ninth and tenth months respectively. *Sextilis* was eventually dedicated to Caesar Augustus, thus becoming August or *Augustus*, while

of the table,[84] he ordered it to be celebrated in veneration of Saint Peter. Also on a similar day, the daughter of a certain Quirinus,[85] a Roman centurion, on the advice of the aforesaid pope who had been thrown in prison by this same Quirinus, kissed the foot-shackles of Saint Peter, and she was cured of a great sickness that afflicted her. [f.161r] Then the holy pope, by satisfying Quirinus, got out of prison. Then Saint Bede, the splendid doctor of the Holy Church corroborated that the Passion of Saint James must be celebrated on that same day, writing and saying in his *Martyrology*:

> *July, at just twice four of the calends,*[86] *enjoys bearing
> The celebration of James, the brother of John, through
> custom.*[87]

And so on the eighth calends of April, he suffered[88]; and on the third calends of January, he was carried from Iria to Compostela and brought to the sepulcher.[89] Procuring the material and doing

---

Quintilis became July in honor of Julius Caesar. See p. XXIX, n. 25, on the months and the Roman year.

84. The Latin is *versa vice*, but this is not so much a case of "opposite" here, but an irony.

85. This is the legendary story of Saints Balbina and her father Quirinus. The Feast of Saint Quirinus was originally on March 25, but was later moved to March 30 and April 30. AASS, March 3:543–54. The Feast of Saint Balbina is on March 31. AASS, March 3:900–03.

86. He uses "twice four" to indicate the "eighth" calends (July 25).

87. Bede the Venerable (c. 672/3–735). This is from the *Poetic Martyrology* (PL 94:604), as opposed to his prose *Martyrology* (PL 94:984–86).

88. March 25. This should be the date of his Passion feast but this chapter explains how it was moved to accommodate other, more important holy days. March 25 was the day on which Saint Quirinus's feast was celebrated, and that may explain the presence of the Quirinus story.

89. December 30 is the date on which his *Translation* and his calling (*vocatio*) are celebrated and was the date of his principal feast in the Mozarabic liturgy of the Iberian Peninsula. This chapter attempts to validate the separation of the feast day of James's *Passion* from the December 30 *Translation* date by implying that his body had been resting in Iria until his sepulcher could be completed in Compostela.

the work on his sepulcher lasted from the month of August up to January. It is just, therefore, that the Holy Church was accustomed to celebrate the solemnities of the Passion of Saint James and the Chains of Saint Peter on the aforesaid days. For, if it should celebrate the feast around Easter, it would unworthily displace an instituted service of either Easter or Lent. This would happen if these feasts occurred on the same day as they do.[90]

Often the Feast of the Annunciation of the Virgin, which must be celebrated on the eighth calends of April,[91] occurred either in the week between Palm Sunday and Easter or in Easter week, and it could not be fully celebrated. Saint Anselm previously ordered the Feast of the Miracles of Saint James to be celebrated on the fifth nones of October,[92] as it celebrates how the holy apostle raised from the dead a man who, on the advice of the devil, had killed himself[93] and how the apostle performed other miracles, and we affirm this order.

It is reported that the *Translation* and Calling of Saint James is celebrated on the third calends of January.[94] The illustrious Spanish emperor Aldefonsus,[95] worthy of good memory, ordered it to be

---

90. Passover is a moveable feast based on the Jewish lunar calendar. Although this chapter establishes that James was killed at Passover, which is generally celebrated the same week as Easter — although occasionally as much as a month later — Pope Alexander moved the feasts for both Saint James's *Passion* and Saint Peter's Chains so they would not disrupt the Lenten or Easter liturgies. In the liturgy of Book I there are special masses listed to be celebrated on the Octave of Saint James (August 1), so that the high mass that day might celebrate Saint Peter's Chains.

91. March 25.

92. October 3.

93. See chapter 17 of Book II, ascribed to Saint Anselm. In Book I, chapter 28 a special mass is listed for this feast of the Miracles, ordered by Saint Anselm and affirmed in language similar to this passage.

94. December 30.

95. This could be Alfonso II (791–842) who first reached out to create a mutually beneficial relationship between the bishops of Iria Flavia, and his political and military defense against the Moslem invasion, and who granted the land around the newly found shrine. See Carlos Baliñas Pérez,

celebrated among the Galicians, before it was corroborated by our authority. He did not believe that the solemnity of the *Translatio* was less prominent than the *Passion*, since the rejoicing Galician people took bodily solace in this follower of the Lord. Certainly at this celebration, the venerable king, with respect for the twelve apostles, was accustomed to offer at mass twelve silver marks and as many gold talents on the venerable apostolic altar; and beyond these offerings, to make gifts and favorable awards to his soldiers and to dress them with silk clothing and mantles; to provide shield bearers with military attire; to equip new soldiers; to feed all those arriving, whether known or unknown; never to close the doors of his court to any poor person, but rather to urge that the heralds call with the sound of the trumpet everyone to partake in the meals in honor of such a great feast.

Indeed, [f.161v] dressed in regal clothing, supported on all sides by multitudes of soldiers and various orders of illustrious men and counts, he marched around the basilica of Saint James in procession in a festive regal manner on this day. The marvelous silver scepter of the Spanish Empire that the venerable king carried in his hands, which was engraved with golden flowers and with varied artwork and

---

"The Origins of the *Inventio Sancti Iacobi* and the Making of a Kingdom," in Antón Pazos, ed., *Translating the Relics of Saint James*. (London: Routledge, 2016) 80–82. It could also refer to Alfonso III the Great "el Magno" (848–910; king from 866) and first Asturian king to be called "emperor." Supporting either of these choices is the image of this king being "worthy of good memory"; they would both endorse the celebration of the *Translation* (supported by the Mozarabic liturgy and the *Pasionario Hispánico*) over that of the Feast of the *Passion* which was promoted as part of the Roman liturgy (as seen in this chapter) to take place of the Mozarabic. For the political-ecclesiastical events that lead to the acceptance of the Roman liturgy in Spain, see Joseph O'Callaghan, *A History of Medieval Spain*, 306–312; and García Turza, "The Formulation," 101–09. Another possibility is that this description conflates Alfonso VII (king 1111–56) with earlier Alfonsos; the description of the number of bishops and other clergy, and the pomp of the ceremony are reminiscent of the Miracles, most of which are set during the kingship of Alfonso VII in support of the permanent transfer of the metropolitan See of Mérida to Compostela by Calixtus II in 1120.

was set with precious stones of all kinds, gleamed. The golden diadem crowning the most powerful king, for the glory of the apostle, was decorated with enameled flowers, with artistic lettering, with all kinds of precious stones, and with brilliant images of cattle and birds. An unsheathed double-edged sword, which was carried before the king, glittered with its gold flowers, bright lettering, a golden pommel and a silver cross-guard.

Before him walked the bishop of Saint James dressed with episcopal robes, bedecked with a white miter, furnished with gilded shoes, adorned with a gold ring, wearing white gloves, with an ivory pontifical staff, appropriately surrounded by his fellow bishops. The cleric who walked before him was assuredly adorned with worthy apparel. The rich capes, in fact, with which the seventy-two canons of Saint James were dressed, were worked marvelously with precious stones, silver knots, gold flowers and the best edgings in front and all around below. Some were covered with silk dalmatics, which were decorated with marvelous beauty with bands having gold fringe from the upper arm downwards. Others were covered above with golden chains decorated with every manner of precious stones, and they were properly embellished with golden knots with the best headbands, with the best sandals, with gold belts, with stoles having gold borders, and with maniples decorated with gems. What more can one say?[96] The choirs of clergy were decorated in an inestimable way with every kind of precious stones and with every delight of gold and silver.

Some happily carried in their hands candelabra, others silver censers, others gilded crosses, others fabrics imprinted with every kind of precious stone, others small boxes filled with the relics of many saints, others phylacteries, others golden or ivory staffs fit for singers, on which onyx or beryl or sapphire or carbuncle or emerald [f.162r] or other precious stones decorated the surface. Others guided two silver tables gilded on the top, placed on silver carts, on which the burning candles of a devout people were placed.

96. This same rhetorical question is found four times in the *Miracles*. See p. 14, n. 42; p. 16, n. 48; p. 35, n. 104; p. 60, n. 167.

THE TRANSLATIO

Devout people — that is to say famous people, governors, nobles, domestic and foreign counts — dressed in festive clothing followed them. The choirs of venerable women who followed were covered and adorned with gilded shoes, with marten, sable, ermine and fox pelts, with blouses, mantels, furs, grey pelts, with rain cloaks red on the outside and varied on the inside, with little gold amulets, with necklaces, with hairpins, with bracelets, with earrings, with ankle bracelets, with small necklaces, with rings, with gems, with mirrors, with golden belts, with silk bands, with summer garments, with headbands, with cottons, with hair twisted with a golden string, and with every other variety of clothing.[97]

CHAPTER 4

CONCERNING THE TRUMPETS OF SAINT JAMES

It is reported that wherever the song of the trumpet of the seas of Saint James, which the pilgrims customarily take with them, sounds in the ears of the people,[98] devotion to the faith increases in them,

---

97. The highly detailed descriptions of clothing and jewelry in this passage use many Late Latin words, including some that were being calqued on the vernacular words. They are notable for their linguistic uniqueness and as examples of Late Latin's ability to assimilate or create new words. They include (using the inflected form found in the text) *esmaldinis* "enameled" (related to the English "smelt"), *nigellinis* "lettering" (from the Latin for black) *pomo* for "pommel" (from the Latin for apple), *cruce* "crossguard" (from the Latin for cross), *cappe* "capes," *fimbriis* "fringe" or "border" or "edgings," *martirinis* "marten," *cembilinis* "sable," *erminis* "ermine," and *murena* "necklace" (from the eel-like fish). The words *bossis* "swellings" was used to mean "knots", and *persceldis* was used for "ankle bracelets"; both of these are explained in the work of John Henry Hessels, *A Late Eighth-Century Latin Anglo-Saxon Glossary* (Cambridge: Cambridge University Press, 1906).

98. The "sound of the sea" would seem to infer a conch shell, while "those that the pilgrims customarily take with them" would seem to indicate the scallop shell, the *pectus maximus*, which has traditionally been the badge of pilgrims to Saint James. Seashell horns or shell trumpets are made from

and all the wiles of the enemy are stricken down from afar. Then also the cold of the hailstorms, the vehemence of whirlwinds, the fury of the storms, the hostile thunder and the fragrance of the wind and the powers of the air are controlled and suspended for their benefit.

HERE ENDS THE THIRD BOOK.

---

the shells of very large sea snails, which are generally found only in tropical waters and are certainly not found on the beaches of Galicia.

APPENDICES[1]

1. Pseudo-Abdias: The "Passion of James"

Book IV

The History and Deeds of the Apostle James the Greater[2]

1. James, son of Zebedee, was a full brother of John who left us the Gospel. Christ our Savior called him when He saw him in a boat with his father and brother and ordered him to follow Him. James, who was compelled by divine love, did this, and he stayed with our Lord from that time on. He was not only a disciple, of which He had many, but he was also called by Him on the mountain to the peak of the apostolate. After the Passion of the Lord, he acquired Judea and Samaria by lot in the apostolic division. As he cultivated these provinces, he went through the synagogues, and he showed that all the things that had been predicted by the prophets according to the scriptures concerning the Lord Jesus Christ were fulfilled in him.

2. When this was done, Hermogenes and Philetus set themselves up in opposition to the holy apostle, and they asserted that Jesus Christ the Nazarene was not the true Son of God, as this apostle reported about Him. James, however, acted confidently in the

---

1. The following texts are included for the reader's interest and in support of the translation and introductory materials. No attempt has been made to do a critical or comparative translation of the texts. No critical apparatus and only minimal footnotes have been added.
2. *Pseudo-Abdias:* "Passio Iacobi." Johann Albert Fabricius, "De historia ac rebus gestis Jacobi majoris Apostoli," in *Codex apocryphus Novi Testamenti* (Hamburg: Benjam. Schiller, 1719), 2:516–31.

Holy Spirit, voided all their assertions and showed from the Holy Scriptures that He was the true Son of God promised to the human race. For this reason, Philetus was moved, since he admired the prudence of James, and he returned to Hermogenes and said to him: "Know that James who asserts that he is a servant of Jesus Christ the Nazarene and His apostle cannot be overcome. For in His name I have seen him casting out demons from possessed bodies and making the blind see the light and cleansing the lepers. My dearest friends have even asserted that they had, in addition, seen him raise the dead. But, why do we delay on many things? He retains all the Holy Scriptures in his memory from which he shows no other to be the Son of God, except the One whom the Jews crucified. For this reason, if you mind my advice, we should go to him and ask his forgiveness. If you do not do this, I am leaving you anyway and will join up with him, so that I may deserve to be his disciple." When Hermogenes heard these things, he was inflamed by wrath and constrained Philetus with magic chains, and said: "We shall see if your James will free you." Philetus, however, quickly sent his boy to James, so that he might tell him what had been done. And immediately Saint James sent his handkerchief to Philetus, saying, "The Lord Jesus Christ raises up the stricken, and He releases foot shackles." However, as soon as the one who had been sent touched him with his handkerchief, he was released from the magic chain, and he came running to James and began to revile the evil deeds of the master.

3. However, Hermogenes the magician, was afflicted for having been reviled by him, and he summoned demons with his art and sent them to James, saying, "Go and bring back to me this James, together with my disciple Philetus, so that I may take vengeance on them, lest the rest of my pupils scoff at me in this way." Thereupon, the demons came to where James was praying and began howling in the air, saying, "James, apostle of God, have mercy on us, for before the time of the fire comes, we already are burning." James said to them, "Why did you come to me?" The demons said to him: "Hermogenes sent us, so that we might bring you and Philetus

back to him. However, as soon as we entered, a holy angel of God bound us with fiery chains, and we are tormented miserably." James said to them, "In the name of the Father and of the Son and of the Holy Spirit, may the angel of God free you again, so that you may return to Hermogenes and bring him back here unharmed but fettered." When they went off, they bound Hermogenes's hands behind his back with ropes, they brought him back bound in this way to the apostle and said, "You sent us to him, when we were burning fiery hot, and, behold, we bring him to you." The apostle of God said to him, "Most stupid of men, when the enemy of the human race had business with you, why did you not consider whom you would send to injure me? However, I have not allowed them up until now to show their fury to you". The demons themselves were also calling out: "Give us power over him, so that we can also avenge your injuries and our burning." The apostle said to them, "Behold, Philetus stands before you. Why do you not hold him?" The demons said to him, "We cannot touch even an ant that is in your room." Then Saint James said to Philetus, "So that you may know that this is the sect of our Lord Jesus Christ in which men may give good things in return for bad things, as he bound you, you are to free him. He tried to bring you to him bound by demons, permit him now, bound by the demons, to go free." And so, as Philetus freed him, and Hermogenes stood dejected and confounded, the apostle of the Lord turned to him and said, "Go, freed one, wherever you would like. For it is our doctrine that no one be converted unwillingly." Hermogenes said to him, "Behold and know that the furies of the demons will hold me and will kill me with various torments, unless you give me something that I may carry." James said to him, "Receive the staff of my journey, and go safely with it wherever you would like." He took the staff of the apostle, and he went to his home.

4. And with hardly any delay, he collected his magic books, and he put full sacks on his and his disciples' necks, and he brought them to the apostle, and he began to burn them in front of him. But James forbad it and said, "Lest perhaps the smell from the fire

might harm those not taking heed, attach stones and lead to the sacks and toss them into the sea." When Hermogenes did this, he returned and began to hold the feet of the apostle and pleaded with him, saying, "Liberator of souls, receive the penitent one whom you have put up with as a detractor until now." James responded and said, "If you have offered true penitence to God, you will receive true forgiveness." Hermogenes said to him, "I offer true penitence to God to such an extent that I have thrown away all my books, in which there were forbidden assumptions, and at the same time I have renounced all the activity of the enemy." Then the holy apostle said, "Go through the houses of those whom you have ruined, so that you may return to the Lord what you have taken. Teach that what before you taught to be false is true and what before you taught to be true is false. And break the idol that you used to adore and the divinations that you thought you offered to it. In addition, spend for a good cause the monies that you acquired through bad works. And just as you were a son of the devil and imitated the devil, you have been made a son of God by following God Who every day freely offers favors even to the ungrateful and Who gives food even to those blaspheming Him. For if the Lord was good to you, even when you were evil toward God, how much more favorable will He be to you if you cease to be a magician and begin to be pleasing to Him through good works?" James said these and other things similar to these, and Hermogenes submitted in all things, and thus he began to be righteous through the fear of God, so that even several wonders would be done through him by the Lord.

5. Therefore when the Jews saw that the apostle had converted this magician, whom they thought invincible, to believe through James in Jesus Christ, and likewise all his disciples and friends who used to convene at the synagogue, they brought money to two centurions who were in charge at Jerusalem, Lysia, and Theocritus, so that they might seize James. Sedition, however, arose from the people, and when he was led into custody, the Pharisees said to him, "Why do you preach about the man Jesus Whom we all know they crucified between thieves?" At these things, James was filled with the Holy Spirit and said:

APPENDICES

> Hear me, brothers, and all you who wish to be sons of Abraham. God promised to your father Abraham that 'all people will inherit in his seed.' However, his seed is not with Ishmael but with Israel. The former, in fact, was cast out with his mother Hagar and was excluded from a share in the seed of Abraham. It was said by God to Abraham 'for in Isaac will your seed be named' [Gn 21:12]. Our father Abraham was indeed called a friend of God [Cf. Jas 2:23] before he accepted circumcision, before he respected the Sabbath, and before he knew of any law of divine ordination. He became however a friend certainly not by circumcising himself but by believing in God, because all peoples would inherit through his seed. If, therefore, Abraham became a friend by believing, it follows that one who does not believe in God, is an enemy of God.

When the apostle had said these things, the Jews said, "And who is it who does not believe in God?

6. James responded:

> "Whoever does not believe that all peoples would inherit in the seed of Abraham. Whoever did not believe Moses when he said: 'The Lord will raise up with you a great prophet. You will hear him as you hear me, by all the things that he will teach you' [Cf. Acts 3:22 and Dt 18:15]. Isaiah predicted this promise and in what order it would occur and in fact said: 'Behold a virgin will conceive in her womb and will bear a Son, and His name will be called Emmanuel' [Is 7:14] 'which means God be with us' [Mt 1:23] and Jeremiah adds: 'Behold your Redeemer will come, Jerusalem, and this will be His sign: He will open the eyes of the blind, He will give back hearing to the deaf, and He will raise the dead with His voice' [Cf. Is 35:4–5], and Ezekiel also pointed to Him, saying: 'Your King will come, O Zion, He comes as a humble one, and He restores you' [Cf. Zec 9:9]. Daniel also said: 'Like the son of a man, so will He come, and He will obtain rule and

power' [Dn 7:13]. And David predicted this: 'The Lord said to Me, You are my Son' [Ps 2:7]. And the voice of the Father said about the Son: 'He will call Me, You are my Father, and I will place Him on high as my Firstborn, among the kings of the earth' [Cf. Ps 88:27–28 / 89:27–28]. And also: 'From the Fruit of your womb I will place upon My seat' [Ps 131:11 / 132:11]. And also the prophets predicted His Passion, and Isaiah in fact said: He was led like a lamb to slaughter.' [Is 53:7] And David said about his human person: They will pierce My hands and My feet, they will count My bones. They will have considered Me and looked into me. And they have divided My garments and cast lots for my cloak' [Ps 21:17–19 / 22:16–18]. And in another place David said: They have given Me bile for food and in My thirst, they have given Me vinegar to drink' [Ps 68:22 / 69:21]. And again he foretold about his death: 'My flesh will rest in hope, for you will not leave My soul in hell nor will you give your Holy One to see corruption' [Ps 15:9–10 / 16:9–10]. The voice of the Son said to the Father: 'I will rise up from here and still I am with You' [Cf. Ps 138:18 / 139:18]. And again: Because of misery of destitution and of the sighs of the poor, now I rise up, said the Lord' [Ps 11:6 / 12:5]. About the Ascension in addition it was said of Him by the prophet: He ascends on high, he brought a captive into captivity' [Cf. Eph 4:8]. And again: 'God ascends in jubilation' [Ps 46:6 / 47:5]. And again: 'He ascends above the cherubim and has flown off' [Ps 17:11 / 18:10]. And many other things are found in the law as witness to His Ascension. As to His sitting at the right hand of the Father, David says: The Lord says to My Lord: *Sit at my right hand'* [Ps 109:1 / 110:1]. And as to His coming to judge the world by fire, [Cf. Is 66:16], the prophet speaks again: 'The Lord will surely come, our God ,and will not be silent. In His gaze, a fire will burn and surrounding Him will be a strong storm' [Ps 49:3 / 50:3].

7. [And James continued:]

All of these things that were predicted were fulfilled in part in our Lord Jesus Christ, and those that have still not occurred will soon be fulfilled, just as the prophets have predicted to you. For Isaiah said: 'The dead who are in the tombs will rise and rise again' [Cf. Is 26:19]. If you ask, 'What is this: that they will have arisen?' David answered that he heard the Lord speaking: 'Once God spoke, I heard two things: *The power is God's and the mercy is Yours, Lord, Who gives to each one according to his deeds*' [Ps 61:12–13 / 62:11–12]. Whence my brothers, let each one of you do penance, so that each of you does not receive according to his deeds, as each knows that he is a participant with those who affixed Him to the Cross, Who has freed the whole world from sufferings. If indeed from His spit, He has illuminated the eyes of one born blind so that He might be proven to be the One who had formed Adam from the slime of the earth, so he made mud with his spit and put it on the eyes and cured them. And when we, His disciples, asked Him who had sinned, the man or his parents, such that he should be born blind, the Master answered us and said: 'Neither did he sin nor did his parents, but it was so that the works of the Lord would be manifest in him.' This means that the Master Who had created him would be made manifest and that He would make whole what had been made less than whole. For the fact that He in His person was to accept bad things as good things was predicted by King David when he said: 'They will give back to me bad things for good, and hatred for my love' [Ps 108:5 / 109:5]. Then after such great favors were offered to the Jews, and He cured so many paralytics and cleansed lepers and cast out so many demons and raised the dead, they all called out with one voice: 'He is guilty of death' [Mt 26:66]. Besides what was to be reported by His disciple, it was also predicted in this order by David: 'Who was eating bread with me, has increased hypocritical deceit against me' [Ps 40:10 / 41:9]. Brothers, the sons of Abraham predicted all these things, with the Holy Spirit speaking through their mouths. If we do not believe these things, will we be able to avoid the punishment of eternal fire, or will we not be deserving of punishment when even the Gentiles believe in the words of the prophets? Will we, however, the people chosen at a certain time, not put any faith in our patriarchs and prophets? Truly, I believe such crimes to be shameful and punishable with so many acts and wicked deeds and to be lamented by us with tearful voices, so that the pious Forgiver may accept our penance lest these things finally come to pass for us as happened to our great people: The earth opened up and swallowed Dathan and covered the synagogue of Abiram. Fire burned in their synagogues and a flame consumed the sinners' [Ps 105:17–18 / 106:17–18].

8. When he had said these things in front of the crowd, not without admiration and a singular grace from God, they all cried out with one voice saying: "We have sinned, we have acted unjustly. Give us a remedy; what should we do?" To this James said, "Brothers, do not despair, just believe and be baptized so that all your sins may be erased." And so, after the sermon of the holy apostle, many of the Jews were baptized. When Abiathar, the priest for that year, saw many people daily believing in Jesus, using money he roused up great civil discord, such that one of the scribes of the Pharisees put a rope on the neck of the apostle and led him to the residence of King Herod. This Herod, who accepted the case, was son of Archelaus, and he ordered Saint James to be beheaded. And when he was led to the place of punishment, he saw a paralytic lying and calling to him: "Holy man, free me from the pains from which my limbs are suffering." The apostle turned to him and said "In the name of Jesus Christ my crucified Lord, for whose faith I am led to death, arise healthy and bless your Savior". And he immediately arose and began to run and praise and bless the name of Jesus the Lord.

9. Then that scribe of the Pharisees whom we said had put the rope around his neck — Josias by name — fell before the feet of the apostle and said, "I beg you that you give me forgiveness and that you make me a partaker of the name of a saint." James turned to him and said, "Do you believe that Jesus Christ the Lord, whom the Jews crucified, is the true Son of the living God?" And Josias

said, "I believe, and it is my belief from this hour that He is the Son of the Living God." Upon seeing these things, Abiathar the Priest ordered him to be seized and said to him, "If you do not leave James and curse the name of Jesus, you will be beheaded together with him." Josias said to him, "May you be cursed, and may all your days be cursed; however, the name of the Lord Jesus Christ whom James preaches, is blessed unto the centuries." Then Abiathar, inflamed with animosity, ordered the scribe to be struck down with blows and sent a report about him to Herod and asked that he be beheaded at the same time and together with James. Therefore, James along with Josias was led to the place of punishment. Before he was beheaded, he asked the executioner about the possibility of water being made available, and a glass filled with water was brought to him. The apostle took it and said, "Do you believe in the name of Jesus Christ the Son of God?" And he said, "I believe." And James poured the water over him and said, "Give me the kiss of peace." And when he had kissed him, he placed his hand over his head and blessed him and made the sign of the Cross of Christ on his forehead. And with hardly any delay, he extended his neck to the executioner. After that, Josias also, having now been made perfect in faith, accepted and exulted in the palm of martyrdom, for Him whom the Eternal God had sent into the world to us for our deliverance. To Him be honor and glory. World without end.

2. Song on the Altars of the Twelve Apostles[3]

Here also James, separated from his ancient father,
Defended the lofty temple with a holy vaulted cover
Who, with Christ calling from the shore to bridge of his filial duty,
Left his own father with his curved ship.
He first converted the Spanish peoples with doctrine
Converting with divine assurances the barbaric multitudes,
Which a short time before revered primitive rites and ghastly temples,
As they had been entrapped by the deception of a horrible demon.
Thus the marvelous bishop brought about many signs,
Which are now solemnly written ritually on square tablets.
Savage Herod, the tyrant and ruler of the kingdom, beheaded and
Killed him with a cruel death by the sword,
The Highest Father, who with justice celebrates the saints,
Transported him with gleaming rewards unto the heavenly heights.

---

3. Translation from Aldhelm. J. A. Giles, ed., *Sancti Aldhelmi, ex abbate malmesburiensi episcopi Schireburnensis: Opera quae extant omnia e codicibus mss emendavit* (Oxford: J.H. Parker, 1844), 122.

APPENDICES

3. O Word of God Revealed By the Mouth of the Father[4]

1.
O Word of God, revealed by mouth of the Father,
Creator and true beginning of things,
Eternal Author, light, origin of light
Brought forth from the womb of the glorious Virgin,
You, O Christ, are, in truth our Emmanuel.

2.
King and priest, to whom sacred stones
Behold, are three times four: onyx, agate
Shining beryl, sapphire, carbuncle
Or amethyst, sardonyx, topaz,
Emerald, jasper, hyacinth, chrysolite.

3.
According to ritual, the sun, the day, with twelve gems each
Gleams with the hours, with the best pearls.
It has illuminated the world in the already fleeing darkness
And with the candelabrum placed above for you
It shines with lamps for the twice-six apostles.

4.
Peter has Rome; his brother, Achaia;
Thomas, India; Levi [Matthew], Macedonia;
James, Jerusalem; and Egypt, the Zealot [Simon].
Bartholomew has Lycaonia;
Mathias, the Pontus; and Philip, Gaul.

---

4. The translation is based on Latin of the PL 86:1306–07 and on the Latin of the http://www.xacobeo.fr/ZF2.02.mus.O_Dei_Verbum.htm (accessed July 2018).

5.
Then the great sons of thunder shine
Having both acquired through the prayer of an illustrious mother
The distinctions of the peak of life:
John guiding alone the right side of Asia,
And his brother placed in Spain.

6.
Shining for their Master, harmless things,
The one acquired the right side after he
Received truces of peace; the other, the left side for his purpose.
Both acquired kingdoms, pledges twice chosen
They hasten to the glory of heaven.[5]

7.
The glorious one, I say, brought to a reward,
The chosen one from this place is brought to the martyrdom
Of Christ, the one called James of Zebedee.
By carrying out the duties of the apostolate
This victor takes also the stigmata of the Passion.

8.
He sowed truly by divine help.
He corrects the offences of the magicians, the rages of demons.
He holds poisons in check. He corrects envious actions.
And finally active in ceremonial robes and in prophecies
A confident and trusting heart may be given as a sign.

9.
Inscrutable, once participating in a wish, he grants
In a flash to the sick person seeking support.
To the one wishing, he opens the gifts of faith,
A banner of peace for the fullness of health,
And discharging with a sword, he strengthens himself in glory.

5.   *Mitridepolis.*

10.
O truly worthy and very holy apostle,
A golden head shining for Spain,
A protector for us and a native patron,
In avoiding pestilence, let there be heavenly salvation.
Banish completely disease, soreness and crime.

11.
Be present and well-disposed to the flock, pious creditor
And gentle shepherd for the flock, the clergy, and the people.
With the heavenly treasure, let us delight in the joy.
When we have acquired the kingdom, let us be dressed in glory
Eternal. Through you, may we avoid the infernal regions.

12.
Be present, we beseech, O Single Power,
Who alone fills the entire world with glory and
Great and everlasting virtue. Let there be eternal
Glory, whose praise, as well as mercy
And honor is living abundantly through the centuries.
Amen.

Acrostic:

O RAEX REGUM REIEM PIIVM MAURECATUM AEXAUDI CUI PROVE OC TUO AMORE PREVE

Standard Latin

O Rex regum, regem pium Maurecatum exaudi, cui probe [h]oc tuo amore praebe.

Translation

O King of kings, listen to the pious king Mauregato; grant this fittingly through Your love.

4. *Pasionario Hispánico*: Saint James, Brother of John[6]

The *Passion* of James the Apostle, brother of Saint John, and of his companions who suffered in Jerusalem on the third calends of January. Thanks be to God.

In those days, James, the apostle of our Lord Jesus Christ and brother of Saint John the Apostle and Evangelist, visited all Judea and Samaria. Going through the synagogues, according to the Holy Scriptures, however, he showed all things predicted by the prophets, which were fulfilled in Jesus Christ our Lord. It happened however that a certain magician, Hermogenes, sent to him his disciple Philetus who, when he came, tried with a few Pharisees to assert to James that Jesus Christ the Nazarene, of Whom James said he was a disciple, was not the Son of God.

James, however, acted confidently in the Holy Spirit, voided all his assertions, and showed him from the Holy Scriptures that He was the true Son of God. Philetus, therefore, returned to Hermogenes and said to him: "May you know that James, who asserts that he is the servant and apostle of Jesus Christ the Nazarene cannot be overcome. For in His name I have seen him casting out demons from possessed bodies. My closest friends assert that they have seen him raise a dead man. But why delay on unnecessary things? He retains accurately in memory all the Holy Scriptures, from which he shows no one else to be the Son of God except Him Whom the Jews crucified. May my advice therefore please you: come to him and ask forgiveness for yourself from him. If you do not do this, know that your magic art will be completely useless to all. Know that I, however, will return to him and will seek that I might deserve to be his disciple."

When Hermogenes heard this, he was filled with zeal and bound Philetus so that he could not move, and he said to him: "Let us see if your James will release you from these chains." Then Philetus sent his boy with haste to James. When the boy had come and told him, James immediately sent his handkerchief to him, saying: "Our Lord Jesus Christ raises those shattered, and He breaks foot

6. Translation from Angel Fabregau Grau, ed., *Pasionario Hispánico* (Madrid: Consejo Superior de Investigaciones Científicas, 1953–55), 111–16.

shackles." Immediately, then, after he had touched him with his handkerchief that he had brought, Philetus was freed from the chain of the magician, and he came running to James and insulted Hermogenes for his evil deeds. Hermogenes the magician, however, was afflicted that Philetus had insulted him, and he summoned demons with his art. Then he sent those demons to James, saying, "Go and bring this James to me, together with Philetus my disciple, so that I may be exonerated by him and so that my other disciples will not begin to insult me in a similar manner."

The demons then came to where James was praying, and they began a howling in the air, saying. "James, apostle of God, have mercy on us, for we are already burning before the time comes for us to burn." James said to them, "Why did you come to me?" The demons said to him, "Hermogenes sent us so that we might lead you and Philetus to him, but as soon as we came in, a holy angel of God bound us with fiery chains and we are tormented." James said to them, "In the name of the Father and of the Son and of the Holy Spirit, the angel of God will free you, so that you may return to Hermogenes, not to harm him, but so you may bring him here to me."

Then they went off, bound his hands behind his back with cords and brought him back this way saying, "You sent us where we were burned and tortured and consumed intolerably." Meanwhile, when he was brought to James, James the Apostle of God said to him, "You are the most stupid of men to have a conversation with the enemy of the human race. Why do you not consider whom you have asked to send his minions to you for harming me and whose fury I thus far have not permitted them to show to you?" These demons also were calling out saying, "Give him over to our power, so that we may be able to avenge your injuries and our burning." James said to them, "Behold, Philetus stands before you, why do you not seize him?" The demons said to him, "We cannot touch even an ant that is in your room." Then Saint James said to Philetus, "So that they may recognize this to be the sect of our Lord Jesus Christ, such that men learn to return good things for bad things, he tied you, but you will free him. He tried to bring you back with the demons, but you will now permit him captured by the demons, to depart."

And then Philetus, confused and humble, freed him, and Hermogenes, dispirited, started to stand up. James said to him, "Go freely where you wish, for it is not our teaching that anyone be converted unwillingly". Hermogenes said to him, "I know the angers of the demons. Unless you give me something to take with me, they will seize me, and they will kill me with various torments." Then James said to him, "Accept for yourself this staff of my journey, and go with it securely wherever you wish." And he took the staff of the apostle, went off to his house, and he put over his neck and the necks of his disciples sacks filled with books, and he brought them to the apostle of God and began to burn them in fires. James said to them, "Lest the odor from their burning harm those who must be safeguarded, put rocks together with lead inside these sacks and make them sink in the sea." When Hermogenes had done this, he came back and began to hold the feet of the apostle and asked him, saying: "Liberator of souls, accept the penitent one whom up until now you tolerated as envious and disparaging." James answered and said, "If you offer true penitence to God, you will obtain His true forgiveness." Hermogenes said to him, "I offer true penitence to God to the extent that I have thrown away all my books in which there was illicit presumption at the same time as I have renounced all the arts of the enemy."

The apostle said to him: "Now go through their houses that you destroyed, so that you may call back to the Lord those you have taken. Teach that what you said was false is true, and what you said was true is false. Also break the idol that you worshipped and destroy the divinations that you thought were answered by it. Spend the monies that you acquired by bad work on good works, so that as you were a son of the devil by imitating the devil, you may be made a son of God by imitating God. For He bestows favors daily even on the ungrateful and provides food for those blaspheming him. For if even when you are bad toward God, the Lord is good with you, how much more will He be benevolent, if you cease to be bad and begin to please Him with good works?"

APPENDICES

Hermogenes complied with these things and with similar things when James spoke. Thus he began to be perfect in fear of the Lord, so that even several miracles were done through him by the Lord. The Jews therefore saw that this magician, whom they considered insuperable, was converted as well as all his disciples and friends who used to convene at the synagogue, and they believed in Jesus Christ through James. Then they offered money to two centurions, Lysia and Theocritus, who were in charge at Jerusalem, and they seized him and they put him under guard.

Sedition was brought about by the people, and it was said that he must be led out and heard according to the law. Then the Pharisees said to him, "Why do you preach Jesus, the man whom we all know was crucified between thieves?" Then James was filled with the Holy Spirit and said, "Hear, brethren, and all you who know that you are sons of Abraham. God promised our father Abraham that all peoples would inherit in His seed. His seed, however, is not on Ishmael, but on Israel, for Ishmael was cast out with his mother Hagar and was excluded from a share in the seed of Abraham. And it was said by God to Abraham: 'In Isaac will your seed be called unto you'" [Heb 11:18]. Our father Abraham was called a friend of God [Cf. Jas 2:23] even before he accepted circumcision, before he respected the Sabbath, and before he knew any law of divine ordination. He, however, became a friend not by circumcising himself but by believing in God, because all peoples would inherit through his seed. If therefore Abraham became a friend by believing, does it not follow that one who does not believe in God is an enemy?"

The Jews, however, said, "And who is it who does not believe in God?" James answered, "Whoever does not believe that all peoples inherit in his seed and whoever does not believe in Moses, when he says: 'He will raise up a great prophet for you, and you will hear as you hear me through all the things whatsoever He will teach you.' [Cf. Acts 3:22 and Dt 18:15]. Indeed Isaiah predicted this promise and in what order it would happen, and in fact said: 'Behold a virgin will conceive in her womb and will bear a son and His name will be called Emmanuel' [Is 7:14], which is interpreted as *God with us* [Mt 1:23]. Jeremiah, however, says, 'Behold your Redeemer will come,

Jerusalem, and this will be His sign. He will open the eyes of the blind, He will give back hearing to the deaf, and He will raise the dead with His voice' [Cf. Is 35:5]. Ezekiel however points this out, saying, 'Your King will come, O Zion, He will come as a humble man and He will restore you' [Cf. Mt 4–5]. Daniel, however, says, 'As the Son of Man, so will He come, and He will obtain principalities and powers' [Dn 7:13]. David, however, said the voice indicates the 'Son of God,' saying, 'The Lord said to me: *you are my son*' [Ps 2:7]. Then the voice of the Father said, 'This one will call me: *You are my Father,*' and I will place Him on high among the kings of the earth' [Cf. Ps 89:27–28 / 89:26–27]. The Word of the Lord spoke to this David, saying, 'From the fruit of your womb I shall place upon my seat' [Ps 131:11 / 132:11].

"Concerning his Passion, however, Isaiah said, 'He was led like a lamb to the slaughter' [Is 53:7], and David said about His human person, 'They will pierce my hands and my feet, and they will count my bones. They have considered Me and inspected Me, they have divided my clothes among them and will cast lots over my clothing' [Ps 21:17–19 / 22:16–18]. And in another place this same David said, 'They have given Me bile as my food, and in my thirst they have given Me vinegar to drink' [Ps 68:22 / 69:21]. About His death, however, He says, 'My flesh will rest in hope, for you will not abandon my soul in hell, nor will you give your Holy One to see corruption' [Ps 15:9–10 / 16:9–10]. The voice however of the Son to the Father said, 'I shall rise from here and be with You" [Cf. Ps 138:18 / 139:18] and again, *'Because of the misery of destitution and the weeping of the poor, I will rise up, said the Lord'* [Ps 11:6 / 12:5]. About his Ascension, however, he said, 'He ascends on high, He brought a captive into captivity' [Cf. Eph 4:8], and again, 'He ascends above the cherubim and has flown off' [Ps 17:11 / 18:10], and again: 'God ascends in jubilation' [Ps 46:6 / 47:5]. Also Anna, the mother of Saint Samuel, said, 'The Lord ascends into the heavens and thunders."[7] Many other things are also found in the law as testimony about His Ascension. As to His sitting at the right hand of the Father,

---

7. Not found.

David said the same thing: 'The Lord said to my Lord, *Sit at my right hand'* [Ps 109:1 / 110:1], and as to His coming to judge the earth by fire, the prophet says, 'God will surely come. Our God will not be silent. In His gaze, a fire will burn and surrounding Him will be a strong storm' [Ps 49:3 / 50:3].

"All these things that were predicted were fulfilled in our Lord Jesus Christ, and those that have still not occurred will be fulfilled, just as the prophets have predicted to you. For Isaiah said: 'The dead who are in their tombs will arise and they will rise again' [Cf. Is 26:19]. If you ask, 'What will it be like when each has arisen?' David said that he heard the Lord speaking about what will be. So that you might judge what it may be, listen to what he says: 'Once God spoke, I heard these two things: that power is God's and mercy is Yours, Lord. You, in fact, give to each one according to his deeds' [Ps 61:12–13 / 62:11–12]. Whence, brethren, let each one of you do penance, and may each not receive according to his word. Each of you, in fact, knows that he has been a participant with those who fixed Him to the cross, Who saved the whole world from sufferings. If indeed He has, with His spit, illuminated the eyes of one born blind, so that He might be proven to be the One who had formed Adam from the slime of the earth, so He made mud with His spit and put it on the places for his eyes that sickness had not blinded but that had been deficient through nature. For we asked Jesus Christ our Lord, saying, 'Who has sinned, this man or his parents, such that he should deserve to be blind?' [Jn 9:2]. And He answered us, saying, 'Neither he sinned, nor did his parents, but it was so that the works of the Lord would be manifest in him' [Jn 9:3]. That means that the Master who had created him would be made manifest and that He would make whole what He had made less than whole.

"For the fact that He was to accept bad things for good things was predicted in His person by David, when he said, 'They will give back to Me bad things for good and hatred for My love' [Ps 108:5 / 109:5]. Then after He had cured the paralytics, cleansed the lepers, given illumination to the blind, cast out demons and raised the dead, all with one voice called out: 'He is guilty of death' [Mt

26:66]. That He was to be handed over by his disciple was predicted in this order by David: 'The one who was eating bread with Me has instigated deceit against Me' [Ps 40:10 / 41:9]. Brethren, the sons of Abraham have predicted all these things, with the Holy Spirit speaking through them. Now if we do not believe these things, will we be able to avoid the punishment of eternal fire, or will we not deserve to be punished, when even the Gentiles believe in the voices of the prophets, and we do not believe our patriarchs and prophets? These crimes of deeds and omissions are to be blushed at and punished. Let us lament them with tearful voices, lest those things that happen to us, the proud ones to whom he said: 'For the earth opened up and swallowed Dathan and covered over the synagogue of Abiram, and fire burned in the synagogues and a flame consumed the sinners'" [Ps 105:17–18 / 106:17–18].

James said these things and things similar to them, and the Lord conferred such grace on the apostle that all with one voice called out: "We have sinned, we have acted unjustly. Give us a remedy. What should we do?" James said to them, "Brethren, do not despair. Just believe and be baptized and all your sins will be erased." After a few days however, Abiathar, who was at that time the priest of the year, saw so many people had believed in the Lord that he was filled with jealousy. He stirred up very great civil discord, such that one of the scribes of the Pharisees put a rope on his neck and led him to the residence of King Herod. Herod, the son of King Archelaus, then ordered him to be beheaded.

And when he was being led to his beheading, he saw a paralytic lying down and calling to him: "Saint James, apostle of Jesus Christ, free me from the pains from which all my limbs are suffering." James said to him, "In the name of my crucified Lord Jesus Christ, for whose faith I am led to my beheading, arise healthy and bless your Savior." And immediately he arose, and he began to run and praise and bless the name of the Lord Jesus Christ. Then that scribe of the Pharisees who put the rope on his neck and was leading him and whose name was Josias, put himself at James's feet and began to say to him, "I beg you, that you give me forgiveness and that you make me a partaker of the name of a saint." James, therefore, understood that his heart had been visited by the Lord and he said to Josias, "Do you believe that this Lord Jesus Christ whom the Jews crucified is the true Son of the Living God?" And Josias said, "I believe, and from this hour forward my faith is in Him, for He is the Son of the Living God."

Then Abiathar the priest had him seized and said to him, "If you do not abandon James and do not curse the name of Jesus, you will be beheaded along with him." Josias said to him, "May you be cursed, and may all your days be cursed. However, the name of my Lord Jesus Christ Whom James preaches is blessed unto the ages." Then Abiathar ordered his mouth to be stricken with punches, and he sent a report about him to Herod and asked that he be beheaded at the same time and together with James. They arrived, however, at the place where they were to be beheaded, and James said to the executioner, "Before you behead us, let some water be given to us." And a full flask of water was brought to him. Then he said to Josias, "Do you believe in the Father and the Son and the Holy Spirit?" And when Josias said, "I believe," James sprinkled him and said to him, "Give me a kiss of peace." When he had kissed him, he placed his hand on his head and blessed him, and made a small sign of the Cross of Christ on his forehead. Thus he was perfected in the faith of the Lord Jesus Christ, and together with the apostle at one and the same hour, he was made a martyr and he went on to the Lord.

To Him is honor and glory. World without end. Amen.

5. Pasionario Hispánico: About Torquatus and His Companions[8]

The Life and Death of Saints Torquatus, Tissefons, Esicius, Endalecius, Eufrasius, Secundus and Cecilius, which is Celebrated on the Calends of May

No human mind can give in detail the names or numbers of the countless throngs of the most victorious blessed martyrs or the innumerable bands of holy confessors that we believe belong to the crowned assemblies of heaven and the company of the angels, with whose help all people overcome the snares of the enemy. Bodies, fallen in death, after being held by a variety of diseases and occupied by various weaknesses, immediately have health as a companion and are restored to growing health, with the sick bodies already easily left behind. For this reason, the plundering of a most atrocious death is not considered to last; and the sleep that is given is rather to be sought for its peace by people, and life is given to the dead, and eternal happiness is brought to those suffering sorrow. But when a glorious story of unadulterated transmission brought so much of this information to me and did not fall short in its knowledge of famous titles and its purity of narration, I think it is fitting to transmit it to following generations. For we must not let this story, found with truthful recollection, be lost through silence, lest we feel guilty in various ways of great negligence after we have hidden a great abundance of rich treasure through concealment.

Therefore, when the most holy confessors Torquatus, Tissefons, Endalecius, Secundus, Eufrasius, Cecilius, and Esicius had accepted the priesthood from the holy apostles in the city of Rome, they went out to deliver the Catholic faith in Spain, which up until now was held by pagan error and abounded in idolatrous superstition. With a divine companion as their guide, they all converged on the city of Guadix. When they were about a mile and a half from the city, and their joints were tired, they rested a little while, so that they might heal their limbs, which were weakened by the length of their journey. They

---

8. Translation from Fabregau Grau, *Pasionario*, 255–60.

were encouraged that the oldest one had prevailed over the journey. By resting they were renewed, and they walked tirelessly on a straight path. While the bodily members with which they moved were visibly worn out, they were nevertheless strengthened with heavenly help and spiritual grace, and they recalled among themselves as an ongoing witness: *The holy ones who hope in the Lord will alter their strengths and will take on wings like an eagle. They will run and not fail* [Cf. Prv 23:5].

And so, as we ourselves learned and in the place where we said, the venerable bishops desired to rest, and they sent followers to the city of Guadix because they needed food. It happened then that it was the day on which they celebrated ritual pagan festivals to Jove, Mercury, or Juno and forgot God sitting on His heavenly throne and they carried out the wicked solemnities to mute and dead images in a vain cult. Then the disciples of the venerable old men entered the city walls and saw the tragic crowds trapped in the snares of greatest deception and immersed by a headlong fall into the unending abyss. It appeared they believed they could be saved by what was being perpetrated by unchaste hands.

And when this pestiferous group met the companions of these holy old men, the group recognized in them the venerable cult of religion and the dress of the pious faith of priests, and this unspeakable enemy pursued them fervidly up to the river on which there was a bridge built in the old style. There, with a divine miracle at work, the structure that no age believed could be destroyed collapsed in a single moment, and the bloodthirsty people and this pagan sedition were submerged in the channel of this river. And the holy men sang: *He has plunged the horse and the rider into the sea* [Ex 15:1]. However, the servants of God were freed. The most of those who saw this event were worn down by a vehement fear. Among them was a certain old lady, illustrious in circumstance and adorned by the kindling of the Holy Spirit, by the name of Luparia. She sent her messengers to them and, through them, said with highest-level entreaties that she wanted to grant a meeting between them and her, so that she might discover the belief of these holy men.

When the woman first got to see them, she had already received heavenly gifts into the depths of her heart, and she boldly asked where the most holy men were from and what regions they were coming to. Then they acknowledged that they were sent by the holy apostles to preach the kingdom of God and that they were commissioned to announce the Gospel of Christ to Spain and to teach them. Then they said that whoever believes in Christ, the Son of God, will not see eternal death, but will possess life with the angels. She, as a new disciple of the holy doctrine, was immediately satisfied and asked for the gift of holy baptism. This was approved but not before she would agree to their requests that she build a basilica for the baptistery where the holy men chose. She accepted these requests and showed continual care over the work for a very long time, until she had brought the whole building of the basilica up to its roof, and she furnished the gables of the undertaken temple.

And when the work was completed and all things were done as ordered and were pleasing to the holy men, they constructed as usual a font, in which the woman of holy devotion might be sprinkled with the water of the bath of salvation. Then the entire people who had revered the emptiness of the idols through superstition followed the example of this woman. They abandoned the temple of venomous crime, and they followed the teaching of the holy old men with avid minds. From then on, the polluted seat of the idols was abandoned, and there they consecrated the church with an altar to Saint John the Baptist. The faith grew, and the people of God increased.

Then they did not separate from each other in mind or in faith but divided themselves up among diverse cities for dispensing the grace of God: Torquatus in Guadix, Tisefons in Vera, Esicius in Carcese, Endalecius in Urci, Secundus in Avila, Eufrasius in Eliturgi, and Cecilius in Heliberri. They stayed in these cities and began to redeem mortals from the beginning of life. And so it occurred that, when the servants of God imparted the gifts of heaven, they acquired greatly the fruits of believers in the holy Church. For that reason, a little after the time of their labors, they carried off the glorious triumphs of the highest palm. Thus, they were secured with an increase of good works and, with the temporal life withdrawing,

APPENDICES

they took possession of the eternal region and migrated with a happy death from this world.

They also left us the venerable treasures of their relics. Anyone who is sick and goes to their holy and sacred tombs out of pious devotion will be delivered with the irrefutable help of these holy confessors. They also expel demons from the bodies of the possessed and restore sight, through their prayer, to the blind who have lost it. All those, however, seeking their help, provided they ask confidently, soon receive from heaven what they requested.

We must not, however, cover with a mantle of silence such remarkable miracles of the Lord as have taken place on their anniversary by the pious and faithful merits of the saints even up to this very day. We all know the persecutors of the Church and the supporters of perfidy also recognize it as true. There is before the doors of the church a moderate-sized olive tree, and the root was planted there by these holy men. On the evening when the feast of these holy men is approaching, such a great abundance is granted to it by the Lord that it appears covered with more fruit than leaves. In the morning, however, the whole assembly — with an equally great horde of pagans and heretics and those of perverse teachings falling in with them — comes together with pious devotion to revere the patronage of the holy men and to harvest such perfect and such plentiful olives adorned with all the beauty of those that matured at the times fixed for this. Thus all the faithful — and even the unfaithful — carry the olives away, to the extent that each one can. Who can say what the abundance of this multitude of the fruit would be? For, if it were possible that it be collected into one place, it would fill a great number of olive baskets.

To Jesus Christ ruling as our Lord, who has taken up His martyrs and His confessors and has glorified them in peace and in virtue, to Him together with the Father is the undivided power and the co-equal essence in the unity of the Holy Spirit. World without end. Amen.

6. Agreement of Antealtares[9]

Agreement of the Bishop don Diego Peláez with the Abbot of Antealtares, Saint Fagildo

In the year 1115 and on the sixteenth calends of September.[10]

There is certainly no doubt, but it remains known to many, as we learned in the witness of Pope Saint Leo, that the most holy apostle James was beheaded in Jerusalem, that he was taken away by the disciples to Joppa, that he was watched over there for no small amount of time by the Lord, that he was transferred finally to Spain in a boat with hand of the Lord guiding, and that he remained buried and hidden for a long time in the farthest regions of Galicia.

However, since light could not be hidden for long in darkness or a lantern under a basket, it is known by provident divine mercy that, in the times of the most serene king and lord Alfonso, who is called the Chaste, it was first revealed through angelic announcements to a certain hermit by the name of Pelagius, who was accustomed to spend time not far from the place where the apostolic body lay. Then by many heavenly lights, it was disclosed to the faithful residing in the parish of San Fiz de Solovio. After they held council together, they presented and revealed the holy vision to Lord Bishop Teodomiro of Iria. After he held a three-day fast and brought together throngs of the faithful, he discovered the tomb of the blessed apostle covered with marble stones. Then he rejoiced with the greatest joy and did not put off calling the aforesaid most religious king.

He was of pious disposition and loved the holiness of chastity. With one church built in honor of this apostle and nearby another

---

9. *Concordia de Antealtares*. Antonio López Ferreiro, *Historia de la Santa Apostólica Metropolitana Iglesia de Santiago de Compostela* (Santiago: Seminario, 1898–1909), 3: 3–7 and José María Zepedano, *Historia Y Descripción Arqueológica De La Basílica Compostelana*, (Lugo: Imprenta de Soto Freire, 1870), 314–19.

10. August 17.

APPENDICES

one in honor of Saint John the Baptist, in front of these altars he immediately hastened to build another moderate-sized church containing three holy altars: the first in honor of the Holy Savior, the second in honor of Saint Peter, the prince of the apostles, and the third in honor of Saint John the Apostle. In this church he placed Lord Abbot Ildefredo, a man of great holiness, along with no fewer than twelve monks assigned to the watch over the apostle and dedicated to the divine office. They sang the divine offices, and they celebrated masses devotedly above the body of the apostle. He also set aside for them a place to the east of these altars, through the charter of this gift, where they built a cloister and workshops according to the Rule of Saint Benedict. Since this place was built in front of the holy altars, it is called the *Antealtares*, and this has remained with the same strong brilliance up to the time of Lord Bishop Diego Pelagio and of the Lord Abbot Fagildo.

Alfonso II wished to construct the Church of Saint James as a work with cut stone walls, and he designed it to be of such a size that it would hold all the aforesaid altar-places along with the church and part of the cloister of the monks. But the most holy abbot, while the church was being built, thought to himself and saw that the monastic office could not be observed there in a perfect way, so he built a very small church for the work of the monks. This church contained three altars, namely one for Saint Peter the Apostle, one for Saint Thomas, and one for Saint Nicholas where Pelagius in former times had a cell. He also built an altar for Saint Pelagius the Martyr.

After this was done, he presented himself together with the same bishop before the face of Lord King Alfonso, and he began to plead for the right of the apostle, that he had thus far held, and of the altars of the Holy Savior and of Saint Peter and Saint John, and how he could possess these in the future after the work on the church was done. Then the king ordered that the abbot and the monastery, for all days should have, by hereditary right, the altar of Saint Peter that was being built in this Church of Saint James, although not in the same place where it had previously stood, but in another one. While work was still being done on these altars, its bishop would have the two other altars along with the monks' portion of the offering from the altar of Saint James. The altar of the Holy Savior and of Saint John the Apostle and Evangelist would be restored to the abbot and the monks to be held in perpetuity.

Finally, while the church was being built, the bishop would have the money of the altar of Saint James, of which formerly the monks acquired half. And when the church was finished, the abbot and monks would have a third of it and the bishop would have two thirds in perpetuity.

For this reason, I, Diego, by divine grace bishop of the See of Iria, holding the chair of the Church of Saint James, with assembly and voice of those present and of those to come in this same church, by the decree of our lord King Alfonso, the descendant of Ferdinand, to you Lord Abbot Fagildo, and to the assembly of the monastery of the altars both in the present and into the future, I have most firmly determined to confirm the decree and also the fine determined at ten pounds of gold. Neither I nor anyone who shall speak in my position, shall breach this decree that you shall hold and possess, from this day into perpetuity, completely and by hereditary right, with all the justices belonging to it, whether ecclesiastical or secular, the altar of Saint Peter, the prince of the apostles that was built of late within the Church of Saint James in the left side at the exit of the door to your chapter and that had formerly been located on the right side, together with the same door and exit both from this altar and from the church, but it is up to you to build this at your expense, so that you may possess it freely, and you may open it and close it from your side.

And after the altars of the Holy Savior and of Saint John are built at our expense, let them be restored to you and to your monastery to be held perpetually. For the building of the work, we may hold your third portion of the offering from the altar of Saint James, of which previously you possessed half. And now, through the agreement of the counts and the good men and by royal authority, you give your portion as a help, which you give both for us and for you, for what we are doing. And when the work on the church is finished, we may restore a part of the revenue of the altar of Saint James to you.

APPENDICES

With your heredity right always being preserved throughout the place, in that place we are to write and place a joining of letters, between the altar of Saint James and those three altars, containing a sign of the type AD, that is an A and a D placed in a line drawn from this same sign to the lower corner of your tower, which is contained within the wall, and from the other sign to the lower corner of your house, which is near the vaulted room of the palace, and then in a circle, as is found in your donation from Kings Casto and Ramiro. May the one who fulfills this be blessed, and may whosoever should act otherwise be cursed and excommunicated and be a participant with the traitor Judas in eternal damnation, and besides, may he be forced to pay a fine to the royal office. In addition, we double the amount for the monastery of what was placed in contempt. And let this writing remain firm for all days.

I, Diego, by divine grace bishop, decree that this be ordered to be done, and I confirm it with my own hand as lasting for all days.

Diego

I, Alfonso, the king, with grateful mind confirm this writing with his authority.
I, Urraca, sister of the king, confirm it.
I, García, the count, confirm it.
I, García Álvarez, confirm it.
I, Ordoño Álvarez, confirm it.
I, Peter Ansurriz, confirm it.
I, Gómez González, confirm it.
I, Martín Flamiz, the count, confirm it.
I, Froilán Díaz, the count, confirm it.
I, Sancho, the count, confirm it.
I, Froila Reimúndez, the judge, confirm it.
I, González, the judge, confirm it.
I, Sarraceno González, the judge, confirm it.
I, González, bishop of the See of Mondoñedo, confirm it.
I, Louis, bishop of the See of Tuy, confirm it.
I, Segeredo, the priest, confirm it.
All of these were present:

Peter, as a witness
Astrario, as a witness
Martin, as a witness
Ramiro, as a witness.
I, Alfonse Peter, have transcribed it.
I, Suarius Fagilat, confirm it.

APPENDICES

7. History of Compostela: Discovery and *Translatio*[11]

In the Name of Our Lord Jesus Christ, Here Begins the *Translatio* of Saint James, Brother of John the Apostle and Evangelist

Chapter 1

As we, therefore, have learned from the truth of the Gospel, our Lord and Redeemer on the fortieth day of His Resurrection would go to heaven, and He ordered His disciples to preach the Gospel through the entire world and to baptize the people converted to the true faith in the name of the Holy and Indivisible Trinity, saying: *Go into the whole world and preach the Gospel to every creature, etc.* [Mt 16:15]. Thus, as the other apostles, at this command of the Lord, went to different provinces and to different cities with an eagerness for preaching the Gospel, Saint James, brother of Saint John the Apostle and Evangelist, preached the word of God in Spain and Jerusalem. There, because of his confession of Christ and his assertion of the Catholic faith, he was beheaded by Herod, and he was the first of all the apostles that suffered martyrdom. For this reason, Saint Luke the Evangelist, in the Acts of the Apostles, says: *King Herod sent his band so that he might afflict some of the Church, and indeed he killed James the brother of John with the sword* [Acts 12:1]. The Jews, led by malevolence and jealousy, did not want to bury the venerable body of this most blessed apostle, nor did they permit it to be buried by the Christians who were living then at the time in Jerusalem. On the contrary, as Pope Leo in the letter that was sent to the Spanish about this *Passion* and *Translation* to Spain, affirmed: "They threw the entire body with the head outside the city, and they exposed it to the dogs and birds and wild beasts to be devoured and eaten." But his disciples were admonished by

---

11. *Historia Compostelana: Inventio* and *Translatio*. PL 170:892–95.

him while he was still alive to transfer his body to the region of Spain for burial. With Pope Leo as witness, they took the entire body along with the head during the night and quickly reached the seacoast via a path. While they were anxious about a boat being there, in which they might go over the seas to Spain, they found on the shore a boat prepared for them by divine intervention. They all gave thanks to God for the boat, placed the most holy body in it, and got in exultingly. They avoided the rock of Scylla and the whirlpool of Charybdis and the dangerous sandbanks of Syrtis[12] with the hand of the Lord steering. Then they arrived first at the port of Iria with their auspicious little boat, then they carried the venerable body to the place that was then called *Liberum Donum* and that is now called *Compostela,* and they buried it there under marble arches in the ecclesiastical manner.

The Christian religion had flourished, moreover, in that place in former times among the supporters of the Catholic faith. However, in the violent time of the persecution and with the haughty tyranny of the pagans trampling the dignity of the Christian name, almost the entire cult of the Christian religion vanished from there a long time ago. In all the time of the Saracens, therefore, and also for a long time after the restitution of the faithful, the venerable tomb of the apostle was not visited by the approach of any Christian. It remained covered over for a long time by the density of the bushes and forests. Until the time of Bishop Teodomiro of Iria, the tomb was not revealed to or known by anyone. However, when it pleased Omnipotent God to visit His working church and to convert mercifully its adversity into the tranquility of prosperity, He immediately changed its state with His powerful control, transformed the kingdom of Spain, and raised up the name and faith of Christ throughout the Spanish region from the pagan superstition, which was trampled and utterly annihilated.

However, before expulsion of paganism, Miro, of happy memory and by divine arrangement king, took the scepters of the kingdom, first set up pontifical sees throughout the provinces of

---

12. The Gulf of Sirte off the coast of Libya.

APPENDICES

Spain according to the standards of the Roman Church and then, with divine grace inspiring him, chose Andreas and elevated him for first time as a bishop of the seat of Iria. We have read assuredly that those written out below succeeded him in order, although we really have no knowledge about them beyond their names: Dominic, Samuel, Gotomarus, Vincibilis, Ilduilfus, Selva, Teodesindus, Bemila, Romanus, Augustine, Honoratus, Quendulfus, and again Quendulfus.

Chapter 2

Concerning the Revelation of the Body of Saint James, Brother of John the Apostle and Evangelist

It is surely reported that Teodomiro was raised to that seat and succeeded the aforesaid bishops, by the arrangement of divine grace. In his time, the omnipotence of divine majesty deigned to illuminate and visit and reveal to the western church the tomb of this great apostle. As to how it was revealed, the following page will make that clear. For certain worthy men of great authority revealed to this bishop that they had seen lights blazing many times in the night above a grove of longstanding age that had grown over the tomb of Saint James, and angels that had frequently appeared to them. When he heard this, he himself went to the place where they claimed they had seen such things and gazed with his own eyes upon the lights blazing in this place with no doubt at all. Therefore, inspired with divine grace, he went quickly to this little grove, looked around diligently and found a certain small house containing a marble tomb within between the forests and the bushes. After it was found, he gave thanks to God and went without delay before King Adefonsus the Chaste who then ruled in Spain. Then he notified him truthfully about what he had heard and had seen with his own eyes. Then the king was indeed filled with the joy of hearing such a thing. He immediately entered these regions by a path, restored to honor the church of this great apostle, transferred the bishop of the See of Iria to the place called Compostela, with the authority of many bishops and of servants of God and of noble men and with a royal privilege. We have heard assuredly, from the accounts given by many people that this happened in the time of Charlemagne. However, Bishop Teodomiro raised his mind's eyes so confidently in contemplation of the heavenly land that he very frequently caught sight of Saint James gleaming with miracles and with powers after a basilica was built for him. Endowed with the hope of the heavens, in a short amount of time he poured out his life securely, as his final fate intervened.

Adulfus, who succeeded him, fed the flock committed to him with the divine nourishment of the word as much as he could and with vigilant care. A second Adulfus also took up the rule of the pontifical office, and he was kindled with so much desire of internal vision that in the presence of the king who then at that time was over Spain, he was accused out of envy by some of his enemies of the vice of sodomy. The king, after hearing of the commission of such a crime, was surely moved by a vehement anger. Before the whole assembly, he ordered Adulfus to be exposed to an untamed and very ferocious bull, in accordance with his most irreverent judgment. For, by law, anyone that was said to be guilty of such a crime should be torn apart completely by the force of a furious bull. However, the one who, in secret judgment, was weighing the situation on the scale of equal justice would not permit the ray of truth to be obscured by the shadow of a lie. Thus he calmed the ferocity of the raging bull. Although the bull was incited by dogs, it could inflict no kind of injury on this religious man. We think, however, it happened for this reason: namely, this person, although he appeared to humankind to be condemned, was confident in divine piety. Before he came to this sentence of such cruelty, he celebrated the office of the Mass, and the uncontestable champion of God, dressed in his pontifical garb, arrived where this public event was happening to protect him from martyrdom through divine intervention. The bull was certainly extremely unsettled by the dogs and the trumpets of the hunters, but when the bull saw him, the untamed was made tame, and he voluntarily placed his horns in the hands of this servant of God, and he thus escaped unharmed. And when the king and all those who were with him saw the miracles of such power, they fell at his feet, and those who had previously wanted to have him condemned by this bit of false testimony confessed with a clear voice that they had been guilty. He, however, granted mercy to them, returning good for bad like the apostle. Then at that hour he set aside the dignity of his bishopric and forsook the transitory things of this fleeting life, and he went to the Asturian region alone to serve God. There he left behind an example of holy conduct toward others, and he paid the debt of nature unto the heavens in 904. Assuredly the chasuble in which he celebrated Mass on the day of the aforesaid trial, was by divine providence of such strength that if anyone at any place were to give an oath and should put it on and if he should by chance be a perjurer, it could certainly in no way be stripped from him.

8. The "Veneranda dies": How the *Translatio* of this Apostle Occurred[13]

How the *translatio* of this apostle occurred is declared from the mouths of many faithful people who say that after he was killed by Herod, his whole body was carried across the sea in a boat from Jerusalem to Galicia with an angel of the Lord accompanying it, with his disciples as sailors, and with various miracles experienced along the way. Galicia and Spain are regenerated by the grace of Baptism, through his *translatio* and the preaching of the apostolic disciples, and the kingdom of heaven is enriched. It is right for this venerable *translatio* to be discussed, since it was once written by a wise man: *A man pleasing to God was made chosen and has been translated from living among sinners* [Ws 4:10]. On this day honoring the apostle, [f.75r] the delighted Church of the faithful is accustomed to sing this verse three times: *James has pleased God and has been transported to paradise so that he may offer repentance to the people.*[14]

But we should consider what there might be for us to understand in his *translatio* and in his being chosen. In his being chosen, then, the setting aside of sins and perseverance in good works are insinuated, and in his *translatio* eternal rest is demonstrated.

Thus, in fact, the blessed apostle, on the day on which he was chosen because of divine love, not only set aside his boat, his father and mother, and his own career, but also the faulty accumulation of the old culture, and from then on he persevered in good works. In this same way, we must eradicate the whole collection of our faults and persevere in good works. For this reason, in fact, the Lord ordered that people set aside all possessions, because he does not wish that those serving him are preoccupied with earthly things, but focused only on the heavenly. As the apostle says: *No one serving*

---

13. Coffey et al., *Miracles*, 9–11.
14. Cf. Eccl (Sirach) 44:16. Here Enoch has been replaced by James. This is the verse that opens the Calixtine sermon, Book I chapter 19, and also the verse of a vespers reading in Book I chapter 19.

under God's banner may involve himself in worldly affairs, so that he may be pleasing only to Him to Whom he has proven himself [2 Tm 2:4].

By the boat that Blessed James abandoned on the waves of the sea when the Lord called, it is right to understand the synagogue of the Jews, which was figuratively tossing about on dangerous laws, just like a ship on the sea's waves, and which humankind abandoned, having heard the evangelic word, just as James abandoned the little boat, and then subjected itself to the Catholic Church. By the nets it is right to understand the ancient law of circumcision and sacrifice by which the Jewish people were caught and held captive like a multitude of fish in a net. Having accepted the Church through the grace of the new baptism, they thus cast off the ancient law, just as James did the nets. By Zebedee, the father of Blessed James, one can interpret the devil, for as James abandoned his father like a fugitive, so the devil himself, leaving God, flees to hell; the human race renounced the devil by taking on the precepts of Christ, just as James renounced his father and ascended to the seat from which the devil had fallen.

By the *translatio* of Blessed James, therefore, eternal rest is signified, since just as the apostle's venerable body is delivered from the place of his martyrdom to the place of his tomb and his soul is carried to eternal rest by the angels, so also are we to be raised from the harshness of our good life to the eternal rest of paradise through perseverance in good works. The Lord makes it manifest that no one can move on to eternal rest except through the labor of this present harsh life, when He says: *Come to me, all who labor and are burdened…and you will find rest for your souls* [Mt 11:28–29]. In the Book of Wisdom [f.75v] it is written: *God will return the price of the labors of his holy ones* [Ws 10:17] The apostle also says: *It is necessary for us to enter into the kingdom of God through many tribulations* [Acts 14:21].

Thus the blessed apostle was chosen this day so that he may tear the world from the devil's jaws by his preaching. He was translated so that he may strengthen with his patronage, bestow with his benefits, look down with his miracles, and prepare seats in the heavenly realm for those loving him with all their hearts, not only for the Galicians but also for those visiting his holy tomb.

At the time when ice is hard like crystal and snow is sowed over the world like flour and everyone is crushed under the pressure of the cold, the *translatio* of Blessed James is celebrated. At the time when the fruit of the earth is collected and the storehouses are replenished with healthful grains, his passion is honored. This is the meaning: it is a fitting time to honor the passion of Blessed James when the fruit of the earth is collected, just as the present age is a fitting time for doing good works. The time when his choosing is honored and his *translatio* is reverenced and every kind of mortal creature is crushed by the pressure of the cold indicates a future age in which no one will be allowed to work. Whoever, therefore, has performed no good works for their souls in this age, will begin the future in an exceptional way.

However, there should be no silence about apocryphal things. On the contrary, these things that many irrational people, torpidly sliding toward heresy, are accustomed to say about James and his *translatio* should be announced so as to be corrected. What is worse, people dare to write about these things with a false pen. Some, for example, think he is a son of the Lord's mother, because they have heard James called "brother of the Lord," both in the Gospel and in the Letter to the Galatians, but this is not so. Others say that he came from Jerusalem to Galicia over the waves of the sea without a boat, sitting on a large stone with the Lord instructing him, and that a certain part of this large stone has remained behind in Joppa. Others say that this very stone arrived on the boat together with his lifeless body. However, I declare both stories to be false. Truly when I once saw the great stone, I knew it was a stone created in Galicia. There are, however, two reasons for which the great stone of Blessed James is to be worthily venerated: first because, as it is reported, at the time of its *translatio,* the apostle's body was placed upon it at the port of Iria Flavia [f.76r] and second — and the greater reason — because the Eucharist was purposefully celebrated on it.

APPENDICES

9. Feast Day of Saint Luparia[15]

For a Feast on February 22

Luparia, in the first century of our era, governed the city of Iria Flavia, in the farthest region of Galicia. She was called "Regula" or "The Little Queen" or else "Primaria" or "The First One." She had a daughter named Claudia Luparia, who had married a certain Agathope, a freed slave of Augustus. When the disciples of the apostle Saint James the Greater carried his body back to Spain, they disembarked in the area of Iria Flavia and asked Luparia for a place where they could fittingly bury the body of the holy apostle, and they obtained it. Luparia, after being moved by miracles that honored the precious remains of Saint James, abandoned idolatry, became a Christian, and after her death, was counted in the number of the saints.

As the place of the holy apostle's tomb was rather isolated, they transferred it later to Compostela. The city of Iria Flavia disappeared little by little, and the place that it occupied was afterwards called Padrón.

Today the feast of this *translatio* of the relics of the apostle, Saint James the Greater, is celebrated in Spain. And in the hymns that one sings on this anniversary, this blessed Luparia is accorded the title of saint. Her daughter, Saint Claudia Luparia, is also honored in Spain.

---

15. M.J. Collin de Plancy, *Grande Vie des Saints* (Paris: Librairie Louis Vivès, 1899), 4: 414–15.

BIBLIOGRAPHY

Acta Sanctorum. Ed. Iohannes Bollandus, et al. Paris: Victor Palmé 1863–1919.

Aldhelm, Saint. *Sancti Aldhelmi Opera Quae Extant Omnia E Codicibus Mss Emendavit.* Edited by J.A. Giles. Oxford: J.H. Parker, 1844.

Allen, Rosamund, ed. *Eastward Bound: Travel and Travellers 1050–1550.* Manchester: Manchester University Press, 2004.

Anselm, Saint. *See* Southern.

Auriol, Achille. "Une illustration d'un épisode toulousain des miracles de Saint Jacques." *Mémoires de la Société archéologique du Midi de la France* 19 (1935): 1–4.

Baliñas Pérez, Carlos. "The Origins of the *Inventio Sancti Iacobi* and the Making of a Kingdom: A Historical Framework, 700–850." In Antón Pazos, ed. *Translating the Relics of St James from Jerusalem to Compostela,* 75–87. London: Routledge, 2017.

Bede, Venerable. *The Complete Works of Venerable Bede.* Edited by J.A. Giles. London: Whittaker and Co., 1843. 8 vols. http://oll.libertyfund.org/titles/bede-the-complete-works-of-venerable-bede-8-vols (accessed July 2018).

———. *A History of the English Church and People.* Edited by Leo Sherley-Price and R.E. Latham. Harmondsworth: Penguin, 1955, rpt. 1975.

Bédier, Joseph. "La Chronique de Turpin et le pèlerinage de Compostelle." *Annales du Midi* 24 (1912): 18–48.

Benton, John F., ed. *Self and Society in Medieval France. The Memoirs of Abbot Guibert of Nogent.* Medieval Academy Reprints for Teaching. Toronto: University of Toronto Press, 1984.

Bibliotheca Hagiographica Latina. 2 vols. Brussels: Bollandists, 1898–99.

Biggs, Anselm Gordon. *Diego Gelmírez, First Archbishop of Compostela*, Washington, DC: Catholic University of America, 1949.

Blaise, Albert. *Lexicon Latinitatis mediae aevi.* Series Corpus Christianorum. Turnholt: Brepols, 1977.

Boschung, Moritz, Jean–Pierre Dewarrat, Edouard Egloff, et al. *Chemins de Saint-Jacques en terre fribourgeoise.* Repères fribourgeois 4. Fribourg: Meandre, 1992.

Bouzas Sierra, Antón. "Aportaciones para una reinterpretación astronómica de Santiago de Compostela." *Anuario Brigantino* 32 (2009): 47–92.

Bucher, François. *The Pamplona Bibles.* New Haven: Yale University Press, 1970.

Caridad Arias, Joaquín. *La lengua romance Vasca: Vocabulario comparado Castellano-Vasco y Vasco-Castellano ante el latín y otras lenguas indoeuropeos.* Lugo: El Tablero de Piedra, 2012.

Cawley, Charles. "Toulouse, Kings, Dukes & Counts." http://fmg.ac/Projects/MedLands/TOULOUSE.htm (accessed July 2018).

Cebrián Franco, Juan José. *Los relatos de la traslación de los restos del Apóstol Santiago a Compostela.* Santiago de Compostela: Instituto Teológico Compostelano, 2008.

Chadwick, Henry. *Priscillian of Avila: The Occult and the Charismatic in the Early Church.* Oxford: Clarendon Press, 1976.

Chaparro Gómez, César. "Notas sobre el 'De ortv et obitv patrvm' seudoisidoriano." *Antigüedad y cristianismo* 3 (1986): 397–404.

Ciril, Mejac. "Galicia en los romances eslovenos." *Cuadernos de estudios gallegos* 3.9 (1948): 81–92.

Codex Calixtinus de la Universidad de Salamanca. Facsimile ed. Burgos: Siloé, arte y bibliofilia, 2012.

BIBLIOGRAPHY

Coffey, Thomas, Linda Davidson, and Maryjane Dunn. *The Miracles of Saint James: Translations from the* Liber Sancti Jacobi. New York: Italica Press, 1996.

Collin de Plancy, M.J. *Grande Vie des Saints.* 3rd edition. Paris: Librairie Louis Vivès, 1899.

Conant, Kenneth. *The Early Architectural History of the Cathedral of Santiago.* Cambridge: Harvard University Press, 1926.

Corrigan, Vincent. "Music and the Pilgrimage." In *The Pilgrimage to Compostela in the Middle Ages: A Book of Essays*, 43–67. Edited by Maryjane Dunn and Linda Davidson. New York: Garland Publishing, 1996.

David, Pierre. "Études sur le Livre de Saint-Jacques attribué au pape Calixte II." *Bulletin des études portugaises et l'Institut français au Portugal* 10 (1945): 1–41; 11(1947): 113–85; 12 (1948): 70–223; 13 (1949): 52–104.

Díaz y Díaz, Manuel. "El *Codex Calixtinus*: Volviendo sobre el Tema." In Williams and Stones, *The* Codex Calixtinus, 1–9.

———. "El lugar del enterramiento de Santiago el Mayor en Isidoro de Sevilla." *Compostellanum* 1.4 (1956): 881–85.

———. "La *Epistola Leonis Pape de translatione sancti Iacobi in Galleciam*." In *Escritos Jacobeos*, 133–81. Santiago de Compostela: Consorcio de Santiago, Universidad de Santiago de Compostela, 2010. First published in *Compostellanum* 43.1–4 (1998): 517–68.

———. "La leyenda hispana de Santiago en Isidoro de Sevilla." In *De Santiago y de los caminos de Santiago*, 87–96. Santiago de Compostela: Xunta de Galicia, 1997. First published as "Die spanische Jakobus–Legende bei Isidor von Sevilla," *Historisches Jahrbuch* 77 (1985): 467–76.

———. "'La *Passio Iacobi*' — Trabajo inédito." In *De Santiago y de los caminos de Santiago,* 17–68. Santiago de Compostela: Xunta de Galicia, 1997.

———. "Literatura jacobea hasta el siglo XII." In *Il Pellegrinaggio a Santiago de Compostela e la Letteratura Jacopea*, 225–50. Perugia: Università degli studi di Perugia, 1985.

———. "El texto y la tradición textual del Calixtino." In *Pistoia e il Cammino di Santiago: Una dimensione europea nella Toscana medioevale*, 23–55. Edited by Lucia Gai. Perugia: Edizione Scientifiche Italiane, 1984.

———. *Visiones del más allá en Galicia durante la alta edad media*. Bibliófilos gallegos. Biblioteca de Galicia 24. Santiago de Compostela: Xunta de Galicia, 1985.

———. "Xacobe en Compostela: primeiros testemuños literarios." In *Escritos jacobeos*, 225–38. Santiago de Compostela: Universidade, Servizo de Publicacións, 2010. First published in *Grial* 161 (2004): 19–27.

———, María Araceli García Piñeiro, and Pilar del Oro Trigo. *El Códice Calixtino de la Catedral de Santiago: Estudio codicológico y de contenido*. Santiago de Compostela: Centro de Estudios Jacobeos, 1988.

Domínguez García, Javier. *De Apóstol Matamoros a Yllapa Mataindios: Dogmas e ideologías medievales en el (des)cubrimiento de América*. Salamanca: Ediciones Universidad de Salamanca, 2008.

———. *Memorias del futuro: Ideología y ficción en el símbolo de Santiago Apóstol*. Madrid: Iberoamericana, 2008.

Dozy, Reinhart Pieter Anne. *Recherches sur l'histoire et la littérature de l'Espagne pendant le Moyen Age*. 3rd ed. Paris: Maisonneuve, 1881.

Dunn, Maryjane. "Historical and Modern Signs of 'Real' Pilgrims on the Road to Santiago de Compostela." In Sánchez y Sánchez, *The Camino*, 13–35.

———, and Linda Davidson. *The Pilgrimage to Santiago de Compostela: A Comprehensive, Annotated Bibliography*. Garland Medieval Bibliographies 18. New York: Garland Publishing, 1994.

BIBLIOGRAPHY

"El himno 'O Dei verbum'." *Pro iter agentibus: Boletín de la asociación gaditana del Camino de Santiago "Via Augusta."* 16 (Sept. 2011): 16–19. www.asociaciongaditanajacobea.org/pia16.pdf (accessed July 2018).

Eusebius. *The History of the Church from Christ to Constantine.* Translated by G.A. Williamson and Andrew Louth. London: Penguin Books, 1989.

Fabregau Grau, Angel, ed. *Pasionario Hispánico.* 2 vols. Madrid: Consejo Superior de Investigaciones Científicas, 1953–55.

Ferreiro Alemparte, Jaime. "El milagro del ahorcado y su representación iconográfica en el portal románico de S. Leonardo en Francfort." *Compostellanum* 34.3–4 (July–Dec. 1989): 297–309.

Fabricius, Johann Albert. *Codex apocryphus Novi Testamenti.* 2nd ed. Hamburg: Schiller & Kisneri, 1719.

Fita, Fidel, and Aureliano Fernández-Guerra. *Recuerdos de un viaje a Santiago de Galicia.* Madrid: Sres. Lezcano, 1880. Rpt. Facsimile edition, La Coruña: Librería Arenas, 1993.

———, and Julien Vinson. *Le codex de Saint-Jacques de Compostelle (Liber de miraculis S. Jacobi). Livre IV.* Paris: Maisonnueve, 1882.

Fletcher, Richard A. *Saint James's Catapult: The Life and Times of Diego Gelmírez of Santiago de Compostela.* Oxford: Clarendon Press, 1984.

Gaiffier, Baudouin de. "Un thème hagiographique: Le pendu miraculeusement sauvé." *Revue belge d'archéologie et d'histoire de l'art* 13 (1943): 123–48.

García Turza, Javier. "The Formulation, Development and Expansion of the *Translatio* of St James." In *Translating the Relics of St. James From Jerusalem to Compostela,* 88–122. Edited by Antón Pazos. London: Routledge, 2017.

Gardener, Steven, Carlos Mentley, and Lisa Signori. "Whose Camino Is It? (Re)defining Europe on the Camino de Santiago." In Sánchez y Sánchez, *The Camino,* 57–77.

Geary, Patrick J. *Furta Sacra: Thefts of Relics in the Central Middle Ages*. Rev. ed. Princeton: Princeton University Press, 1990.

Gerson, Paula. "France and Spain on Five *Nummus* a Day: A Medieval Travel Guide." *Topic: A Journal of the Liberal Arts* 35 (Fall 1981): 3–10.

———, Annie Shaver–Crandell, Jeanne E. Krochalis, and Alison Stones. *The Pilgrim's Guide: A Critical Edition*. 2 vols. London: Harvey Miller, 1998.

Guerra Campos, José. "Notas críticas sobre el origen del culto sepulcral a Santiago de Compostela." *Ciencia tomista* 88.279 (July–Sept. 1961): 417–74; 88.230 (Oct.–Dec. 1961): 559–90.

Guibert of Nogent. See Benton.

Hämel, Adalbert. *Uberlieferung und Bedeutung des Liber Sancti Jacobi und des Pseudo-Turpin*. Sitzungsberichte, Philosophisch-historische Klasse 2. Munich: Bayerischen Akademie der Wissenschaften, 1950.

Haskins, Susan. *Mary Magdalen: Myth and Metaphor*. New York: Harcourt, Brace & Co., 1993.

Hauschild, Theodor. "Archeology and the Tomb of Saint James." In Williams and Stones, *The* Codex Calixtinus, 89–103.

Herbers, Klaus. *Der Jacobuskult des 12. Jahrhunderts und der* Liber Sancti Jacobi. In *Studien über das Verhältnis zwischen Religion und Gesellschaft im Hohen Mittelalter*. Historische Forschungen 7. Wiesbaden: F. Stiner, 1984.

———. "The Miracles of Saint James." In Williams and Stones, *The* Codex Calixtinus, 11–35.

———, and Manuel S. Noya. See *Liber Sancti Jacobi*.

Hermida, Xosé. "La Catedral compostelana retira una imagen de Santiago 'Matamoros.'" *El País*, 2 May 2004. https://elpais.com/diario/2004/05/02/cultura/1083448804_850215.html (accessed July 2018).

BIBLIOGRAPHY

Hessels, John Henry. *A Late Eighth-Century Latin Anglo-Saxon Glossary.* Cambridge: Cambridge University Press, 1906.

Historia compostelana. Edited and translated by Emma Falque Rey. Madrid: Ediciones Akal, 1994.

Historia silense. Edited by Francisco Santos Coco. Centro de estudios históricos. Madrid: Rivadeneyra, 1921.

Hohler, Christopher. "The Badge of Saint James." In *The Scallop: Studies of a Shell and Its Influences on Humankind,* 49–70. Edited by Ian Cox. London: Shell Transport and Trading Co., 1957.

Iacobus de Voragine. *See* Jacobus de Voragine.

Al–Idrisi. *Geografía de España.* Edited by Antonio Ubieto Arteta and translated by Eduardo Saavedra. *Geografía de España.* Textos medievales 37. Valencia: Anubar, 1974.

Isidore of Seville, Saint. *De ortu et obitu patrum: Vida y muerte de los santos.* Translated by César Chaparro Gómez. Paris: Société d'éditions "Les Belles Lettres," 1985.

Jacomet, Humbert. "Un miracle de Saint Jacques: le pendu dépendu." *Archeologia* [Brussels] 278 (Apr. 1992): 36–47.

———. "Santiago: En busca del gran perdón." In *Santiago, Camino de Europa: Culto y Cultura en la Peregrinación a Compostela,* 55–81. Edited by Serafín Moralejo Álvarez, Fernando López Alsina, and Rosa Alcoy. Madrid: Fundación Caja de Madrid, 1993.

Jacobus de Voragine. *The Golden Legend: Readings on the Saints.* Translated by William Granger Ryan. Princeton: Princeton University Press, 1993.

———. *Jacobi a Voragine Legenda Aurea: Vulgo Historia Lombardica Dicta.* Edited by Johann Georg Theodor Graesse. Wroclaw: Köbner, 1890; rpt., Osnabrück: Otto Zeller, 1969.

Kemp, Brian. "The Miracles of the Hand of Saint James." *Berkshire Archaeological Journal* 65 (1970): 1–19.

Ladić, Zoran. "Some Remarks on Medieval Croatian Pilgrimages." Presented at the International conference on Christian civilization in Lublin (Poland), 1996. https://hrcak.srce.hr/file/120800 (accessed July 2018).

Lewis, Agnes Smith. *The Mythological Acts of the Apostles, Translated from an Arabic MS in the Convent of Deyr–es–Suriani, Egypt, and from MSS in the Convent of Saint Catherine on Mount Sinai and in the Vatican Library.* London: C.J. Clay and Sons, 1904.

Liber Sancti Jacobi. Codex Calixtinus. Edited by Walter Muir Whitehill, Germán Prado, and Jesús Carro García. 3 vols. Santiago: CSIC: Instituto Padre Sarmiento de Estudios Gallegos, 1944.

Liber Sancti Jacobi: Codex Calixtinus. Translated by Abelardo Moralejo, Casimiro Torres, and Julio Feo. Santiago: CSIC. Instituto Padre Sarmiento de Estudios Gallegos, 1951. Rev. ed. with new notes by Juan José Moralejo and María José García Blanco, Santiago de Compostela: Xunta de Galicia, 2004; rev. ed. by María José García Blanco, Santiago de Compostela: Xunta de Galicia, 2014.

Liber Sancti Jacobi: Codex Calixtinus. Edited by Klaus Herbers and Manuel S. Noya. Santiago de Compostela: Xunta de Galicia, 1998.

Liber Sancti Jacobi: Codex Calixtinus de la Catedral de Santiago de Compostela. Madrid: Kaydeda, 1993.

Lima, Fernando de Castro Pires de, and Ramón Otero Pedrayo. *A lenda do senhor do galo de Barcelos e o milagre do enforcado.* Lisbon: Fundaçao nacional para a alegria no trabalho, 1965.

Lipsius, Richard A. *Die Apokryphen apostelgeschichten und apostellegenden.* Braunschweig: C.A. Schwetschke und Sohn, 1883.

López Alsina, Fernando. *La ciudad de Santiago de Compostela en la alta edad media.* Santiago: Ayuntamiento de Santiago de Compostela, 1988.

BIBLIOGRAPHY

López Ferreiro, Antonio. *Historia de la Santa Apostólica Metropolitana Iglesia de Santiago de Compostela.* 11 vols. Santiago: Seminario, 1898–1910.

Ludus Sancti Jacobi: Fragment de mystère provençal. Edited by Camille Arnaud. Marseille: Arnaud, 1858.

Magallón, Ana Isabel, and José Carlos Martín. "La leyenda de la venida de la Virgen a Zaragoza (BHL 5388): Edición crítica y estudio." *Hagiographica* 21 (2014): 53–84.

Malan, S.C., trans. *The Conflicts of the Holy Apostles, an Apocryphal Book of the Early Eastern Church. Translated from an Ethiopic MS.* London: D. Nutt, 1871.

Márquez Villanueva, Francisco. *Santiago: Trayectoria de un mito.* Barcelona: Edicions Bellaterra, 2004.

Mascanzoni, Leardo. "Un miracolo Emiliano-Romagnolo nel *Codice Callistino* di Compostela." *Studi Romagnoli* 63 (2012): 509–24.

Melczer, William. *The Pilgrim's Guide to Santiago de Compostela.* New York: Italica Press, 1993.

The Met [Metropolitan Museum of Art]. "A Full-Scale 3D Computer Reconstruction of the Medieval Cathedral and Town of Santiago de Compostela." https://youtu.be/SmVJSmLA7BU (accessed July 2018).

Moralejo Álvarez, Serafín. *Arquitectura románica de la Catedral de Santiago de Compostela: Notas para una revisión crítica de la obra de K.J. Conant.* Santiago: Colexio de Arquitectos de Galicia, 1983.

Moralejo, Abelardo, Casimiro Torres and Julio Feo. See *Liber Sancti Jacobi.*

Nasrallah, Nawal. *Annals of the Caliphs' Kitchens: Ibn Sayyār al-Warrāq's Tenth-Century Baghdadi Cookbook. English Translation with Introduction and Glossary.* Leiden: Brill, 2010.

O'Callaghan, Joseph F. *A History of Medieval Spain.* Ithaca: Cornell University Press, 1975.

Pack, Sasha. "Revival of the Pilgrimage to Santiago de Compostela: The Politics of Religious, National, and European Patrimony, 1879–1988." *The Journal of Modern History* 82 (June 2010): 335–67.

Pazos, Antón, ed. *Translating the Relics of St James from Jerusalem to Compostela.* London: Routledge, 2017.

Piccat, Marco. "Il miracolo jacopeo del pellegrino impiccato: riscontri tra narrazione e figurazione." In *Il Pellerinaggio a Santiago de Compostela e la Letteratura Jacopea,* 287–310. Perugia: Università degli studi di Perugia, 1985.

Plötz, Robert. *"Peregrinatio ad Limina Sancti Jacobi."* In Williams and Stones, *The* Codex Calixtinus, 37–50.

Poole, Kevin. *Chronicle of Pseudo-Turpin: Book IV of the* Liber Sancti Jacobi (Codex Calixtinus). New York: Italica Press, 2014.

Puy Múñoz, Francisco. "Santiago abogado en el 'Calixtino' (1160)." In *Pistoia e il Cammino di Santiago,* 57–92. Perugia: Edizione scientifiche italiane, 1984.

Riesco Chueca, Pilar. *Pasionario Hispánico (Introducción, Edición Crítica y Traducción).* Sevilla: Universidad de Sevilla, 1995.

Robert, Ulysse. *Bullaire du Pape Calixte II.* 2 vols. Paris: Imprimerie Nationale, 1891; rpt., Hildesheim: G. Olms, 1979.

———. *Histoire du pape Calixte II.* Paris: Alphonse Picard; Besançon: Paul Jacquin, 1891.

Sánchez, y Sánchez, Samuel, and Annie Hesp, eds. *The Camino de Santiago in the 21st Century: Interdisciplinary Perspectives and Global Views.* New York: Routledge, 2015.

Santiago, Camino de Europa: Culto y Cultura en la Peregrinación a Compostela. Edited by Serafín Moralejo Álvarez and Fernando López Alsina. Madrid: Fundación Caja de Madrid; Santiago de Compostela: Xunta de Galicia, Consellería de Cultura

BIBLIOGRAPHY

e Xuventude, Dirección Xeral do Patrimonio Histórico e Documental; Arzobispado de Santiago de Compostela, 1993.

Santos Coco, Francisco. See *Historia Silense.*

Schermann, Theodorus. *Prophetarum vitae fabulosae: indices apostolorum discipulorumque Domini Dorotheo, Epiphanio, Hippolyto: aliisque vindicata : inter quae nonnulla priumum edidit recensuit schedis vir. cl. Henr. Gelzer usus prolegomenis indicibus testimoniis apparatu critico instruxit.* Lipsiae: In aedibus B.G. Teubneri. 1907. "Breviarum apostolorum," 207–11. http: // public.eblib.com/choice/publicfullrecord.aspx?p=935163.

Shaver–Crandell, Annie, Paula L. Gerson, with Alison Stones. *The Pilgrim's Guide to Santiago de Compostela: A Gazetteer.* London: Harvey Miller Publishers, 1995.

Sicart Giménez, Angel. "La figura de Santiago en los textos medievales." In *Il Pellegrinaggio a Santiago de Compostela e la Letteratura Jacopea,* 271–86. Perugia: Università degli studi di Perugia, 1985.

Southern, R.W. "The English Origins of the Miracles of the Virgin." *Mediaeval and Renaissance Studies* 4 (1958): 176–216.

———, and F.S. Schmitt, eds. *Memorials of Saint Anselm.* Auctores britannici medii aevi 1. London: The British Academy, Oxford University Press, 1969.

Southey, Robert. "The Pilgrim to Compostela: Being the Legend of a Cock and a Hen to the Honour and Glory of Santiago." *The Poetical Works of Robert Southey.* London: Murray, 1829.

Spencer, Brian. *Pilgrim Souvenirs and Secular Badges.* London: The Stationery Office, 1998.

Sulpicius Severus. "Writings," "Life of Saint Martin, Bishop and Confessor," 7:101–40; and "The Second Dialogue," 201–24. In *The Fathers of the Church.* Edited by Roy Joseph Deferrari and translated by Bernard M. Peebles. New York: Fathers of the Church, 1949.

Taylor, Melina "South Korea promotes Jeju Olle Trail as Major Tourist Destination." *American Trails Magazine*.http://atfiles.org/resources/international/Korea-tourism-Jeje-Olle-Trail.html (accessed July 2018).

Torres Rodríguez, Casimiro. "Arca Marmórea." *Compostellanum* 2.2 (1957): 323–39.

———. "Notas sobre 'Arca Marmórea.'" *Compostellanum* 4.2 (1959): 341–47.

Uitti, Karl D. "The *Codex Calixtinus* and the European Saint James the Major: Some Contextual Issues." In *De Sens rassis: Essays in Honor of Rupert T. Pickens*, 645–66. Edited by Keith Busby, Bernard Guidot, and Logan E. Whalen. Amsterdam: Rodopi, 2005.

Van Dam, Raymond. *Saints and Their Miracles in Late Antique Gaul*. Princeton: Princeton University Press, 1993.

Van Herwaarden, Jan. "Saint James in Spain up to the 12th Century." *Wallfahrt kennt keine Grenzen*, 235–47. Edited by Lenz Kriss–Rettenbeck and Gerda Mohler. Munich: Schnell & Steiner, 1984.

———. "The Origins of the Cult of St James of Compostela." In *Between Saint James and Erasmus: Studies in Late Medieval Religious Life*, 311–54. Leiden: Brill, 2003. First published in *Journal of Medieval History* 6.1 (March 1980): 1–35.

———. "The Integrity of the Text of the *Liber Sancti Jacobi* in the *Codex Calixtinus*." In *Between Saint James and Erasmus*, 355–78. Leiden: Brill, 2003.

Villa-Amil y Castro, José. *Descripción histórico-artístico-arqueológica de la Catedral de Santiago*. Lugo: Soto Freire, 1866.

Voragine. *See* Jacobus de Voragine.

Ward, Benedicta. *Miracles and the Medieval Mind: Theory, Record and Event, 1000–1215*. Philadelphia: University of Pennsylvania Press, 1982.

Whitehill, Walter Mui. See *Liber Sancti Jacobi.*

Wilkinson, Isambard. "Public Outcry Forces Church to Keep Moor Slayer's Statue." *The Telegraph*, 22 July, 2004. https://www.telegraph.co.uk/news/worldnews/europe/spain/1467621/Public-outcry-forces-church-to-keep-Moor-Slayers-statue.html (accessed July 2018).

Wilkinson, John, Joyce Hill, and W.F. Ryan, eds., and trans. *Jerusalem Pilgrimage, 1099–1185*. Hakluyt Society. 2nd ser. 167. London: Hakluyt Society, 1988.

Williams, John, and Alison Stones, eds. *The Codex Calixtinus and the Shrine of Saint James*. Jakobus–Studien 3. Tübingen: Gunter Narr, 1992.

Zepedano, José María. *Historia y Descripción Arqueológica de la Basílica Compostelana*. Lugo: Imprenta de Soto Freire, 1870.

INDEX

A

Abdias (Pseudo-Abdias) XXVII, XXXV, XXXVI, LX, LXIII, 97
Abiathar the Priest XVII, 85, 104–5, 116–17
Abiram 104, 116
Abla, see Avila.
Abraham 101, 103, 113, 116
Acci [Spain], see Guadix.
Achaia [Greece] XXIX–XXX, 107
Adam 103, 115
Adefonsus, King 70, 129. See also Alfonso II, Alfonso III.
Adriatic Sea 2, 61
Adulfus, Bishop 130
Africa 8, 61
Agabus the Prophet 88
Agathope, son-in-law of Luparia 135
Alberic of Vézelay LIII, 64
Aldefonsus, King 92–93. See also Alfonso II, Alfonso III
Aldhelm of Malmesbury XXX, 11, 106
Alexander I, Pope Saint LXV, 90, 91, 93
Alexander II, Pope 90
Alexander of Canterbury XLIX, LII
Alexandria [Egypt] 61
Alfonso I, King XXXI

Alfonso II, King, "the Chaste" XXXI, XXXVI, 13, 70, 92–93, 122, 123, 124, 125, 129
Alfonso III, King, "the Great" LXII, 93
Alfonso VI, King, "Emperor" LI, LXII, 8–9
Alfonso VII, King 62, 93
Alfonse Peter, scribe 126
Allobrogia[n] [France] 37
Almería [Spain] 8, 61–62, 73
Altina [Italy] 89
Anna, mother of Samuel 114
Andreas, Bishop 129
Andrew, Saint XXI, LVII, LXI
Anselm, Saint XLVI, XLVIII–XLIX, LI–LIII, LVIII, 41, 44–45, 52, 92
Antioch [Turkey] 71, 88
Apulia [Italy] 33, 36
Archelaus, King 104, 116
Arles [France] 22
Arnaud du Mont, monk XXXVII, XXXIX
Asia XXVIII, 70, 108
Astrario, witness 126
Asturias, Asturian [Spain] XXXI, XXXVI, 86, 93, 131
Atapuerca [Spain] 15
Athanasius, disciple LXIII, LXV, 73, 74, 87
Augustine, Bishop 129

Augustus (Caesar), *see* Caesar, Augustus
Augustus, slaveowner 135
Avila (Abla) [Spain] 73, 120
Avitus Maimon 28–29, 61
Aymeric Picaud XL

B

Babylonia XXVII
Balbina, Saint 90–91
Barcelona [Spain] LII, LIV, 8, 60, 61, 62
Bartholomew, Saint 107
Basques 20
Beatus de Liébana XXXI
Bede, Saint XLVIII, 11, 91
Bemila, Bishop 129
Berber [Africa] 61
Berja, *see* Vera.
Bernard of Clairvaux XLVIII, 17
Bernard of Sauvetot (abbot) 8
Bernard, pilgrim 5, 35
Besançon [France] XLV, XLVIII, 18
Biskra [Algeria] 61
Blasia 61
Boanerges, *see* Sons of Thunder.
Bougie (Béjaïa) [Algeria] 28, 61
Burgundy [France] XXXVII, 18, 41, 57, 59, 64
Burgos [Spain] 15

C

Caen [France] 41
Caesar, Augustus (Augustus Caesar) 90
Caesar, Julius (Julius Caesar) 91

Caesar, Claudius (Tiberius Claudius Augustus Caesar) XXV, 88
Caesarea [Israel] XXV
Calixtus II, Pope (Guy of Burgundy) XXXVII, XXXIX–XL, XLIV–XLV, XLVII–XLIX, L, LII–LIII, LVIII, LX, LXII, 1, 2, 7, 14, 18, 22, 25, 28, 30, 32, 34, 35, 36, 37, 38, 39, 41, 50, 52, 54, 57, 59, 60, 70, 88, 93
Canterbury [England] XLIV, XLVIII, LVIII, 41, 45
Carcese (Cazorla) [Spain] 73, 120
Castille [Spain] LI, 8
Cazorla, *see* Carcese.
Cecilius, Saint XXXV, 73, 76, 118, 120
Charlemagne XVI, XXXVIII, XL, XLV, XLVIII, LV, LXVI, 13, 18, 19, 25, 40, 70, 130
Charles Martel XLVIII
Charles the Bald XLVIII
Chavannes [France] 37
Chromatius of Aquileia 72, 89
Cize Pass [France] LVIII, 3, 19–20, 25
Claudia, daughter of Luparia 135
Claudius, *see* Caesar, Claudius.
Clement of Alexandria XXIV–XXV
Cleopatra, Queen 90
Cluny, Cluniac [France] XVII, XL, XLII, LI, LII, 8, 14, 45, 50–51
Coimbra [Portugal] XL, LI, LVI–LVII, 54, 56
Corociana (Corsica) 61
Corsica [France], *see* Corociana.
Corzanum [Italy] 35
Ctesiphon, *see* Tissephons.

INDEX

D

Dacia XLV, 1
Dalmatius, soldier 5, 37
Dathan 104, 116
Diego Peláez or Pelagio, Bishop XXXVI, 122–25
Diego Gelmirez, Bishop XXXIX, XL, 28
Dominic, Bishop 129
Donzy [France] 41, 44
Dugium (Duio) [Spain] 79

E

Egypt 61, 80, 107
Elias, Prophet 65
Elvira (Heliberri) [Spain] 73 120
Eliturgi, *see* Urci.
Endalecius, Saint (Indelecius) 73, 76, 118, 120
Enoch 132
Ermengotus, Count (Ermengol IV or V) LI, 8, 57
Esicius, Saint (Isicius) XXXV, 73, 118, 120
Estella [Spain] LI–LII, 63
Ethiopia 61
Etruscan Sea, *see* Tyrrhenian Sea.
Eudoxia, *see* Licinia Eudoxia.
Eufrasius, Saint XXXV, 73, 76, 118, 120
Eusebius of Caesarea XXIV, XXV, 17, 89

F

Fagildo, Saint XXXVI, 122–24
Ferdinand I of León, King LI, LVII, 56, 120, 124
Forcalquier LI, 57
France, French XV–XVII, XXXIV, XXXVIII, XL–XLII, XLV, LIV, LXVIII, 1, 8, 14, 18, 19, 20, 22, 25, 32, 37, 41, 44, 45, 52, 64, 78
Frisia, Frisian [Holland/Germany] XLII, 28
Frisonus, sailor 4, 28–30
Froila Reimúndez, witness 125
Froilán Díaz, witness 125

G

Galicia/n XIII, XV–XVI, XXX, XXXII–XXXIII, XXXVIII, XLIII, XLV–XLVI, LXI–LXIII, LXV–LXVI, 1, 11, 12, 14, 18, 30–31, 34–36, 38, 41, 45, 52, 54, 60–61, 71–72, 75, 77, 82, 85, 93, 96, 122, 132, 134–35
Galilee (Gennesaret) XXII, LVII, LXI, 32
García Álvarez, witness 125
García the Count, witnesss 125
Gascony XLV, 19
Gaul [France] 16, 107
Gerald, pilgrim 45
German/Germany XV, XLII, XLV, LIV, 1, 22
Gennesaret, *see* Galilee.
Gethsemane XXII
Giberga XL
Gilles, Saint XLVIII, 13, 22, 52

Girinus the Bald LI, 44
Gómez Gonzalez, witness 125
González the Bishop, witness 125
González the Judge, witness 125
Gotomarus, Bishop 129
Gregorio Papareschi, *see* Innocent II.
Gregory VII, Pope 8
Gregory of Tours, Saint XLIV, 16–17
Guadix (Acci) [Spain] XXXV, 73, 80, 118–20
Guibert of Burgundy 59
Guibert of Nogent 45
Guy of Burgundy, *see* Calixtus II.

H

Hagar 101, 113
Heliberri, *see* Elvira.
Heliodorus, Saint 72, 89
Hermogenes XXVII-XXVIII, XXXV-XXXVI, LXIII, 70–71, 97–100, 110–13
Herod Agrippa I XXI–XXII, XXV, XXIX–XXX, XXXII–XXXIII, LXIV–LXV, 7, 58, 71, 77, 85, 88–90, 104–6, 116–17, 127, 132
Hesychius, *see* Esicius.
Hillary of Poitiers 16
Honoratus, Bishop 129
Hubert of Besançon XLV, XLVIII, 18
Hugh, Saint LI, LII, 50–51
Hugh, Abbot 52
Hungary XLV, 1, 16

I

Iberia, Iberian XI, XIV, XVII, XXI, XXVII–XXVIII, XXX, XXXIII, XXXV, XXXVIII, XLI, LIV, LIX, LXIII, 60–61, 70, 76, 81, 91
Ilduilfus, Bishop 129
Illicinus, Mount, *see* Pico Sacro.
Indalecius, *see* Endalecius.
India XXVI, LII, 61, 107
Innocent II, Pope (Gregorio Papareschi) 64
Iosias, *see* Josias.
Iria Flavia [Spain] XXXVI, LXI, LXIV–LXV, 11–13, 77, 86, 91–92, 122, 124, 128–29, 134–35
Isaac 101, 113
Ishmael 101, 113
Isicius, *see* Esicius.
Isidore of Seville XXX, 11
Israel XXVI, XXX, 86, 101, 113
Italy, Italian XLII, XLV, XLIX, LIV, 1, 11, 33, 35, 39, 60, 76, 89

J

Jacobus de Voragine XXVII, XLVIII, 18, 70, 74
Jairus, priest XXII, 17
Josias, Saint IX, XX, XXIV–XXVIII, XXXV–XXXVI, LXIII, 71, 85, 104–5, 116–17
Jerome, Saint LXV, 71–72, 89–90
Jerusalem XXI-XXII, XXIV, XXVIII, XXXII–XXXIII, XXXIX, XLII, XLVI, LIV, LVII, LXI–LXIV, 7, 9, 28–32, 34, 49,

INDEX

58, 70, 71, 75–76, 90, 100-101, 107, 110, 113–14, 122, 127, 132, 134
Jews, Jewish XXI, XXV, 85, 88, 92, 98, 100–101, 103–4, 110, 113, 117, 127, 133
John, Saint XXI-XXII, XXIV-XXV, XXIX-XXX, XXXII-XXXIII, XXXVIII, LVII, LXI-LXII, 72, 75, 87–89, 91, 97, 108, 110, 120,123–24, 127, 129
John the Baptist 120, 123
Joppa (Jaffa) [Israel] LXIV, 86, 122, 134
Judas XXII, 125
Judea 77, 97, 110
Julius Caesar, *see* Caesar, Julius.

L

Labicum [Italy] 48
Lazarus 17
Leo, Pope Saint XXXIII–XXXIV, XXXVI, LX–LXII, LXIV, 69–70, 73, 85, 122, 127–28
León [Spain] 8, 21
LePuy [France] 19
Lérida [Spain] LIV, 8, 9
Liberum Donum (Libredón) LXV, 86, 128
Libya 61, 128
Licinia Eudoxia (Eudoxia) 90
Lisia, *see* Lysia.
Logroño [Spain] LI–LII, 63
Lorraine, *see* Lotharingia.
Lothaire, King 18
Lotharingia, Lotharingian (Lorraine) [France] 3, 18
Louis VI, King 25, 64

Louis the Bishop, witness 125
Lupa, *see* Luparia.
Luparia (Lupa) XXXV, LXIV, LXVIII, LXXII, 78, 119, 135
Lycaonia [Turkey] 107
Lydia [Turkey] XXVI
Lysia, centurion 100, 113
Lyon [France] LI–LII, 41, 44–45

M

Macedonia 107
Mark Anthony 90
Martín Flamiz, witness 125
Martin of Tours, Saint XLIV, L, LIX, 16–17
Martin, witness 126
Mary, Mother of Jesus LVIII, 5, 9, 49, 88, 101, 107, 113
Matamoros (Saint James) XXIII, LIV, LV, 23, 43, 54
Matthew, Saint (Levi) 107
Matthew, Count XLVI–XLVII
Matthias, Saint XXII, 107
Mauregatus, King XXXI, XXXVI, 109
Mediterranean Sea LII, LIV, LXIV, 2, 28, 60–61
Miro, King 128
Moabites 3, 8, 28
Modena [Italy] 35
Mondoñedo [Spain] 125
Mont-de-Narsan [France] 19
Monte de Gozo [Spain] 21
Montpellier [France] XLV, 22
Moors, Moorish XXIII, XXXVIII, XLI, LIV, LVIII, 8–9, 62
Moorslayer, *see* Matamoros.

Moses 80, 101, 113
Moslem(s) XXXII, XLIX, LVII, 8, 29, 60, 92

N

Narbonne [France] XXVII
Nicholas, Saint 123
Nogent [France] 45
Notker Balbulus XXXII

O

Oca Montes de [Spain] 3, 15
Ordoño Álvarez, witness 125
Ostia [Italy] LIII, 64

P

Palestine XXXII
Pamplona [Spain] XL, XLV, LV, 25–27
Pannonia [Hungary] 16
Pelagius, Hermit, see Pelayo
Pelayo (Pelagius), hermit XXXVI, LX, 122–23
Persia, Persian 8, 61
Peter Ansurriz, witness 125
Peter, witness 126
Peter, Saint XXI-XXII, XXIV-XXVI, LVII, LXI, LXIII, LXV, 49, 72, 75, 88, 90–92, 107, 123–24
Pharisee LXIV, 76, 100, 104, 110, 113, 116
Philetus, magician XXVII, LXIII, 71, 97–99, 110–12
Philip I, King, of France 25
Philip, Saint 107
Pico Sacro (Illicinus), (Mons Sacer) XV, XVIII, XXXIV, 81–82

Poitiers [France] 3, 16, 25
Pontius, Count, of Saint-Gilles 5, 52
Pontus [Turkey] 107
Porta Clusa [France] 19
Portugal 22, 56,
Priscillian of Avila, Bishop XXXII, 16, 71
Pseudo-Abdias, see Abdias.
Puente la Reina [Spain] 22, 25
Pyrenees 19, 22

Q

Quendulfus, Bishop 129
Quirinus, Saint 90–91

R

Raimbert, pilgrim 5, 37
Ramiro, King 125
Ramiro, witness 126
Ramón Berenguer 8, 62
Roland XVI, XXXVIII, 13, 19
Romanus, Bishop 129
Rome [Italy] XXIV, XLII, XLIX, LII, LXIII, 48–49, 64, 72, 90, 107, 118
Roncesvalles [Spain] 19, 25
Rouen [France] 74

S

Sacer, Mons, see Pico Sacro.
Sadducee LXIV, 76
Saint-Michel [France] 19
Saint-Gilles [France] LII, 5, 22, 52
Saint-Jean-Pied-de-Port [France] 19, 25
Samaria, Samaritan XXII, 97, 110

INDEX

Samuel, Bishop 129
Samuel, Prophet 114
Sancho VII, King XXVI
Sancho the Count, witness 125
Santo Domingo de la Calzada [Spain] XV, 22
Saracen LVI, 8, 25, 28–29, 32, 56, 60–62, 128
Sarraceno González the Judge, witness 125
Secundus, Saint XXXV, 73, 76, 118, 120
Sagredo the Priest, witness 125
Selva, Bishop 129
Seven Apostolic Men, *see* Saints Torquatus, Tissephons, Secundus, Cecilius, Endalecius, Esicius and Euphrasius.
Sicily [Italy] 60
Simon the Zealot 107
Slovenia [Croatia] 61
Somport Pass [France] 22
Son(s) of Thunder XXII, LVII, 108
Spain IX, XII, XV–XVI, XXIII–XXIV, XXVI, XXVIII–XXXV, LI, LIV–LV, LXIII–LXIV, LXX 8–9, 11, 16, 19, 22, 25, 55, 61, 71–72, 76, 82, 85, 87, 90, 93, 108–9, 118, 120, 122, 127–30, 132, 135
Spanish XXVII, XXX–XXXI, XXXIV, XLI–XLII, XLIX, 19, 40, 92, 93, 106, 127–28
Stephen, Bishop LVI, 5, 54–56
Suarius Fagilat, scribe 126
Sulpicius Severus 16
Switzerland 22

Syrtis Sandbanks [coast of Libya] 128

T

Tabor, Mount 75
Tertullian 71
Teodesindus, Bishop 129
Teodomiro, Bishop XXXVI, XLVIIII–XLIX, LI, 11–12, 122, 128–30
Teverya, *see* Tiberias.
Theocritus, centurion 100, 113
Theodorus, disciple LXIII, 73, 87
Theophilus XXVI
Thomas, Saint 107, 123
Thomas Becket, Saint XLIV
Tiberias (Teverya) [Israel] 4, 32
Tisefons, *see* Tissephons.
Tissephons (Tisefons) XXXV, 73, 76, 118, 120
Torquatus, Saint XXXIV–XXXV, LXIV, 73, 76, 118, 120
Toulouse [France] XV, 22, 52
Turkey, Turks XXIII, XXVI, 4, 32, 61
Turpin, Archbishiop (Pseudo-Turpin) XVI, XXXVII–XLIII, XLV, LV, LXVI, 8, 19, 25, 28, 70, 73
Tuy (Tui) [Spain] 125
Tyrrhenian Sea (Etruscan) 2

U

Urci [Spain] 73, 120
Urgel [Spain] LI, LIV, 8, 57
Urraca, witness 125
Usuard of Saint-Germain-des-Prés XXXII

V

Vendôme [France] 16
Vera (Vergu), (Verga), (Berja) [Spain] 73, 120
Vézelay [France] LIII, 19, 64
Vienne [France] XL, 37
Villafranca [Spain] 15
Vincibilis, Bishop 129
Voragine, *see* Jacobus de Voragine.

W

William of Poitiers 11, 25, 57
William, Patriarch XXXIX

Z

Zadar [Croatia] 61
Zaragoza [Spain] XL, XLIX, LI, 9, 57
Zebedee XXII, XXIX–XXX, XXXIII, 1, 18, 97, 108, 133

*Production of This Book Was Completed on
September 8, 2018 at Italica Press, Bristol,
United Kingdom. It Was Set in
Adobe Garamond &
Charlemagne.*

✣   ✣
✣

www.ingramcontent.com/pod-product-compliance
Lightning Source LLC
Chambersburg PA
CBHW030400100426
42812CB00028B/2781/J